# BAD BOY

Also by Ronin Ro

*Street Sweeper*
*Have Gun Will Travel*
*Gangsta*

# BAD BOY

The Influence of

## SEAN "PUFFY" COMBS

on the Music Industry

RONIN RO

POCKET BOOKS
New York   London   Toronto   Sydney   Singapore

POCKET BOOKS, a division of Simon & Schuster, Inc.
1230 Avenue of the Americas, New York, NY 10020

ISBN: 0-7434-2823-4

First Pocket Books hardcover printing November 2001

10  9  8  7  6  5  4  3  2  1

POCKET and colophon are registered trademarks of
Simon & Schuster, Inc.

For information regarding special discounts for bulk purchases, please
contact Simon & Schuster Special Sales at 1-800-456-6798 or
business@simonandschuster.com

Printed in the U.S.A.

For
Sean John Combs,
Christopher George Wallace,
and Susan and Rachel

# contents

# preface

IN EARLY 2001, WEARING A DARK, CONSERVATIVE SUIT AND TIE, SITTING at the defense table, and facing up to fifteen years in prison, Sean "Puffy" Combs watched attorneys and Judge Charles H. Solomon bicker over pretrial matters. The suit he wore was as far as one could go from the regalia of his *No Way Out* heyday, which included outlandish jewelry, earrings, and designer sunglasses. Though some of the people closest to him told reporters he was a fiery control freak, Puffy's face was impassive when the judge said the trial was officially active and media coverage might taint the jury pool. The thirty-one-year-old rap mogul, a powerful figure in his industry for nearly a decade, offered no protest, despite the fact that the order meant he'd no longer be able to proclaim his innocence during press conferences or interviews.

For a year, magazines such as *People* and *Newsweek* had focused on his relationship with Jennifer Lopez and his criminal charges. He complained often about reporters, but the truth is he thrived on interviews and on seeing his name in gossip columns. He continued to tell reporters he was a changed man. He appeared at a Harlem high school with his disgruntled artist Black Rob to hand out one hundred free computers. He told reporters he was working on a gospel album. He invoked the names of his late father, Melvin, and the late rapper Biggie Smalls while facing a grand jury in January 2000, and added that he'd never own or carry a gun. He even invited a writer to his East Hampton home, appeared in sweats and sneakers, and kept the Bentley and bodyguards out of view.

After his years of arrogance and excess, he announced that he really wasn't all about the Benjamins, as his hit song once claimed. His so-called Hampton estate was actually much smaller than other houses on the street, he explained. It only had three bedrooms, and didn't even have much furniture. He also wasn't a gangster.

Unlike his codefendant, Anthony "Wolf" Jones, who left through a back door, Puffy paced in front of the courthouse. Reporters yelled questions, but the gag order barred him from speaking. He stepped to the curb and hailed a cab. Usually he traveled in a limousine, one of his Bentleys, or in one of his record company's vehicles. Sometimes he'd relax in a private jet. Other times in the Bahamas, on a chartered boat with guests at his New Year's Eve parties. Typically, he had bodyguards with him. Now, waiting for a cab, alone, his name seemingly over in rap circles, he heard a fan call out his name. He turned and saw a young girl in a red leather coat and large gold earrings. He approached, embraced her for a second, and then entered the taxi waiting at the curb. Before the trial, newspapers and columnists described him only as a mogul, and did so mainly to spice up stories about his possible fifteen-year prison term.

The day of his next pretrial hearing, after the weekend, he got into a brown pin-stripe suit and put an ivory handkerchief in his breast pocket. He walked out of a sports utility vehicle that cold winter morning and did his morning walk past the cameras gathered by the court entrance. He tried to project determination and innocence. Reporters were on either side of him, like a gauntlet. They had been hounding him for years now, unfairly, he claimed.

Inside, he met with his attorneys: Johnnie Cochran of O. J. Simpson fame, a short, square-shouldered man who told reporters this would be his final criminal trial, and Benjamin Brafman, a confrontational speaker who had faced this prosecutor in court before. After hanging up his coat in a metal locker in the back of the courtroom, Puffy took his place at the defense table.

The judge told Court TV they couldn't film his criminal trial. Then Brafman argued with Matthew Bogdanos, a stocky, white senior assistant district attorney with a crew cut and a résumé that included serving in the Marines' reserve and practicing his boxing in a gym downtown. Brafman complained that shooting victim Natania Reuben, a day after the gag order was imposed, had granted an interview to the New York *Daily News*. The newspaper also had run a story that cited unnamed sources claiming a mystery witness would testify that Puffy had fired a gun in Club New York.

Puffy had been facing these accusations since December 27, 1999. He was standing near his rap artist Shyne in a crowded New York nightclub. Someone threw money in Puffy's face, and Shyne, in an effort to defend Puffy's honor, some said, opened fire with a handgun. Puffy and his then girlfriend, movie star Jennifer Lopez, fled the scene in a Lincoln Navigator; police chased them through several red lights, arrested them, and found a stolen gun in the vehicle.

In court, Brafman was livid; he blamed police officials for planting stories, and then asked the judge to lift the gag order so he could respond.

Puffy watched Brafman and Bogdanos find a way around the order by discussing undisclosed information in open court. Reporters in the stands scribbled notes when Brafman railed against this "secret witness." Brafman said he had thirty witnesses ready to testify that this witness was lying about Puffy having a gun. "We have a lot of 'secret witnesses' who'll blow the government's case right out of the water."

Bogdanos brushed this aside. Not one of the four hundred witnesses interviewed by the state offered evidence to exonerate Puffy, he said.

Brafman asked for their names and said Bogdanos would eat his words when some witnesses told the jury they personally had told Bogdanos that they "never saw Puffy with a gun." Brafman then accused him of trying to taint the jury pool by leaking information to the press.

Bogdanos's response was crushing. He said Puffy was the one who'd been "playing the media like an instrument for a decade." After describing Puffy's blow-by-blow description of events to the Associated Press, he said the defense actually had leaked the story about a secret witness. They did it, he added, so the judge would "release the gag order so they can go out and try the case in the streets."

At the defense table, Johnnie Cochran shook his head and laughed.


THE FIRST DAY OF JURY SELECTION, PUFFY DIDN'T LOOK WORRIED. He had a worn miniature copy of the New Testament with him and the very best lawyers that money could buy. While the judge questioned panelists for the trial, Puffy made sure every one could see him thumbing through the Good Book. Before that day, none of the two hundred and sixty prospective jurors had known he was the defendant. When they entered the room he noted the shocked expressions on their faces. At one point, standing near Johnnie Cochran in his conservative, pin-striped blue suit, he heard one young black woman say, "Oh, my God!"

Mostly he sat quietly and thumbed through his Bible. If Brafman's questioning of a witness led to insults and performances for spectators in the stands, Puffy'd look up and watch the show. After Bogdanos removed five blacks and four Hispanics from a panel of eighteen prospective jurors, Brafman accused Bogdanos of trying to exclude people of color.

When Cochran came up to bat, he wisely avoided the issue of race. Johnnie Cochran instead used his time in court to claim Matthew Bogdanos was targeting Puffy because of his celebrity.

Bogdanos presented another humiliating comeback. The only person who wanted special treatment because of fame, he said, was Puffy. He said Puffy had used publicists to downplay his previous troubles, and claimed that the night of the triple shooting, the flamboyant rapper was "being his manipulative self, trying to control things on the street like he controls so much else."

The second day Puffy sat at the defense table and watched potential jurors take the stand and describe him as a rap mogul, a Hamptons' resident, a restaurateur, and the owner of the successful Sean John clothing line. One panelist said friends in the Hamptons had called Puffy a good neighbor. Another, a white woman in her thirties, gushed that Puffy's "I'll Be Missing You," set entirely to The Police's classic "I'll Be Watching You," had touched her heart.

The third day he put on a conservative blue suit with a pink tie. He shoved a pink handkerchief into one pocket, then left for court. Potential jurors took the stand and recalled news stories, his appearance on *Who Wants to Be a Millionaire,* and video footage of him with Jennifer Lopez in the almost see-through Versace dress on the red carpet at the 2000 Grammy Awards show. Each prospective panelist claimed they'd ignore his fame and treat him like any other defendant. While they spoke, he took notes in a tiny spiral notebook. When one woman said he was a "good dresser," he stopped writing, faced her with a smile, then nodded. Puffy was a star, and fame would be an issue in his trial. Everyone in the room, including the judge, seemed to know this.

DURING HIS CRIMINAL TRIAL, PUFFY LATER CLAIMED, HE REALIZED that he had to change his life. The bullets that had struck three people in Club New York also put an end to his image as a mainstream-approved superstar, business mogul, and trendsetter.

The trial would shatter the image he had spent a decade maintaining, and put an end to the myth of Puff Daddy and his merry Bad Boy Family.

Even now, in 2001, it's hard to grasp the magnitude of the damage Puff Daddy has done to hip-hop. Puff Daddy did more to ruin the once proud genre than MC Hammer, the "Cop Killer" controversy, gangsta rap, sampling lawsuits, a disapproving mainstream media, and promoters who refuse to book rap concerts.

Until a certain point, Puffy really was the rap mogul that newspaper reporters had continued to describe in print. Before forming Bad Boy, he was an intern at Andre Harrell's Uptown label. After Harrell fired him in 1993, Puffy formed Bad Boy, signed a distribution deal with Arista Records, and began his meteoric rise in the industry. He was talented, he had an ear for hits and an eye for packaging, and he knew how to supervise the production of hit records. He also introduced the world to The Notorious B.I.G., born Christopher George Wallace, and to Biggie's album *Ready to Die,* which introduced a new level of quality and emotion to rap music.

Hip-hop magazines like *The Source* and *Vibe* supported Puffy's work back then—and wound up aiding in the destruction of a music and culture they claimed to love. Magazines believed Puffy would continue recording authentic hip-hop and staging his career in revolutionary terms.

But support soon turned to shock when they realized Puffy's revolution would amount to nothing but buying himself $375,000 Bentleys and platinum jewelry, and to blowing more money on ostentatious parties on Wall Street and in East Hampton. Even so, magazines continued to promote him as the savior of hip-hop.

After his top draw, The Notorious B.I.G., died in March of 1997, after being shot in a drive-by shooting that continues to pain the hearts of many black youth, Puffy shocked his fans by seeming to exploit the murder. He tied it to his solo album and concert tour.

Ultimately, Puffy's greatest gift seemed to be for promotion, particularly for self-promotion. He made sure the media knew he was a production genius, the "king of sampling," even though real players knew he wasn't always a hands-on producer. Former schoolmate, business partner, and producer Deric Angelettie remembered that in 1997, "Puff came to me with this record and wanted me to do something with it. It was really fast, and I slowed it down and laid some more shit on top of it, and it was ready."

That song, "It's All About the Benjamins," went from an initial pressing of one hundred copies to become one of 1997's biggest hits and the basis for a chart-topping rock-flavored single. When reporters praised Puffy for the song, he gave the impression to the media and at award shows that he was Bad Boy's chief producer.

Puffy also shocked people by tailoring his black artists and their music to suit the tastes of a white teenage suburban audience. This changed the Bad Boy sound from classic soul and hard-core rap to passive mainstream pop. Unquestioning white fans supported his new sound, and MTV called Bad Boy "the Motown of the nineties."

Nevertheless, by 1998, black fans were crying "sellout," much as folk fans had when Bob Dylan began playing an electric guitar. Despite what some called a staggering 75 percent dip in sales, his distributor, Arista, gave him a reported fifty-million-dollar advance against future earnings. Puffy seemed to be unstoppable. He thought so too, telling reporters he would outdo David Geffen. But as soon as the ink on the Arista deal was dry, he abandoned the Bad Boy Family image and hip-hop pose, became flamboyant and demanding, and lost touch with his audience. "I'm not going to go down in history as a black music-maker," he told a reporter. "I'm going to go down as a music-maker that was so incredible that he represented all of culture. You're not going to be able to label me."

If Puffy ever regretted losing Bad Boy's audience, arguably, by releasing three R & B albums during a year in which *rap* sales soared to a historic eighty-one million albums, he didn't show it by exercising restraint. He spent big from the jump, setting off a round of inflation that is still taking a toll on the music industry today. By 1999, Puffy saw himself as the rap mogul described in newspaper stories. He wore expensive European clothing, spent big, traveled in a Gulfstream jet, and continued to lose touch with rap fans. In the office he was a typical executive; barking orders and treating many of the people who helped him reach the top as expendable. The more he partied in the Hamptons, the more disgusted his fans became, especially since Puffy had little cause to celebrate. Other labels, including Roc-a-fella and Ruff Ryders, offered genuine hip-hop, and rendered his sound obsolete.

Bad Boy was out of step. When Puffy should have been focusing on his career, he was partying in East Hampton, focusing on other businesses, and spending millions on a twelve-story building on Park Avenue, a mansion, a little-known magazine, and a Notorious B.I.G. impersonator. He didn't realize that his bad decisions, his hubris, and his legendary temper were all about to catch up to him. *Bad Boy* will explain what happened, how it happened, what caused it to happen, and why Bad Boy Entertainment worked, but can no longer work the way it used to.

# PART 1

# MONEY, POWER, RESPECT

"Puffy owes no one any apologies for his success."

—*MC Hammer*

# ONE

# Party and B.S.

IN 1988, NINETEEN-YEAR-OLD SEAN "PUFFY" COMBS GRADUATED from high school, packed his belongings, and moved to Washington, D.C. A thin teenager with his hair styled in a "Gumby," Sean was majoring in business administration at Howard, a predominantly black university filled with New Yorkers who enjoyed hip-hop. On campus, Sean wore his polka-dot shirts, played his hip-hop loud while driving his Jetta, and displayed exceptional dance skills in front of the school cafeteria. After the novelty of being in a new place wore off, however, the driven young student from Mount Vernon, New York, threw himself into his studies. By this point, however, he knew he wanted more: "I knew I didn't want to just get a degree, like I was reaching to be the greatest stockbroker or the greatest lawyer. I had made up my mind that I was going to be successful, a multimillionaire."[1]

He had inherited his drive for success and love for fashion from his parents. Puffy's father, Melvin, had worked for the Board of Education and as a cab driver. "My mom was modeling," he said. "She was always like the fly girl of the neighborhood, and my pops was the fly guy of the neighborhood. That's what attracted them. That's how they got together."[2]

When Sean was born in Harlem on November 4, 1969, one million

---

1. Susan L. Taylor, *Essence,* 1998.
2. Sean "Puffy" Combs, *Rolling Stone,* 1997.

people of color were squeezed into four square miles. Many middle-class families had fled the area nine years before, forcing property owners to lower rent, lose interest in buildings and the neighborhood, and inadvertently create what the media called one of the most feared ghettos in America. Unemployment and the infant mortality rate soared. Rampant poverty encouraged riots, drug abuse, and despair. While neighborhood organizations requested federal funding to rebuild the community and create jobs, no help arrived.

The Combs family, however, lived in a cleaner, relatively safe middle-class section, while Sean's grandmother Jessie lived in the well-kept, government-subsidized cooperative building Esplanade Gardens.

Sean's interest in performing seemed to come from his mother. She'd been interested in fashion since she was six, when her mother, Jessie, had turned a brocaded slipcover into an elegant dress. When Sean was two his mother included him in a fashion show she staged at a day-care center. "I came out and tried to steal the show," said Puffy. "As soon as that spotlight hit me, I just embraced it." An executive from the Baskin-Robbins chain in the audience hired him to appear in a print ad, and since then, his aunt Geri Garcia remembered, "He was such a ham."

In 1972, Sean's sister, Keisha, was born, adding yet another mouth to feed. His father had gone from playing cards and shooting pool at the Rhythm Club to running numbers and dealing drugs. He bought the family a Mercedes and developed a reputation as a Robin Hood figure, but Sean's mother, Janice, claimed his life in the drug trade was "a new thing": "I never knew about the drugs stuff because he always worked. He did it in between times."

Soon after giving Sean a birthday party—tossing him in the air, Sean recalled—his father went to meet some people near Central Park. It was January 26, 1972, and he was sitting in his car. Someone else arrived, something went wrong, and this person shot him in the head. Janice had to identify his body. After his father's death, Puffy remembers, "my mom and grandmom pulled together and kept me off the streets."

Today Janice is a fashionable woman with platinum Lil' Kim–styled tresses and a penchant for designer clothing and boots; she charms reporters, supports her son, associates with his ex-girlfriends, and attends fashion industry events.

Back then, she was a young woman with two kids to feed, a high school diploma, bills to pay, and concerns about the future. Back then, she recalled, "I wasn't going to be homeless. I wasn't going to be on welfare, if I had to work all day and all night." She threw herself into work, becoming both mother and father to Sean and Keisha. She found part-time work as an assistant teacher at a local day-care center and as a school bus driver, and a night job as an attendant for children with cerebral palsy while her mother watched the kids.

Sean continues to count his mother as a major influence, and some of her behavior seems to have inspired his own. When she drove the school bus and kids left their seats, she used lollipops and candy as incentives for good behavior. "When I told them, 'sit down'," she said, "they sat down." Later, critics like Jeru and The Lox would accuse him of using champagne, designer clothes, jewelry, and cars in like fashion with his artists.

The drive to be a millionaire also seemed to come from her; she'd tell him conformity would guarantee success. "Go to school and pay close attention to your teachers if you want to be a millionaire," she'd say.

By age eight, Sean was aggressive and stubborn. "He wouldn't take no for an answer," said Garcia. He was already a loner when his mother enrolled him in the Fresh Air Fund, a nonprofit organization that arranges for city kids to vacation with host families in the country. He spent a summer among the Amish in Pennsylvania Dutch country, wandering through empty fields and roads, then returned to Harlem, where he got into a few personality-shaping confrontations.

One afternoon, while leaving a store with a pack of his grandmother's cigarettes, he saw a kid approach; the kid asked for a dollar. Sean put his grandmother's change away, put his hands up, and started fighting. The other kid hit him in the face a few times, took his money, and left him thinking, Before I get into a fight, I gotta make sure I can win it.

Another day he came home in tears and told Janice that another kid had beaten him up and taken his skateboard. She forced him to leave the house and not return until he got it back. Outside, he ran into an older, taller kid and asked him to handle the job. Thus began his habit of forging alliances with tougher kids. He ran with a crew of rap fans called The 7-Up Crew, but viewed himself as a loner.

In 1982, his mother moved Sean and Keisha to Mount Vernon, a working-class suburb in Westchester County, north of the Bronx. Sean was able to escape Harlem's claustrophobic, tenement-lined streets and tougher residents. He had room to breathe, trees, private houses, car culture, well-trimmed lawns, and a less congested, racially integrated Montessori school to attend. He was also enamored with hip-hop: "From Run-D.M.C. to KRS-One to the Beastie Boys to L.L. Cool J, I was there. I seen that." At age twelve, he claimed, "I'd be out until three, four in the morning, seeing the music. I had to sneak out to do it, but I was doing it."

Soon he started looking for a job. His mother was already holding down two of them—at the day care center and driving a bus—and searching for a third; she later began selling clothing in a shop: "Like a lot of kids who grow up in single-parent homes, I had to get a job much quicker and start thinking about the future much earlier. I had to help out and become the man of the house sooner, so I had my paper route when I was twelve."

When the newspaper delivery service said he was too young to apply for work, he added a year to his birth certificate and got his route. He had another student apply for a second route and took that one as well. Seeing his mother work numerous jobs inspired his own legendary work ethic.

At age fourteen, Janice enrolled him in Mount St. Michael Academy, a private Catholic school in the Bronx that expected him, as she put it, to "dress accordingly," in a suit and tie. Each morning, he put on his school sweater, slacks, and dress shirt and accepted lunch money from her.

At school, sheltered suburban white and Asian classmates praised the music of Ozzy Osbourne and other rock musicians. He liked hip-hop records, including 1979's Top 40 hit "Rapper's Delight" by the Sugarhill Gang. He also liked having extra money.

During lunch each day, he later told *Rolling Stone,* he would put away the money his mother had given him and wander the cafeteria to "ask everybody for fifty cents." Soon he was earning money from two or three jobs, including one at an amusement park. Other students laughed at the sight of him working at the park when they came there to relax and enjoy the rides, he said, "but I would always say to myself that I wanted to be somebody who makes history, and not selfishly, not for me. I just wanted to make a change. I didn't want to be a person who just lived and died." He ignored taunts from schoolmates and asked his employer to let him work double shifts.

After school, he traveled to Harlem to attend an afterschool program, hang with old friends, and keep up with developments in hip-hop. He was coming of age during a time when the genre was rising. At the same time, many kids were beginning to deal crack cocaine, to earn fortunes, and to become ghetto celebrities.

Sean immersed himself in hip-hop, having a barber carve trendy musical notes into his Gumby, dancing in clubs, rocking then-fashionable polka dot shirts, and answering to the nickname Puffy. Later, he'd be evasive about his stage name, but finally said, "It came from a childhood friend. It's a silly reason. Whenever I got mad as a kid, I used to always huff and puff. I had a temper."

It was at age fourteen, when he "knew about street life [and] knew who was hustlers," that he learned what really happened to his father. While his mother told him Melvin had died in a car accident, people in Harlem alluded to his father's stint as a dealer, his father's furs, and his family being "the only people in Harlem to have a Mercedes-Benz." Soon, he says he wondered, "Come on, man, my pops was hustling or something?"

Determined to learn the truth, he went to a public library, did some research, and found old newspaper stories that described Melvin Combs as "the biggest of his time when he was here."

The articles also attributed his murder to people eager to take over his number-running and drug operations. "It was just a transition," Puffy decided. "He was the ruler. It was time for a new ruler. That's the life that he led."

By now, hip-hop was boosting his self-esteem. He had dreams of turning his love of hip-hop into a business of some sort. He began to hang out at The Rooftop nightclub on 155th Street, a place where up-and-coming rap producer Teddy Riley, old school rappers like Kool Moe Dee, and future celebrities rubbed shoulders with their fans. After a week at his restaurant job, cleaning dirty stoves, mopping floors, and waiting on tables, Sean would sneak out of his suburban home, travel to the club, and wait outside. After a while, bouncers would let him in and he'd draw attention with his dancing.

At first, one employee at MTV revealed, he planned to form a group with another dancer. But he also dreamed of recording albums. At the time, hip-hop was moving from message rap and toward the stripped-down hard-core of L.L. Cool J's *Radio* and Run-D.M.C.'s *Raising Hell*. "Everybody has a dream when they're watching Run-D.M.C. or L.L. Cool J," he told one interviewer. "And I was always somebody who closed my eyes and dreamed, but then opened my eyes and saw what I had to do."

He harbored dreams of performing, and continued to attend a racially mixed private school and an afterschool program in predominantly black Harlem. He wore a school sweater and well-pressed slacks and shirt, played on the school football team, and began to play suburban class-mates the latest rap records. He also hung out with rap fans, met artists like Doug E. Fresh, and practiced dance moves while listening to WBLS-FM, to many of the records he'd later set his music to. By the time he graduated, he had danced in music videos by Doug E. Fresh, Babyface, the Fine Young Cannibals, and singer Stacy Lattisaw.

When he arrived at Howard, he felt, "I was nurtured into wanting to be somebody special." Ron Gilyard, who would later work with him, re-membered fellow students seeing his videos and idolizing him even more. They had their own dreams and believed hitching a ride on his coattails would bring them closer to achieving them.

He soon had an entourage but wanted more than their adulation. During this period he was so ambitious he later described himself as a "savage." He was single-minded about making history and earning his fortune.

Seeing a promotional video for the compilation album *Uptown's Kickin' It* strengthened this desire. During one scene, Uptown CEO Andre Harrell, a young, clean-cut former rapper in wire-rim glasses and corpo-rate attire, marched into a conference room and methodically signed a stack of contracts for the camera. Puffy later said this businesslike image inspired him to pursue a career in music.

Another day, on the set of a video, an imposing limousine deposited well-dressed executives with cell phones and briefcases. To his young eyes they exuded as much power as Harrell. Watching them coordinate details of the shoot, he thought, I don't know what they do, but I want to do that! The "Puff Daddy" persona was born.

He formed a company with schoolmate Deric Angelettie, who was impressed by Puff's ability to cater to voids in the marketplace and by his drive to earn money. Though he was flamboyant, loved being the center of attention, and was pursuing a degree, he still found time to run a shuttle service to the airport, to allegedly sell old term papers, and to even hawk T-shirts and sodas.

Most telling was his reaction to an incident in which rebellious students took over an administrative building. That day, reporters took notes for stories as students protested. After the incident, Puffy collected magazine and newspaper clips that described the event, turned them into poster-size collages, and sold them to the "revolutionary" students.

In Puff, Angelettie saw someone who could profit from even "a crazy situation," and Puff's idea to throw and promote parties could pay off, especially since Howard had a built-in audience just waiting for these events. As Howard alum Ron Lawrence remembered: "At the time, probably seventy percent of Howard was New Yorkers. So we brought the music with us; we brought the style of dress with us. And in trying to keep that vibe, we would throw parties all over the campus. You had guys like Puffy and Deric forming their little team as party promoters just to keep that New York spirit alive."

"When Puffy came, he was a very flashy guy," Angelettie remembered. "He was always out at the clubs, and the young girls loved him. He'd be in the middle of the floor doin' all the new dances. And his style of dress was a little more colorful, bolder. Everyone took notice of this cool, overconfident young dude. I was deejaying at the time, and one night he came up to me and said, 'I'd like to throw a party with you. You're pretty popular.' "

Operating under the name "A Black Man And A Puerto Rican Productions," Sean and Deric prepared for their first event. Sean wanted to invite as many celebrities as possible, and reached out to twenty-one-year-old Heavy D, a Mount Vernon–based rapper who recorded for Uptown Records. Puffy overwhelmed Heavy with his interest in music, his ambition, and his constant flattery, and Heavy accepted his invitation. Almost immediately, Puffy included his name on promotional materials with Slick Rick, Doug E. Fresh, and the R & B group Guy. Remarkably, every celebrity appeared. "And ever since that first party, everyone made it a point to go to Puff's parties," said Gilyard.

Puff's success united music-minded students Ron Lawrence, Chucky Thompson, Nashiem Myrick, and Harve Pierre. Soon they formed a group that held events on campus or in nearby clubs, and drew paying customers by promoting and advertising the events as an ongoing movement. Puffy also was promoting himself heavily. On his first business card, in the bottom left-hand corner, he had engraved "Sean (Puf) Combs." He was officially in business. "For the next two years, we threw one damn [party] near every week," Angelettie remembered. "Even Howard came to us to do their parties. Our biggest was Homecoming Eighty-nine at the Masonic Temple. I expected maybe fifteen hundred. Forty-five hundred people came. The D.C. police shut down the whole block and brought out the dogs. We had to get on our knees and beg them not to lock us up."

If Puffy learned a popular group was in town, he'd travel to where they were staying and personally invite them to a party. He focused less on his studies, which he felt were keeping him from his dream. "I was like, 'Four years?' " He says he told himself, "I got to get my hustle on now."

Since people from the industry attended his events, he reached out to them first. He took the four-hour train ride to New York to let industry executives know he was looking for work but learned no record company would hire him.

He adapted to the situation by lowering his sights. When he approached Def Jam, he asked for an internship. Executive Lyor Cohen, who helped Run-D.M.C. land their lucrative endorsement deal with Adidas, agreed to meet with him. Puffy got into his Sunday best and made the trip. He sat with Cohen, discussed what he was doing, and announced his reasons for wanting to work for Def Jam. The meeting ended, and he figured he'd hear from Cohen within days. "I didn't get a callback. I had on a polka-dot tie at the time. It wasn't hip-hop enough for them."

He returned to Howard and learned that his friends Ron Lawrence and Deric Angelettie were leaving to form a rap group. As Two Kings and A Cipher, or Amen-Ra and D.O.P., they would record a single and achieve minor success in a glutted rap market. That people he knew entered the industry, when he'd been rejected, inspired him even more.

STINGING FROM WHAT HE CONSIDERED REJECTION BY DEF JAM, Puffy reached out to Heavy D, who was working as vice president of artists and repertoire (A & R) at Uptown Records. Heavy agreed to speak with Andre Harrell and do what he could to get Puffy an internship at the label.

At the time, twenty-nine-year-old Andre O'Neal Harrell was an up-and-coming music executive. In 1984, Harrell had performed with high school classmate Alonzo Brown as the group Dr. Jekyll & Mr. Hyde. They wore suits and ties onstage, rapped about office politics over crossover R & B tracks, and saw their 1984 album, *The Champagne of Rap,* sell a mere seventy thousand copies. It probably would have sold more if Harrell had not tried to foist his version of Chic's suit-and-champagne image on an audience that wanted drum machines and loud horn blasts. But Harrell, raised in a Bronx housing project by a grocery store supervisor and a nurse's aide, needed more; he "wanted the music to be fabulous, ghetto fabulous."

Later he claimed that he wore a suit on stage because, at age twenty-four, after graduating from Lehman College, he was working as an account executive at radio station WWRL. Wearing the suit made his life easier; after a night of performing, he didn't have to change clothes; he'd make it to the station's daily 8:00 A.M. meeting on time. Either way, rap fans rejected his album, and Harrell, sharing an apartment with rap manager Russell Simmons, soon took a job at Simmons's management firm, Rush.

In 1985, Harrell promoted Simmons's crossover client Run-D.M.C., but also tried to promote his own flamboyant group, Dr. Jekyll & Mr. Hyde. Simmons recalled that "he booked himself in a show in the Beacon Theater on top of L.L. Cool J!"

Harrell paid attention to how Simmons ran his company and decided he could also run a business, but his company would be "fabulous." It would shun rap's working-class pretensions, make black music "star-studded," and promote his "ghetto fabulous" marketing strategy as an exclusive philosophy. In short, he'd present music "that made champagne popular."

When Harrell received a demo tape from Heavy D & the Boyz, he saw that his dream was possible. Myers, born in Jamaica and raised in Mount Vernon, wrote songs with his deejay, Eddie F, and had his friends Trouble T-Roy and G-Wiz dance behind him. Anxious to leave Rush, Harrell quit his day job in 1986 and formed his own production company, Uptown Entertainment. He hired staff members with an affinity for R & B, including A & R man Kurt Woodley, signed seventeen-year-old Heavy to a deal, and funded the recording of his best-selling album.

Though Simmons claimed that Harrell had a vision for R & B "when R and B was worth zero, nothing," Harrell simply continued in the vein of early commercial rap groups like Whodini. Instead of yelling insults, that Brooklyn trio had recorded mild-mannered story raps over R & B and had sold millions of copies of "Freaks Come Out at Night" to a receptive white audience. Harrell wanted the same success for Heavy and his production company, Uptown.

Uptown's first deal was with MCA for a one-off compilation album called Uptown Is Kickin' It, which introduced middle-of-the-road rap groups Finesse and Synquis and Groove B Chill. Next Harrell had producers fill Heavy D's debut album with swing beats, James Brown samples, and R & B keyboards. Away from the studio, the former salesman developed a marketing campaign around the phrase "The Overweight Lover M.C." and contrived an image that fused L.L. Cool J's angry young man pose to the historically effective dapper "big shot" image.

Heavy D's clean-cut image and mild-mannered rap style helped sell half a million copies of his group's debut, Livin' Large. But Harrell's next project, an album by Teddy Riley's first new jack swing group, Gyrlz, flopped, then MCA passed on singer Al B. Sure!'s debut. Harrell sold Sure!'s album to Warner Brothers Records; it became an immediate hit and Warner offered him a deal for A & R and production.

By 1989, Harrell was enjoying success with Heavy D's second album, *Big Tyme.* Heavy had replaced his designer tracksuit with a suit and tie, and delivered pithy raps over commercial new jack swing. While white listeners enjoyed his million-selling single "We Got Our Own Thang," hip-hop's core audience rejected his glossy rap and viewed Heavy as a sellout.

It was at this point that D asked Harrell to meet with Puffy.

Harrell had to travel to Washington, D.C., anyway, to visit Rare Essence, a go-go band he signed in 1988. By the time he met with the group, Harrell had Puffy by his side. According to guitarist Andre Johnson, Harrell said, "This dude is probably gonna be interning with me, and I'm gonna have him work with you."

Puffy's first project was to find music producers willing to travel to Washington, Johnson added, "because Andre wanted to use a hip-hop producer with a go-go beat. We tried that a couple of times and it didn't really work, and Puffy ended up going to New York."

Puffy had arrived right after MCA signed Uptown to a deal that gave Harrell money, major distribution, offices, and checkbook power to sign, record, and promote new artists. Guy's debut album—driven by the hit single "Groove Me," which Harrell called the most important record of his career—quickly sold two million copies, and the group drew more fans with a look that Harrell instantly dubbed "ghetto fabulous."

As Harrell's intern, working in the office two days a week, Puffy had to take a four-hour train ride each weekend from Washington, D.C., to New York to make it to Uptown on time. In the office he was one of many young college students handling menial tasks in the hope that they would rise through the ranks or make profitable connections.

In the beginning, Puffy was a compulsive note-taker, trying to learn everything he could about the industry; he was one of the most devoted interns industry veteran Harrell had ever seen. Once, Harrell asked him to pick up a tape from another building. Puffy returned within minutes, out of breath and disheveled. Harrell asked him what was wrong.

"I ran," he answered.

"Even at nineteen, Combs was natty: crisp polo shirts, khakis, tight coif," Barry Michael Cooper once wrote. "I don't ever remember him wearing sneakers. What I can't forget is how he watched everything and everybody."

Back then, Cooper added, "Harrell would lead the drunken revelry of his Champ(agne) Pack, of which I was a temporary member, in the lobby of Manhattan's tony Royalton Hotel." Puffy watched flashy people drink Cristal and Veuve Cliquot champagne,[3] and listened to Harrell explain why "Harlem drug kingpin Leroy 'Nicky' Barnes," actor Wesley Snipes, and Duke Ellington were "ghetto fabulous." Soon, Cooper claimed, after not speaking with him for two months, Puffy approached him outside of Uptown/MCA's headquarters and broke the ice by saying he had lived near Cooper in Esplanade Gardens. Then, Cooper recalled, Puffy said, "When you write your next movie, keep me in mind. My name is Sean, but they call me Puffy. And I'm gonna be a big star. Remember that."

"For some reason," Cooper added, "I knew he was deadly serious. And he was."

By May of 1990, Puffy was asking Harrell to let him handle A & R chores for new artists. By now, Guy had imploded; members had feuded with each other and producer Teddy Riley, who had tried to sing with them on their follow-up, *The Future*. Just as Guy had disbanded, the group Jodeci arrived at Uptown's offices, from North Carolina, with twenty-nine songs on three cassette tapes.

While sitting in the waiting room, they decided to practice their singing. Heavy D, working in the office and walking by, heard them, then rushed to Harrell's office to urge him to listen to this group. Harrell did, and signed Jodeci on the spot. A & R man Kurt Woodley reportedly was unimpressed by their sound. Puffy, who told coworkers he had "platinum ears," felt they were superstars in the making. After helping the group find a place to live in a Bronx housing project, he monitored their progress.

By now, Puffy's hard work and self-promotion had paid off. Andre Harrell realized he was working eighty-hour weeks and commuting

---

3. Years later, he'd ask a reporter, while pouring a glass of the stuff, "You like Veuve Cliquot?"

weekly and decided to mentor him. Puffy dropped out of Howard, much to his mother's dismay, and "Andre became like my big brother. He bought a mansion, gave me a room—not a mansion, a big house."

Andre invited Puffy to live in his New Jersey home, which was replete with two BMWs and a swimming pool. Puffy's living arrangement with Harrell, similar to Harrell's own living arrangement with Simmons back in 1984, gave Puffy his own room, a pool to swim in, a salary, and endless networking opportunities at Harrell's industry parties.

Puffy also accompanied Harrell wherever he went, publicly supporting Uptown but striking some people as too competitive. When Harrell introduced him to Russell Simmons in a Brooklyn gym, Puffy bet Simmons he could outlast him on the StairMaster. When Simmons agreed to the bet, Puffy, who'd never been on a StairMaster before, spent a grueling ninety minutes on it. He won seven hundred dollars, which he used to have his car repaired.

When Kurt Woodley resigned from Uptown in 1991, Harrell tapped Puffy for the A & R position. As head of artists and repertoire, Puffy had to shape artists' careers, predict trends, discover new groups, and help everyone personally and professionally. At the time, Uptown's roster consisted of singer Christopher Williams, the groups For Sure and Key West, and rap acts Finesse & Synquis, white rapper Lucas, and Father MC. Heavy D was the label's only bona fide star.

Puffy began working with Father MC. Born Timothy Brown, Father had grown up in Brooklyn and Queens, drifted into rap at an early age, and won a 1985 talent contest at a local roller rink. By 1989, when Harrell signed him to Uptown, Father had a number of nonthreatening love raps written. In the studio, Puffy had the new group Jodeci sing on Father's "Treat Em Like They Want to Be Treated."

As with Heavy D, hip-hop fans viewed Father as corporate pap. For one, Father was a Big Daddy Kane clone right down to his name. His raps serenaded the ladies, during a time when hip-hop was in its black nationalist period. Eric B. and Rakim were promoting Islam on *Let the Rhythm Hit 'Em*. Kool G. Rap and DJ Polo warned about street life on *Wanted: Dead or Alive*. Brooklyn group X-Clan and Public Enemy encouraged political activism on *To the East Blackwards* and *Fear of a Black*

*Planet.* NWA and Ice Cube railed against brutal police on *100 Miles and Runnin'* and *AmeriKKKa's Most Wanted.*

Father, meanwhile, borrowed half of "Treat Em's" title from Slick Rick's classic "Treat Em Like a Prostitute," bit Kane's rap style, and dressed like Hammer in one video. In fact, Hammer's 1990 album, *Please Hammer Don't Hurt 'Em,* and record-breaking hit "U Can't Touch This" informed much of Puffy's work with Father.

Puffy was targeting the same audience that liked seeing Heavy D & The Boyz wear matching suits and dance to tame numbers like "We Got Our Own Thang." For "I'll Do 4 U," he put Father's love rap over Cheryl Lynn's familiar "Got to Be Real," had then new artist Mary J. Blige sing backup, and saw the single reach Number 20. Despite initial success, rap fans rejected *Father's Day,* disposable love songs "Lisa Baby" with Jodeci, and "Why U Wanna Hurt Me," and Father's Hammer-styled posturing.

Puffy signed producer Hitman Howie Tee's wife, Lady Kazan, discovered Dave Hollister (later of BLACKStreet) in Central Park, and prepared to work with Jodeci after Andre Harrell decided the group could use a bit of development.

He had his work cut out for him. Jodeci had a unique sound, but major labels had glutted the market with the glossy boy bands Color Me Badd, Milli Vanilli, and Motown's market leader, Boyz II Men. "They were like a piece of clay I thought I could help mold into something," Puffy said of Jodeci, "so I just decided to take the way I was seeing kids dressing in the streets."

Actually, he asked his then girlfriend, Misa Hylton, to think up a few ideas. Hylton, who hailed from Mount Vernon, would later make a name for herself by styling Lil' Kim. But at this point, styling artists were something new; she had only been doing it for two years, since leaving her 1989 internship at Def Jam. However, at seventeen years old, Misa had reached her own conclusions about how R & B artists should look. "At the time," she recalled, "R and B singers were really dressy." Misa told him to style Jodeci in baseball caps and jerseys, jewelry, leather outfits, and sunglasses. He added the bright-colored hair, the cell phones as fashion accessories, and the Harrell-like champagne-and-swimming-pool pose.

Many coworkers didn't understand the image, but Puffy urged them to have faith. Through his racially mixed "Daddy's House" parties, held every Wednesday night at the Red Zone nightclub for street kids and preppy students from Columbia University and New York University, he saw what fans were dancing to and wearing. He continued shaping Jodeci to fit his personal vision.

Until this point, the pop audience had revered their singing idols. After seeing Michael Jackson's regalia for *Thriller,* fans of both sexes had rushed to buy corny red leather jackets, hair gel, sunglasses, and glittering gloves. The same with Madonna: Teenage fans quickly copied her raunchy outfits and blunt makeup. With Jodeci, Puffy planned to turn the tables; the stars would now resemble the audience. In rap music, Run-D.M.C. had already shown the way. The Queens-based duo, which included Russell Simmons's brother, Joe, had shunned the leather outfits, thigh-high boots, spiked bracelets, and outlandish costumes that characterized old school rap. Instead, Run-D.M.C. won their devotees over by appearing on stage, in videos, and in photos in working-class gear: black jeans, black-hooded sweatshirts, *Godfather* hats, and Adidas footwear. Their working-class image aided in the downfall of the old school look and became the new embodiment of rap culture.

But in R & B some labels refused to relinquish the image of the slick-haired, champagne-swilling lover. R & B singers continued to dress in square-shouldered suits, holding flowers in one hand and a mike in the other. But Puffy knew that era had ended and that kids wanted something more in tune with their tastes and their world. Actually, a few of his coworkers felt Puffy was simply styling Jodeci to look exactly as he looked, but he ignored them.

Puffy succeeded in getting Jodeci out of cheap blazers and into the baggy jeans, boots, hooded sweatshirts, vests, and jewelry their target audience preferred.

Later, Puffy's approach would become standard operating procedure for boy bands 'N Sync and Backstreet Boys and soloists such as Sisqo. But in the early 1990s, the look he designed for Jodeci—bright orange hair, army fatigues—was nothing less than shocking. When their debut, *Forever My Lady,* was about to ship to stores, they no longer resembled gospel singers, R & B artists, or even a rap group. Puffy also asked them to build their mystique by posing for photos with their backs to the camera, which he borrowed from Guy's stage show.

His other marketing ideas were just as shocking. He assembled a team of twenty teens and asked them to spread the word about Jodeci, Mary J. Blige, and Christopher Williams. While most record labels felt standing in the middle of a nightclub and handing out stickers was enough, Puffy dispatched his new "street team" to housing projects. If his team appeared at a nightclub, it was to personally hand copies of a new song to a deejay, charge onto the dance floor, and dance as if Uptown's new song was the greatest hit ever recorded. "Supa" Mario Pizzini, a member of the team, told reporter Denene Millner: "We would just go out and make it seem like Uptown was putting out the dopest shit in the world." Soon, labels with bigger budgets would imitate this relatively simple concept; eventually, street teams would wander from label to label, indiscriminately promoting any album, whether it was good or bad. Still, Puffy originated the concept while at Uptown Records and sold a few more albums.

Thanks to him, Jodeci now had the right image. But while their album brimmed with sensitive themes and haunting melodies, Puffy felt they needed to move past the R & B market and into hip-hop, where young people bought millions of albums and viewed R & B musicians as "suckers." Musically, they had a way with words. But their music confused him, especially since they openly enjoyed beat-driven hard-core rap. Since Jodeci already had a producer, he would have to improve their sound through the format called the "remix." Before this time, the remix had been essentially reserved for dance music. In that genre, a remix producer typically would bring a copy of the original song into a studio, strip off every track but the vocal, then add his or her own elements and backing track.

Sometimes a remix could revive sales of an album; other times, it inspired listeners to scratch their heads in confusion. At worse, a remix went ignored and became a complete waste of time and money, since record companies charged them directly to an artist's royalty account.

For Puffy, the remix was a way in. He wanted to produce records but didn't know much about actually creating a song. At Daddy's House events he heard what contemporaries in hip-hop did with old break beats and decided that he could do the same, even though he couldn't play in-struments or program a "pattern" into a drum machine. At those parties he paid special attention to which songs made guests move and decided that "I would figure out a way to bring that record to life. Make it like it was some brand-new shit."

In short, he was about to try to outdo Teddy Riley, who had set new jack swing to bouncy rap-style shuffle beats. Puffy would have Jodeci vo-cals set to melodies already market-tested on hip-hop songs.

He was soon in the recording studio, replacing the drums and melodies from Jodeci's ballad "Come & Talk to Me." He added his favorite record of the time: EPMD's "You're a Customer," itself set to the obscure breakbeat "Five Minutes of Funk."

With the remix, Puffy learned that his idea of adding hip-hop samples to traditional R & B songs could move records from both genres higher on the *Billboard* pop chart. Thus a formula was born, and Puffy went from acquiescent team player to ambitious young executive who felt he under-stood the audience and could run Uptown better than Harrell did. He be-came increasingly vocal and assertive and, much like Harrell at Rush Management, dreamed of running his own company.

In addition to silencing his critics in the office, the Jodeci remix showed Harrell that the Father MC hit had not been a fluke. With Riley gone, Puffy could develop a sound that would make hip-hop more com-mercial, R & B tougher, and Uptown the market leader.


AT THE SAME TIME THAT HE WAS MAKING A NAME IN MUSIC, HE increased his visibility on the party circuit. By March 1991, Puffy and Jessica Rosenblum, who promoted events for the downtown nightclub Nell's, were drawing larger crowds at his weekly "Daddy's House" party. They moved the event from Wednesday to Thursday night and continued to attract over a thousand guests. In addition to street kids and college students, Puffy rubbed shoulders with Ice Cube and Doug E. Fresh, exec-utives such as Russell Simmons, and editors from the national rap maga-zine *The Source,* which had begun to promote him heavily. When fights broke out, Puffy would mount the stage with mike in hand and remind guests that police shut many clubs down because of violence. Already, the club's neighbors were complaining about the noise, and the NYPD was wary of large crowds attending rap-related events. Puffy, meanwhile, already was envisioning a larger event.

After "Magic" Johnson's revelation about having HIV, Puffy worked to arrange a basketball game featuring rap artists as a way to raise awareness of the AIDS crisis. Heavy D decided to help.

Puffy asked a woman named Tara Geter to ask City College of New York to host the game. She told him the gym was available if he gave the Evening Students Group (ESG) a check for $1,850 to cover the cost of the gym and add to their evening student scholarship fund.

On December 19, 1991, he gave her $850 as a deposit for the ESG. She handed the money to an ESG rep and signed a contract on Puffy's behalf that said he would give the student group $1,850 total, "provide a minimum of 20 celebrities," and cover the cost of insurance.

When Tara returned to Puffy's office at Uptown with the signed contract, he was on the telephone. She placed an envelope on his desk and left. He looked it over but didn't give it a detailed reading. This was why he never paid insurance to cover the event, he said.

Next, he asked a man named Louis Tucker to contact KISS-FM; Tucker received ad rates from an account executive. Puffy said they would buy ten commercials that would run from December twentieth to the twenty-eighth. He also gave KISS twenty free advance tickets and allowed the station to hang posters in the gym in exchange for eighteen thirty-second spots at no extra cost.

Next, he authorized the printing of two thousand advance-sale tickets, despite the fact that the gym could only hold 2,730 people. Multiple flyers were then printed. One called the event, "OUR FIRST ANNUAL CELEBRITY HOLIDAY BASKETBALL CLASSIC," and listed dozens of famous performers near the words "A Video Music Box Presentation."

Another promised that "Heavy D's team" of stars would play Puff's squad, which included Jodeci, Father MC, Mount Vernon group Brand Nubian, and Guy. Near the bottom of this flyer, a sentence claimed portions of the proceeds would be "Donated for AIDS Outreach Education Programs."

Before the game, Puffy asked Louis Tucker to arrange security. Puffy would bring seven guards, but wanted more to handle frisks and crowd control. Tucker ultimately called X-Men Security, a licensed firm run by corrections officer Anthony Richard, and Richard agreed to send fifteen to twenty men for fifteen hundred dollars. Tucker arranged for X-men to conduct frisks of the audience entering the building. On the eve of the game, Puffy and Heavy D traveled to KISS-FM to talk the game up on a daily countdown show.

At 2:00 P.M. the next day, three hours before the doors opened and four before the game was to begin, people began to arrive at the venue. At 3:00, Anthony Richard and his X-Men employees positioned wooden barricades to form a ticket line. By 3:45, Jessica Rosenblum had arrived to arrange for ticket distribution, sales, and collection. Puffy arrived within minutes, and two tables were set up in a lobby with two women at each. Rosenblum pulled out two rolls of numbered tickets and a clicker that would determine how many people arrived without an advance ticket and paid to enter.

By 4:00 P.M., fifteen hundred people were outside. An hour later, police arrived and watched people enter the building. In the lobby, after X-Men frisked them, unarmed guests approached the tables, bought their tickets, had their hands stamped, and walked down a flight of stairs. Entering a tiny vestibule, they saw four metal doors up ahead. To control the flow of the crowd, only one, on the far left, was open, and near it, one of Puffy's employees took tickets, checked hands for stamps, then let them in.

By 5:30, the crowd outside watched Puffy's assistants escort celebrities into the building and became anxious about getting into the show. The New York Police Department and X-Men cordoned off the front area, but within fifteen minutes the crowd had knocked barricades over and charged the door.

At a second entrance, the sight of people sneaking into the building drew complaints from ticket holders on line. As Puffy stood in the lobby with his cashiers, the crowd surged forward, shattering a glass door. It all went wrong from there. He asked police to clear the lobby, demanding that they use their bullhorns. Instead, the police and the X-Men tried to control the crowd by leading them from one entrance to another, or by trying to block the doors. But nothing worked. The crowd pushed forward, dragging several people—many of whom had passed out—

through the doors. When one guard leaned forward to help a woman who had fallen, the crowd knocked him down. After the crowd trampled him, it carried the guard toward the entrance, through a doorway, and into the lobby. By now the frenzied crowd had yanked the outer door off its hinges.

At 6:20, more cops arrived to clear the sidewalk in front of the gym and barricade doors. Within thirty minutes they seemed to have the crowd under control, but Puffy and Rosenblum decided to remove the money from the ticket tables.

Rosenblum lifted the two cashier trays filled with money and carried them downstairs to the gym. Puffy and other staff members stayed in the lobby collecting tickets. At the other entrance, on 138th Street, no one was at the tables. One person present remembered a crowd in the lobby and another facing the metal doors downstairs. At this point, every metal door was shut. Without warning, 150 people pushed into the lobby behind him, threw him up against a wall, then ran down the stairs and into the people waiting in front of the doors.

The crowd pushed forward, crushing people directly into doors. Inside the gym a table had been wedged "as leverage to force the door closed," Judge Louis Benza would later report. Even worse, a heavy man stood on the table to keep it from budging. The crowd kept shoving and "people were banging on the doors, yelling and screaming for someone to open the doors, but to no avail," said another ticket holder.

Eventually, someone inside opened a door and began to pull bodies into the gym, already 75 percent filled. On stage, Doug E. Fresh asked the crowd to clear the area in front of the doors, to use their cell phones to call for ambulances, to use CPR and help the injured. The first call to 911, at 7:04, found a man frantically reporting that "people are dying inside of City College."

Some guests tried to perform CPR on victims lying on the floor immediately inside the doorway. At 7:28 P.M., EMS ambulance workers arrived and tried to revive victims. People were grabbing them and asking them to attend to relatives and friends. Twenty-one other ambulances arrived, and by 7:55 P.M. victims were being transported to the hospital. Within a minute, however, EMS workers pronounced six people dead. In area hospitals, doctors pronounced two more people dead. A ninth victim was stabilized on life support but pronounced dead on January 1, 1992. The cause of death for each was asphyxia due to compression of the chest.

Puffy would claim that "after the frenzy, I looked up and everybody was gone." He would say that he didn't leave the gym because he didn't do anything wrong. "I knew I would have to explain what was going on and what happened. I was there with nine bodies on the ground. Nobody else was there. No police, nobody. Just me and nine bodies."

Police Officer Sean Harris told a different story. After climbing a banister and reaching the crowded space at the bottom of the stairs, he had to push the table aside and open the door to the gym. "After falling through the door [and] into the gym," Benza continued, "[Harris] saw Combs standing there with two women, and all three had money in their hands."

WHEN HARRELL LEARNED ABOUT THE TRAGEDY, HE GOT HIGH-profile lawyers William Kunstler and Michael Warren on the telephone for Puffy. The story was all over the local media, and published reports claimed that promoters had sold five thousand tickets although the gym could only hold 2,730 people.

Puffy didn't get much sleep that weekend. Dream Hampton remembered that he and Heavy spent much of this time crying, pacing, or speaking on the telephone. They called lawyers, took calls from their friends, or called the families of the victims after locating telephone numbers. Puffy's girlfriend, Misa Hylton, was with him, though one of her friends had died at the event and her friend's mother was grieving. Puffy claimed he was getting closer to God. "When I was in my crib losin' weight and cryin', feelin' sorry, and thinkin' everybody was against me, and sayin' I didn't do nothin' wrong, I started talkin' to Him," he said. "And I started getting to know Him better." While his faith in God might be sincere—he was an altar boy in high school—Puffy soon would develop a pattern of reacting to negative headlines by hiring powerful lawyers, and invoking religion.

By Monday morning, December 30, 1991, he was sitting in the conference room at Uptown with Andre Harrell, Heavy D, and his lawyer

Michael Warren. They were going over a statement he would give to reporters. Later he would tell a supportive journalist, "Nobody can know what I went through. Everybody was saying, 'Did he oversell the tickets? Did he kill those kids?' The world turned against me."

Eventually he did what he had to do. He sat at the conference table, faced a stack of index cards, and tried to memorize the speech he had written. He had to sound sincere. Harrell and the lawyers were there to edit the statement. He began to read aloud: "It has always been my dream to throw parties where young black people—"

Andre cut in. The word "dream" was pretentious.

Michael Warren agreed.

"But I would say that," Puffy snapped. "Wouldn't I say that?"

By the time the meeting had ended, Harrell told him that he should stay away from the office until things died down. Puffy began to feel that even his friends were shying away from him, that only his immediate family and Misa were on his side. "It was too much for me to handle," he later said. "After the incident, it was like I was crazy, losing my mind . . . thinking about the people who died, thinking about the families, thinking about their pain. For a while I was probably clinically insane."

He made it to that afternoon's press conference at the St. Regis hotel and provided the *New York Post* with ammunition for the next morning's story—the *Post* blamed the deaths on a "FOOL NAMED PUFF DADDY."

Though it was Misa's birthday, and her friend's death had depressed her, he was obsessed with what the tragedy could mean for his name. He dragged Misa down to *The Source,* where editors were writing a story about the event, and hid in the hallway until a friend, *Source* employee Dream Hampton, appeared. Hampton was a talented writer whose alleged antics included dating Heavy D.

During their conversation, she later wrote, Puffy mentioned suicide and death threats from people claiming to be related to the victims, then opened his black coat and said, "But I feel protected by God. See, I don't have anything on me, no guns, vests. If they kill me, they kill me. It's meant for me to die."

Eventually, the mainstream media began to research the AIDS Education Outreach Program listed on Puffy's flyer and found that no AIDS service organization had ever heard of it. It wasn't a registered charity, every state and city agency reported. Some reporters claimed the charity worked with the city's health department, despite the fact that the health department could not accept charitable funds.

When Deputy Mayor Milton Mollen reported on the tragedy, he revealed that Puffy and other promoters—including Heavy D—hadn't set any of the proceeds aside for any specific charity. The city wanted to learn more about the ticket sales, but the money was missing. On December 30, 1991, attorney Martin Garbus wrote Mayor David Dinkins to say he was representing Puffy, who would cooperate with the investigation, but the money was still missing.

Deputy Mayor Mollen called Garbus the next morning to ask about the estimated twenty-five thousand dollars the party had pulled in. Garbus said Puffy had given him permission to turn the money over to the city, and sent Mollen a check for $24,581 the next day.

The CCNY tragedy would haunt Puffy for years to come. He would defend his actions that night by saying that he had entered the gym that night to help others get in as well. It was impossible to let people in, he'd explain, because the metal doors opened out into the crowded hall, and out there the crowd was slamming into the doors. In 1998, Judge Benza decided that Puffy was lying. Puffy's guards knew there was a crowd in the tiny seven-by-twelve-foot space outside and purposefully shut the only door that could have allowed them into the gym, Benza wrote. By doing this, they created a barrier that forced people to crush into each other and squash the life from young bodies. Police officer Sean Harris's statement, Benza felt, "places a strain on the credibility of Combs' testimony that he was caught up in the melee and attempted to help the people who were trapped in the stairwell."

# TWO

# Gimme the Loot

NEGATIVE HEADLINES DID NOT KEEP PUFFY DOWN FOR LONG. HE returned to Uptown Records in 1992 with a new attitude and image. With Misa's help, he moved past caring what anyone thought of him following the CCNY event. Lucky for him, other atrocities displaced the story from the front page. When he returned to Uptown it was to get back to work, and Harrell, impressed by the Jodeci remix, gave him more and more responsibility at A & R.

Another thing that had changed was his interest in jewelry. He bought a chain and a golden medallion and told people the medallion—shaped like a man's head and filled with diamonds—was Lazarus, another man who'd died and been reborn.

He also developed his first entourage in the music industry. Some coworkers felt these characters—some of whom carried guns—were around to give him credibility in hip-hop circles, but he didn't care which way the gossip ran. According to Russell Simmons: "He was a young kid. He needed management. Andre would be, like, 'Yo Puff, you can't beat up people and do this and do that!' Andre stood by Puffy through a lot of shit."

The payoff was the success he had with Father MC and Jodeci. In fact, Puffy was becoming one of the "ghetto fabulous" people his mentor wanted to target. With his promotion to head of A & R had come a white BMW and fancy rims. He became more flamboyant, dying his hair first a honey blond shade, then platinum, and wearing his sweatpants with one leg rolled up to the knee. One person claimed that he stood in the hallway outside of the office without a shirt telling people, "Puff Daddy is my name as an artist, Sean Combs is my name for the movies."

He continued to live in Andre's house in New Jersey and to watch Andre live in style. At first, he was low-key at the lavish parties Andre threw. Eventually, while Veronica Webb swam in the pool and Andre ate ribs and held court, Puffy would dart from guest to guest like a traveling salesman, trying to cultivate friendships. After telling some guests about his future company, Bad Boy, his version of Uptown, he'd open his suitcase and pull out a logo he designed, an infant in a baseball cap, brim tipped rebelliously to the side.

At Uptown, his next project was Mary J. Blige. In her earliest days on the roster she had provided a chorus for Father MC's "I'll Do 4 U." Since then she had not been doing much. Blige, born January 11, 1971, was raised in a Yonkers housing project by her mother, who worked as a nurse and exposed Mary and her sister to records by Otis Redding, Gladys Knight, Al Green, and Donny Hathaway. Mary sang in a church choir and during school talent shows but never thought a record label would sign a girl from a suburban housing project. During a trip to the Galleria Mall in White Plains, New York, friends encouraged her to enter a karaoke booth. She recorded a rendition of Anita Baker's "Caught Up in the Rapture" so stirring that her stepfather passed it to MCA executive Jeff Redd. "Well, the next thing I know, Jeff and some other people spoke to Andre Harrell and there was a lot of hype about it," Mary said. "They made me real excited." Puffy heard the tape and urged Harrell to move quickly. Harrell called Mary to say he and Puffy were coming by her house to hear her sing live.

Puffy saw his ideal of music and image personified in seventeen-year-old Blige—even more so than in Jodeci. Her exposure to classic soul and hip-hop resulted in an extraordinary style and lyrics that addressed topics like domestic abuse and teen pregnancy.

By 1992, Puffy was part of an office clique led by Heavy's deejay, Eddie F, and unofficially dubbed the Untouchables. Initially this loose association consisted of F, newcomer Pete Rock, and Nevell Hodge. Then it grew to include producer Dave Hall, Kenny Smoove, Kenny Green, and Jodeci. Eddie now inducted Puffy and Mary. Thus, when Puffy spent eighteen months working on Mary's music, Eddie F let him move into his home and use his studio. "That's when all the Mary J. stuff came together with Dave Hall and Kenny Green," Eddie remembered.

To Mary the album would be a way to pay tribute to classic soul, but Puffy had other ideas. To him, her music would highlight hip-hop sounds and bring an R & B artist even closer to the audience buying millions of hard-core rap albums.

Ultimately he asked her to embrace a tough working-class culture that had given her nothing but hell, heartache, and a scar under her left eye.

Her first recording, a cover of Patrice Rushen's "You Remind Me" included on the soundtrack of the movie *Strictly Business,* topped the R & B chart and reached Number 29 on the pop chart, confirming for Puffy that they were on the right track.

He invited Brand Nubian's Grand Puba, Busta Rhymes from Leaders of the New School, old school pioneers Kool DJ Red Alert and Clark Kent, and new rappers Little Shawn and CL Smooth into the studio to perform on her songs. Devante Swing of Jodeci played instruments while K-Ci provided harmony. L.A. Reid, who would soon play an important part in Puffy's life, added keyboards and vocals.

The first single from her album, "Real Love," paved the way. Set to an entire drum pattern from The Audio 2's hit "Top Billin'," it topped the R & B chart and soared to Number 7 on the pop chart. While she was outwardly willing to go along with Uptown's plans, privately Mary viewed the new image with disdain. She just wasn't into promoting this "ghetto fabulous" image. She later said, "I'm from the element of the streets that says that once you've made it, it's yours. But keep it to yourself."

For her cover shot she wore a pleated tennis skirt with Doc Marten boots. On the sidelines, Puffy repeatedly told her to "feel it." Instead, she had a stylist fetch a baseball hat from a rack, pulled it low over her eyes, and gave the camera a squinty-eyed stare. Even so, the image—boots, hockey jerseys, blonde hair, and bandannas—appealed to hip-hop fans.

Her album *What's The 411,* released on July 28, 1992, quickly sold two million copies and ranked at Number 30 on the *Village Voice*'s list of the forty best albums of the year. *Entertainment Weekly* wrote that her powerful voice "conquers everything she tackles," then called her "a new-Jill comer with her eyes on the prize."

Another critic felt "Blige is Aretha's heir apparent." Kierna Mayo of *The Source,* impressed by Mary's cover of "You Remind Me," wrote, with uncanny foresight, "She, without a doubt, will become to us what Aretha and Gladys Knight are to our mothers."

*What's The 411* succeeded on every level possible. Mary paid tribute to the oldies she had enjoyed during her girlhood, including Chaka Khan's "Sweet Thing," and became one of 1992's biggest natural crossover acts. After fusing R & B to hip-hop, Puffy saw an R & B album reach Number 6 on the pop chart.[1] Harrell profited even further from best-selling singles such as "Reminisce," shipped a million copies of her debut to record stores, and ultimately sold twice that amount.

Mary eventually decided she deserved better pay. Away from Uptown she faced jealous neighbors in her housing project. If she held her head up and felt pride in her accomplishments, they immediately crowed that this "star" didn't even have enough money to move from the projects. They didn't "understand how you can record and be on the radio but still live in the ghetto," she said later. "I had to keep fighting all the time." Her need for more money would soon cause problems for Puffy.

AS 1992 CONTINUED, PUFFY TIRED OF HAVING A MENTOR: "WHAT started to happen is, I started to have other dreams. At the same time, Uptown was growing and getting bigger, and Andre was having to deal with corporate concerns."

He was tired of waiting for Andre to help launch Bad Boy. He believed his projects were responsible for Uptown's success. In fact, his approach, fusing R & B melodies to rugged hip-hop beats, had energized both genres and gotten rap records into higher positions on the *Billboard* charts. Similarly, his approach also benefited R & B artists. The media

---

1.  Reaching the pop chart was important because it meant a white audience was buying your work. More money was coming in.

promoted some horrible singers as part of the Puffy-hyped "hip-hop soul" trend.

As a mentor, Harrell had protected, guided, taught, tested, and trained Puffy. He also had provided many gifts: a place to live, a base of operations, introductions to industry leaders, and the opportunity to make a name for himself through music production. Though Andre had a big ego and was very flamboyant, his example had taught Puffy how to get people on the telephone, set up meetings, and secure the best product for the right price. Still, Puffy needed Andre to do more than *talk* about Bad Boy.

Whenever they discussed Bad Boy, Andre seemed to be in his corner. He helped define a business plan and seemed enthusiastic about hosting the imprint, especially since Uptown would receive a chunk of the profits.

Puffy would do his part. He had a photographer snap a photo of his godson in huge Doc Marten boots with one hand holding his privates and the other pointing skyward. He then turned the photo into postcards that bore the phrase "THE NEXT GENERATION OF BAD MOTHAFUCKAS" and ordered his street team marketers to dole them out at hip-hop events.

However, summer turned to autumn and autumn to winter and Puffy realized that not much had happened with Bad Boy since their discussions. Finally, in December 1992, Andre rectified the situation.

He promoted Puffy to vice president of A & R, making him one of the youngest people to ever hold this position in the industry, then announced that Uptown would host Puffy's new management, record, and production company. Said one coworker: "Puffy went from being an intern to being our boss."

Flush with success, he said, "I'm gonna be right, I'm gonna be loyal, and we'll try to continue the legacy of Uptown." Publicly, Harrell was just as happy. He told reporters he gave Puffy his own company because of his success with Mary and Jodeci. Privately, however, Harrell had different reasons for finally pushing forward with Bad Boy.

"I think at times I was hard to work with," Puffy told *Rolling Stone* in 1995. "Possibly I was doin' shit that an asshole would do, just abusing the power. But that was only a little bit of the time."

Even so, Puffy faced accusations of trying to work his way into artists' songwriting credits. By having his name in credits, he would accomplish two things: He would be entitled to a portion of the publishing rights and money, and have impressive credits to show future employers if he ever left Harrell's enterprise. He got away with it, an MCA employee told *Vanity Fair* reporter Steven Daly, because "there were enough kids that would keep quiet about it because they needed the money." While everyone at Uptown knew, few dared speak out against Harrell's favorite.

Next he reportedly demanded to have his name appear wherever Harrell had his listed, and developed a reputation for being a tyrant in the studio. A tape made the rounds in which studio engineers were heard saying, "Keep Puffy away from the board!"

He also reportedly booked expensive studio time and then didn't show up, or arrived hours late, despite the fact that Harrell had to pay for every second of a recording session. If anything exacerbated tensions between him and Harrell it was his allegedly casual attitude toward money. The bills he ran up attracted the attention of MCA executives, and Harrell's parent company asked him to account for some of these expenditures. Harrell didn't like it. Later, Puffy's business lawyer, Kenny Meiselas, who took him on in 1992, tried to minimize the situation by claiming both Uptown and MCA signed off on Puffy's various budgets.

Even so, the situation was serious enough to merit MCA arranging a meeting with Harrell. As Harrell tells it, he felt the need to create a solution that kept Puffy's moneymaking ability tied to Uptown but distanced Harrell from his budgets. This was why he gave him his own company, Bad Boy, Harrell said later, to "satellite Puff out."

PUFFY'S NEXT MOVE WAS TO CALL MATTY C, WHO REVIEWED reader-submitted demo tapes in *The Source*'s "Unsigned Hype" column. Matty, who went on to become a successful A & R person, described a tape by new artist Biggie Smalls that was passed to him by Mister Cee, a deejay for Big Daddy Kane. "At that time, I used to go by Mr. Cee's crib to check him out," said producer Easy Mo Bee. "And he would always holler about Biggie Smalls and Outloud, who became the group Blahzay Blahzay. He'd play me these cats and tell me, 'These niggas got some shit.' "

As Biggie remembered it, "The demo was basically freestyle lyrics. Fifty, sixty bars of just straight rhyming over 'Blind Alley,' EPMD instrumentals, and shit like that. Just showing niggas I had skills." *The Source* planned to include Biggie on a compilation album with Mobb Deep and Common Sense.[2]

Once Puffy received Biggie's tape, he couldn't stop playing it. Biggie's lyrics were smooth enough for program directors at radio stations and aggressive enough for *Source* readers. "Biggie was somebody who came into my life right on time," he said later. "When I met him, I had this dream of a company, and all he wanted to do was be a rapper. I thanked God, not because he sent me a dope rapper, but because he sent me somebody who cared for me. I needed that."

Signing him to Uptown, which specialized in peaceful rap such as Heavy D or Father MC, was an uphill battle, but ultimately, Puffy laid the facts out plainly: If Harrell didn't sign Biggie, then another label would. Harrell, an R & B man at heart, trusted Puffy's instincts. Now Puffy had to find the guy.

He called people he knew in Brooklyn, and then traveled out there to conduct his search. Once they connected, he took the six-foot-three, over-three-hundred-pound rapper to lunch. As he described his plans for Bad Boy, Biggie hung on every word: "I had just got finished working on Jodeci and Mary J. Blige and Father MC and Heavy D, so I was kind of known a little bit." By the time a waiter brought the check, Biggie had verbally committed to signing with Uptown.

Before this agreement, Christopher Wallace didn't have as much to offer the world as he might have thought. Like Puffy, he grew up without a father. His mother, Voletta, a devout Jehovah's Witness, attended night school and worked two jobs to pay for their apartment in a drug-infested section of Brooklyn. In third grade Big had shown an interest in art, and, like Puffy, had attended Catholic school. After being enrolled at age six, he spent nine years excelling in math, English, and science. Then he fell in with a group that sold drugs and spent three years trying to hide this from his mother. If he wanted to wear clothes purchased with drug

---

2.    Instead, Mobb Deep signed to Island and Common signed to Relativity.

money, he'd "leave for school in the busted shit my moms gave me and change my whole outfit on the roof." Voletta eventually discovered what he was doing and, he later said, told him that no drug dealer would live under her roof.

Before signing with Uptown Biggie had spent his days watching television in his yellow-walled bedroom, smoking marijuana with his buddies in front of his building, or selling crack on the corner. Biggie coldly sold drugs to his neighbors but also rapped his sidekick, James "Lil' Cease" Lloyd, on the head if he skipped school. After lecturing him about the importance of an education, he'd send Cease to the store for cigars, which he'd reroll with marijuana and smoke as a "blunt."

One night, playing with a gun at home, he blasted the closet door. When his friends Damien and Gutter dropped by to visit him, Voletta lectured both about bringing guns into her home. Biggie blamed them for the hole in the door, appearing behind her to add, "I told him, Ma!"

Other times he'd upset his mother by performing lyrics. For a beat, he'd bang his fist on the wall. She'd complain about the noise and he'd say this noise would someday make them rich. Away from her, he perfected his music in a neighbor's house, rapping over Chic's disco record "Good Times." One witness said, "Every rap ended with him making it big, having money and success and going away from here."

The relationship with his mother continued to sour. "He was just not the son I wanted," she said. "When he quit school I wanted to kill him."

Then he further upset her. He planned to continue to sell drugs to earn enough money to invest in a legitimate business, but police arrested him in 1989 for carrying an unlicensed gun. Since he was seventeen, with no prior arrest record, a lenient judge gave him probation. But Biggie went back to hustling, and his mother often would see him dealing on the corner when she left the house for work. Within a year, police arrested him again for a probation violation.

The real tragedy happened in 1991, when he moved to North Carolina to sell drugs and the police arrested him. For nine months, he didn't call her. He was facing five to fifteen years. Finally, he asked her to pay his bail. To do this, she had to use the nest egg she had been saving for his future. It came from an accident Biggie had as a toddler: He had broken his foot while leaving a city bus, and New York City settled with her for ninety thousand dollars. When he returned to New York at age eighteen, she told him, "If you can't live by my rules, you can't live under my roof." He didn't listen. He kept selling drugs, impregnated a neighborhood girl named Jan, and refused to get his diploma or go to college.

He began to aspire to a career in rap. According to Lil' Cease: "He never told nobody, and one day he just let it out." Many of his friends were in a basement, cracking jokes, smoking marijuana, drinking, and listening to DJ Fifty-Grand play records. Biggie stood up from his seat, plugged a microphone into the mixer, and started to rap. His friends were shocked. When they sold drugs all night, he'd now entertain them by rapping over beats from a nearby radio. His friends told him to pursue a record deal, but he'd say, "I don't have time to be going to nobody's label, standing in the hallway trying to get them to hear me." Yet he recorded the demo that led to the meeting with Puffy and a record deal.

When he told his mother about Puffy, she wasn't impressed. She wanted him to "excel academically." He told her Puffy said he'd make him a millionaire at age twenty. She resented Puffy even more. But despite her protests, Biggie said he was going to sign with Uptown.

"For what?" she asked.

To earn money and make something of himself. He wouldn't be a doctor or lawyer but would make an honest living. "I don't have to go to college to do that," he said. "I can do my music and be successful. This is the life I choose; this is what I want, Mama."

She said, Fine.

Puffy signed Biggie to Uptown, paid him a modest advance, and searched for opportunities in which to present his new signing.

Puffy later would claim he told Biggie to stop selling drugs and consider himself an artist, and that he tried to teach Biggie the rudiments of business. To Biggie, he added, this last part was especially important. This was why, when he accompanied Jodeci to a concert in Washington, D.C., Puffy brought Biggie with him.

During the trip Puffy joined Jodeci member Mr. Dalvin, Biggie, and Chuck Bone, Puffy's childhood friend, Uptown's national director of rap promotions, and Biggie's manager on a trip to a local mall. A female Jodeci fan spotted them and a crowd formed. The group ducked into a clothing store, but security guards entered, and one of them said, "Listen, we got to get y'all out of here. You got about a thousand girls out there waiting for you to come out." Biggie couldn't wait for this to happen to him.

Music was his path out of the ghetto, and even when he wasn't recording, Biggie stayed close to the industry. He became a fixture in Uptown's office, which Chuck Bone described as "ghetto to the utmost." Puffy would watch as Biggie arrived during lunch hour to draw employees into games of chance. During these games Puffy saw that Biggie's determination to earn a buck equaled his own. "Biggie didn't really have money," he said later. "And you can't really gamble with somebody who don't have money, 'cause they want to win more than you do. He'd come to the office with like two thousand dollars and wind up leaving with a couple thousand [in winnings]."

A frequent loser in these games was Father MC. According to Bone, "No matter what happened, Father MC would lose, 'cause he didn't know Biggie gave him loaded dice. He got Father MC for at least ten or fifteen thousand dollars over the years."

Since he was already in the city, Biggie also would visit friends like Bonz (pronounced "Bones") Malone. "He came up to Island Records [my base of operations at the time] with ten bags of cheeba and a bottle of Alize," Malone wrote. "We rolled dice on the roof for an hour and a half; not for money, for push-ups."

From time to time, Biggie also stopped by deejay Clark Kent's house. Kent, who had been involved with hip-hop since before there were records, had produced a number of artists, including Dana Dane, or toured as their deejay. By the early 1990s he was making inroads as a producer. When Biggie visited, he would type lyrics into Kent's computer, such as "How We Roll," or record vocals over tracks created by Kent or EPMD member Erick Sermon, whose use of funk sounds had inspired Dr. Dre.

Though most associates remember Biggie as someone who loved to tell jokes, Puffy claimed he was a close-mouthed person who entered a room and stood in a corner—a timid and bashful wallflower. Puffy also would claim Biggie's shyness stemmed from him not wanting his "street side" to frighten executives, and that he had to frequently draw Biggie into conversation.

The whole time Puffy was preparing to record his music. He called Rush Producers Management, the division of Def Jam that managed some of the same producers who created Def Jam songs. He told Francesca Spero that he was seeking producers. Spero assembled tapes from various producers, including Easy Mo Bee, who had started his career with Big Daddy Kane in 1989, producing "Calling Mr. Welfare," and who had won a Grammy a year later for his work with Miles Davis.

Puffy told Mo Bee to drop by Uptown's offices at 1775 Broadway. "So I went up there to the meeting," said Mo Bee. "He had this little office. We sat, we talked, played the beats, and then we ended up doing the tracks for Biggie. I'll never forget that Puffy went back to Fran and said, 'Thank you so much for hooking me up with Mo Bee. I didn't know he was that dope or he had that much to give.' From that point on, I just did as much as I could with Biggie." In fact, Mo's six contributions to Biggie's debut—"Warning," "Gimme the Loot," "Friend of Mine," "The What," "Ready to Die" and "Machine Gun Funk"—would establish Biggie as rap's most popular draw.

Puffy wanted Mo Bee to produce a song he had arranged for Biggie to contribute to the soundtrack for the film *Who's the Man.* He booked time at Soundtrack Studios, and Mo arrived and saw Biggie on a couch in Studio F, the biggest room. His old drug-dealing crew, some of whom were forming a rap group called Junior M.A.F.I.A., was also there. Mo went to a tape recorder and played a few beats. During one track Biggie sat up on the couch. "Yo, I like that," he said in his deep voice. "Mo, I feel that. I wanna use that shit right there."

"What Big wanted Puff wanted, so he agreed," Mo explained.

"My instructions were to track the track and put it to tape. After the track was done, a producer could still sit at the board and watch the booth through the glass—watch the MC do his lyrics—and help coach them. Or if they had a manager, a 'man' that be with them in their clique or a person who's his most personal supporter, they'd come up to the board with you. You'd sit there just watching everything, but they'd be the one giving the real vocal or moral support. That's what Puffy used to do."

If Biggie delivered a low-grade vocal, Puffy would say, "Yo, bring it back. I don't like that line. Do that shit over."

As this first session continued, Mo played a tape of The Last Poets's

"Niggas Are Scared of Revolution." Biggie heard its closing moments, a chant that accuses black people of wanting to do nothing but "party and bullshit," and yelled, "Yo, *put* that shit in there! We'll make some jumping *party shit* offa that!"


BIGGIE'S SINGLE BEGAN WITH MEMORABLE AUTOBIOGRAPHY. "I was a terror since the public school era," he rapped. "Bathroom passes, cutting classes, squeezing asses." He told the listener that he smoked every day. Since thirteen, he had been "a chubby nigga on the scene." He used to have a handgun in his jacket but now carried a Mac-10 in his knapsack. He asked a woman, "Where the party at?" Could he bring his gun?

He described a party. Women hugged him and neighborhood thugs shook his hand. He saw an old friend from the projects. The friend asked if Biggie had a gun he could borrow. Biggie had two .22s in his shoes. He went to drink champagne. "Ain't no stopping Big Poppa, I'm a Bad Boy," he said.

As the song continued, he described dancing with a sexy woman. His friend Big Jacque had a gun in his waistband. Biggie wanted to take this girl home, but a fight broke out. At this point on the record, Puffy stopped the music. Listeners heard what sounded like a fistfight, then Biggie yelling, "Yo, chill, man, chill!" When he rapped again, it was to say he had left the party with his girl. Then the "Party and Bullshit" chant came in, and he gave shout-outs to Junior M.A.F.I.A., Uptown, Bad Boy, "Brooklyn Crew," and Third Eye.

After Puffy edited out Biggie's obscenities, "Party and Bullshit" became a hit on radio stations and in nightclubs. That it sold a half million copies amazed Biggie. That famed rappers approached him to shake his hand and offer flattery in nightclubs was staggering.

He continued to record his album, and in 1993 became inspired by the work of Death Row Records performers Snoop Doggy Dogg and house producer and rapper Dr. Dre. The year before, Dre's landmark *The Chronic* had been the biggest rap hit, and Snoop's *Doggystyle* was more of the same. "Yo, these guys," Biggie told his friend Damien. "This is hot! These guys are competition. I like how they coming off and doing their thing."

In the studio, this translated into Biggie recording useable vocals in one take. "In the beginning, he was on fire," Mo recalled. "I used to watch them do things like 'Gimme the Loot.' At this point, Puffy was overseeing what he thought would be Biggie's debut album on Uptown. "Biggie would just go in there and just bust it," Mo said. "He'd finish and walk out and tell someone, 'Light up one of them things, man.' He'd get it right in just one lick."

Before recording the song "Warning," Mo played more tracks, including one created for Big Daddy Kane. "Kane was into Barry White and Isaac Hayes, and that was an Isaac Hayes sample." While creating the track, Mo was thinking, "This would *really* bring Kane out." In the studio, Biggie's vocals were even more climactic.

Puffy, meanwhile, was working with Craig Mack, a former roadie for the group EPMD who had handled baggage during their 1992 tour. "I used to rhyme in the hotels, battling other kids that wanted to see [EPMD rappers] Erick and Parrish." After the tour, he tried to land a deal of his own.

One night in 1993, Puffy saw Craig in a Manhattan nightclub. "We went outside in the back of an alley, up against an old garbage can, and he asked me to bust a freestyle for him," Craig recalled. "I did, and he thought it was the illest he ever heard. He was, like, 'Come down to the office the next morning.' I went down, talked, and he wanted to sign me. But he was getting ready to leave Uptown. So he said, 'You can get a deal with Uptown or come with me. I'm about to start a new label. I'm talking to distributors now. There are no guarantees, but if we do it it's gonna be the dopest thing ever.' "

Craig said, "Without a doubt! You the one that picked me up and said I was dope, so I'm rolling with you."

Next, Puffy went to Mo Bee and said, "I got my artist Craig Mack."

"That's exactly what he used to call him," Mo explained. "He said, 'My artist. My artist Craig Mack.' " Puffy wanted Mo to create a first single for him.

At home, Mo faced his equipment and contrived a melody. "It's just a guitar flooded with mad reverb, and the reverb was already on the record," he revealed. "I took the stab and pitched it high and low." Next, he set the melody to "drums that have been in front of our faces for years.

I took the drums and just chopped them up. Broke it down to a kick, snare, and high-hat." Mo included the track on a tape for Mack.

Together they selected which numbers would appear on his first album. His first session at the prestigious Hit Factory studio on Fifty-fourth Street was for a song called "Flava in Ya Ear." Mo explained, "Craig did one vocal he didn't like." Puffy listened to it, then cut it off. "Nah" was his verdict.

Puffy had to step out for a minute. "Craig keep working on the vocals," he said.

"By the time Puff came back, Craig had done the vocals," Mo said. "They were banging and everything. Puff came back in and was, like, [impressed] 'Yo!'" But he rushed over to the board. "Turn some of this shit right here up more," he said. "Turn more, turn this." This was part of his creative process: adjusting sound levels and lowering the beat to emphasize certain lyrics for dramatic effect.

"Anything that says Easy Mo Bee on it was definitely produced by Easy Mo Bee," Mo says. "But I'm not afraid to say Puffy would have come to the board, which is where he lived whether you were the producer or not. He lived there. That was his home. Regardless of you being the producer, no matter what, he was always good for saying, 'Why don't you turn this up more? On the other hand, why don't you give this more level?' He had good mixing ideas."

He also knew how to juggle multiple tasks. Puffy was aware of Biggie's need for money. He also wanted to get Bad Boy beyond the verbal stage and into existence. He handled the two problems, and a third—positioning Mary J. Blige further into the hip-hop market—with a second Mary J. Blige project. Whether Uptown issued an album of remixed versions to sell the same music to the audience—without paying as much for talent—or to maintain her presence in record stores is unknown. What's clear is that Puffy used the occasion to highlight his artists and his Bad Boy concept, and to promote himself on her songs.

After introducing "Real Love," urging the producer to "Take 'em uptown to the Polo Ground," he featured Mary's verse, followed by Biggie's rap. "Look up in the sky, it's a bird, it's a plane," it began. "Nope, it's Mary Jane, ain't a damn thing changed." The rest of the verse found him saying he was "Teflon Don," flattering Mary, then referring to Brooklyn and his friend, producer Daddy-O. The remix of her title track, however, showed that he was far from another fat jolly rapper in the Heavy D mold.

On this one, Puffy again opened the song. "Check it, yeah, mutha-fuckas," he said. "What we about to do right about now, we gonna get kind of funky. I am the Puff Daddy and rolling with my man Biggie Smalls, Mary J. Blige, and K-Ci from Jodeci, and we about to do some-thing new." Biggie then rapped about smoking marijuana and drinking beer and screwing Patti LaBelle, Regina Belle, Jasmine Guy, and Mariah Carey, having a crush on Mary since "Real Love," and threatening to show her he was "the boss of intercourse." The song ended with Puffy saying, "Yeah, it's a Bad Boy thing." That the album received unenthusi-astic reviews and only its cover of "Sweet Thing" reached the pop singles chart to peak at Number 28 didn't matter. Puffy had taken the first step in introducing the world to the sound they'd hear once Uptown shipped completed Bad Boy albums to record stores. Between appearances, Big-gie would go through his money quickly, then discuss his drug-dealer days in nostalgic tones. He'd tell anyone who'd listen that making records didn't pay anywhere near as well as his former vocation. Puffy, having to keep seeking remix projects, managed to arrange for Biggie to appear on a remix of reggae artist Supercat's "Dolly My Baby," a recording that served as another commercial for his nascent company.

On this song Puffy rapped with Biggie and Uptown artist Third Eye, who allegedly coined the term "bling bling"[3] back in 1993. During Eye's Heavy D–styled verse, he mentioned, "It's a Bad Boy thing, ninety-three, we coming through." Within seconds, Puffy rapped that he was "on your radio, it's the Bad Boy, look!" Biggie used the occasion to introduce his trademark phrase, "I love it when you call me Big Poppa," then wrapped things up with another blurb for the upcoming company, "Yes, it's Bad Boy." To top it off, Puffy then chanted the words "I'm a Bad Boy" until fade out.

Before long, Heavy D asked Puffy to produce songs for his next album, *Blue Funk,* a departure from his neighborly pop style. He agreed, but under one condition—Heavy had to include Biggie beside Gang Starr and Busta Rhymes on his song "A Bunch of Niggas." Heavy approved,

---

3. "Bling bling" refers to the shine caused by platinum, diamond-covered jewelry.

Puffy helped with Heavy's album, and subsequently Biggie earned more money and prominence.

Biggie's appearances ultimately proved too radical a departure from Uptown's house sound: MCA took exception to some of Smalls's raunchy lyrics and Harrell felt he was dragged into yet another imbroglio not of his making.

Uptown's employees chose sides. Some defended Harrell and his vision and understood that it was his company. Others felt Puffy had a better sense of the market. "It became a situation where it was two kings in one castle," Puffy said later, "and it was his castle, so I found myself in the moat."

By July 1993, after a meeting with a general manager from MCA, Harrell decided to fire Puffy. While he may have valued his artistic decisions, he also had to maintain sociable relations with his parent company. Exactly how he reached his decision remains in question. While Harrell claims that he had dealt with Puffy's "lack of respect for authority" and budgets, an unnamed music-industry executive later told *New York* magazine that Russell Simmons "told Andre to fire Puffy. Russell separated Andre and Puffy. He thought they were too formidable as a team." The same article quoted another unnamed executive: "If Russell told Andre to fire Puffy, it was because he thought Puffy was going to get him in trouble. Andre was Russell's [close friend]." This person added: "If Russell told Andre anything, it was probably: 'That kid [Sean] is gonna get you killed.' And I think Russell didn't like the way Sean had started treating Andre. In front of Andre, Sean was saying things like 'You wouldn't be shit without me.' In public and shit."

Barry Michael Cooper, meanwhile, expressed his own theory: "Combs was so successful with Blige that Harrell got jealous—or, depending on whom you talk to, became so demanding on her behalf that Harrell got fed up—and his mentor fired him."

Either way, Puffy was in his office when it happened. That night, he told his friend, *Source* writer Dream Hampton, "This nigga walked into my office and said there can only be one lion in the jungle."

He couldn't believe Andre had dismissed him. He was scared to death despite other labels already calling to express interest in Bad Boy.

Leaving Uptown was like being involved in a divorce, he said. He was used to working with, and being near, Andre Harrell every day. "It's just so crazy," he said. Even worse, Andre asked him to move out of the New Jersey home they had shared. He later told a reporter: "It was like I was forced to handle a situation, and then I had to grow up real quick."

# PART 2

# NO WAY OUT

"Remembering Biggie is never going to stop."

—*Sean "Puffy" Combs*

# THREE

# Victory

GETTING FIRED PUT PUFFY RIGHT BACK AT THE BEGINNING. "I cried for a coupl'a days and felt like I wanted to jump off a building," he said. "I felt like I didn't know everything to be able to make educated decisions."

He began to run Bad Boy from his mother's home in Westchester and listed Janice Combs as the company's official owner. He hired Kirk Burrows as general manager and his old college friend Deric "D-Dot" Angelettie—whose group 2 Kings and A Cipher had failed commercially—and two of his other fellow Howard alumna, Harve Pierre and Nashiem Myrick. At the time, Pierre and Myrick had lost their deal with independent label Payday Records; they called themselves Stixx en Stonz, but were given the boot before any of their music had arrived in stores.

Puffy asked Deric and Harve Pierre to handle various duties while sharing one computer; Nashiem Myrick acted as a studio intern and another Howard alumni, Chucky Thompson, produced music.

In its earliest days, Bad Boy filled the coffers by managing Heavy D, producer Jesse West, and rapper Third Eye, who joined Puffy on a number of remixes. As an employer, he demanded that Deric and Pierre be awake by 8:00 A.M. and at work on time. Most days ended with them giving a daily progress report. Pierre thought it was the hardest job he had ever held. One day blurred into another. "Every day, all day long, twenty-four hours a day," he remembered.

Puffy had to keep Biggie happy. The night Harrell fired him, Biggie went through an entire gallon of Hennessey liquor. Biggie also had lost his deal with Uptown. "Party and Bullshit" had been a hit, Biggie said, but Harrell didn't know what to do with a hard-core rapper. "He was more expecting another form of Heavy D." His music was not "that Uptown, Guy, Mary J., Heavy D" pap. "It wasn't that glossy feel. It was darker."

Puffy called to buoy his spirits, but Biggie continued to smoke marijuana and wallow in self-pity. He was sad about his friend Damien being jailed for a work release violation, about not being able to provide for his newborn daughter T'Yanna, and about his mother's breast cancer diagnosis. Puffy urged him to keep writing lyrics.

Biggie continued to be embarrassed, especially when he overheard neighbors saying, "That fat black ugly nigga ain't comin' out with no records. 'Party and Bullshit'—that's it. Nigga need to be happy for that."

Puffy decided to meet with him. In the past, while at Uptown, Biggie had complained frequently about Harrell stalling the release of his album. Puffy took him to Junior's restaurant in Brooklyn and, over cheesecake, said that together they'd be unstoppable: "I'm a visionary. You've got to trust me."

Now that Biggie was without a deal, Puffy met him at the Shark Bar. Writer and friend Dream Hampton, also seated at the table, mentioned that Biggie was heading out of town. Puffy told him, "I swear to God, Big, if you going out of town to do one illegal thing, if you run a red light in North Carolina, I'm never fucking with you ever again." Outside he gave Biggie money for a cab ride home, but no cab would stop for him. Biggie told Hampton, as he walked toward the train station, "This nigga, he stay sweating me. He's from fucking Westchester. He ain't never been broke in his life. Man, if this shit don't happen soon . . . if this shit don't happen by the end of the summer, which it's not, I'm taking this train right uptown and buying some fucking weight. Fuck Puff."

Puffy overcame his initial fear and put the word out that he was seeking a distributor. When he had an appointment to meet with record company executives, he'd squeeze everyone into the tiny Volkswagen Rabbit he was driving at the time. Employees sat motionless during the ride to the city. Kirk Burrows had it the worse, Chucky Thompson recalled. Burrows "would be in the backseat with his briefcase, with papers everywhere."

Despite firing him from Uptown, Andre Harrell publicly supported Puffy. Other black executives did as well. L. A. Reid, a producer who ran Arista-distributed LaFace Records, put him in contact with Clive Davis.

Davis started his career in 1960 as assistant legal counsel for CBS Records.[1] But in 1976, CBS executives accused Davis of expense account violations and fired him. He also pled guilty to tax evasion. Still, the industry loved him: He was given control of Columbia Pictures's record label, he renamed it Arista, and he was given 20 percent of the label's equity. In 1979, BMG bought Arista, and Davis went on to sign Barry Manilow, Neil Diamond, Aretha Franklin, and Whitney Houston in 1983. In certain ways, Davis was like Puffy. Some people said he was egotistical—one person joked that he thought the industry named the CD in his honor—but Davis had an undeniable talent for choosing hits.

Davis didn't know what had happened between Puffy and Harrell. "All I knew was that Puffy was a young black entrepreneur whose credentials were told to me on the phone by Bert Padell, Puffy's [then] accountant." He knew Puffy wanted his own label. Davis called L. A. Reid, who had steered Davis to producer Dallas Austin's Rowdy Records. "L.A. had also been in touch with Puffy separately," Davis said. "Indeed, the first meeting that took place with Puffy, L.A. was there. Neither felt threatened. Puffy was more street, and L.A. and 'Face were working more, they felt, for blue-collar workers." Davis claimed that instead of discussing money, "Puffy and I found a *music* connection."

During the meeting, Puffy was an excellent salesman. Davis later said he found Puffy "grounded in practicality," and that he was "unusual in his marketing perspective, creative visions, sense of himself, and the music he wanted to do."

He played Davis some music by Craig Mack and Biggie. Davis felt Puffy could carry Arista into the lucrative hip-hop market. Even better was how Davis felt Bad Boy fit with the other Arista-backed labels, LaFace and Rowdy. "Puffy was into the street, he was into rap. He was into a whole kind of edgy urban style." L. A. Reid, who played on *What's the 411,* and

---

1.  Clive Davis once said, "I grew up with no money, and the only way to rise above your station was to get a profession, so I studied law."

Kenneth "Babyface" Edmonds, the star of one music video in which Puffy danced while in high school, were saying the "cross-pollination" between the labels "could only benefit all of us," Davis explained.

Moreover, Puffy was a young man he could mentor. He put an estimated fifteen million dollars on the table and reportedly included a clause in the contract that said Puffy had to spend a certain amount of time with him each month, learning the business. Puffy's annual salary would rise to a reported seven hundred thousand dollars. He'd have creative control and BMG's powerful distribution network behind him.

After signing the deal, he wanted to thank L. A. Reid for his assistance. Reid took what he called "a small, small piece of it." More important, "I got the satisfaction of seeing it happen." Puffy, he claimed, had offered a large percentage of the company. "And I said, 'You know what, Puff? I would be a very wealthy man if I took you up on your offer, but what I'd rather do is to have you never forget that I did it, and someday you reach out and help somebody.'"

Puffy took his advice and called Biggie on the telephone, finally reaching him in North Carolina. True to his word, Biggie had returned to North Carolina, ignoring Puffy's objections, to rent an apartment with some associates and obtain drugs from a new connection. During their conversation Puffy told him not to destroy his life; contracts for a new deal would be ready the next day; he would even send him a train ticket: "Come on up and I'll have the check waiting for you."

Biggie boarded the train to New York just as North Carolina police raided the apartment and arrested his new roommates. One had been a wanted fugitive for seven years. Police charged the other two with conspiracy.

Bad Boy has never divulged publicly the details of the contract Biggie signed, but the industry standard might provide a sense of what he and many rap artists agree to. While Biggie appreciated the one-hundred-thousand-dollar advance he received, the reality is that most musicians, even rappers with a six-figure advance, don't earn much money from royalties. Most artists promoting the image of success in videos might buy nice clothing, cars, jewelry, and homes, but they might also never receive a penny in royalties. For an artist to see a penny he has to sell a large number of copies. Only artists who sell millions of albums live the life seen in music videos. Then again, the group TLC once sold ten million albums, then filed for bankruptcy. Whether an artist sees royalties depends on how much their label spent on creating and promoting their work and what terms they negotiated in their contract. Either way, most recording contracts in any genre of music don't benefit the artist.

When a rapper signs with a record label, he's the last person to receive money from his advance. In most cases he has to pay his manager 15 to 20 percent of his advance. The musician must also pay a lawyer, who either bills by the hour or accepts anywhere from 5 to 10 percent of the deal. An accountant also bills by the hour but might accept 5 percent of the advance. The Internal Revenue Service also expects to receive anywhere from 28 to 41 percent of all income.

In negotiating his deal, an artist tries to receive as many "points" as possible. Points are percentages of the retail price of an album. Most artists receive eight to thirteen points on every record sold. Each album contains only one hundred points. Each point is worth eight cents. For example, an artist with seven points receives fifty-six cents from every CD sold.

An artist receives royalties only after the label recoups what it has spent. This means that a record company will charge an artist for his huge advance, samples, big-name producers, extravagant music videos, and loans given from time to time. Even if his album sells a million copies, the artist might not receive any royalties. He might even end up owing his record company money. The label has been keeping track of every penny it paid the artist from the minute he signed on the dotted line. The artist might now be living in a huge home, driving a fancy car, wearing the best clothing and jewelry, and have his work topping the *Billboard* album chart. But a record label is deducting what they paid him upon signing, his sample clearance budget, the money they paid producers and guest stars, half the costs for any videos filmed, and any cash advances. Record companies deduct these amounts from the artist's tiny share of all revenues. The label collects their lion's share of the money, itemizes the artist's bill, then repays itself from his eight to thirteen or more points. This is the case for an artist whether he sells ten copies or ten million copies.

In short, the artist pays for almost everything a record label does for him. If an artist looks rich in ten videos, the artist is paying half of the costs for each clip. If his album doesn't sell millions of copies, he won't get rich from royalties. If a record label releases a remix of a song, the artist's share of the royalties pays for the producer, recording costs, and what the label spends on marketing and promoting this single.

If the label hires independent promoters to convince radio station program directors to add his song to the playlist, the artist is charged. If the artist has to meet a reporter and the label sends him to the interview in a limousine, the label charges the limousine to his royalties. The label gladly pays costs for tour support, wardrobe, out-of-town promotional tours and recording costs, but meticulously adds each cost to the artist's bill.

In addition, if an act has more than one member, as in the case of groups, every member sees even less money. For each member to earn royalties for their work, the group must sell more albums. One way to offset costs is to produce your own work. By doing this the label won't have to hand three points, or twenty-four cents, on each song the group produces to producers.

And yet other hidden costs further reduce the amount of royalties an artist might receive. If the suggested retail list price of a cassette is $10.98, 15 to 20 percent of this price might be credited as a packaging deduction that lowers the amount of money actually credited to an artist's royalty account. And artists only receive royalties from a certain percentage of total albums sold. If one million albums are shipped, some labels may decide that 150,000 of them will be set aside as "free goods" to major chain stores. This is intended as an incentive to have them order more albums from the label. Already the record company has given away 15 percent of the money. This happens at the discretion of the record label and, in all cases, the money comes out of an artist's pockets.

In addition, the label also keeps a certain amount of an artist's share of royalties in reserve in case it has to repay itself for any items that retail stores have returned. The record label usually holds this money, as returns against reserve, for two to four years, depending on the length specified in the recording contract.

But even this reserve money is up for grabs. If a record label deducts costs from the artist's royalty account and learns the artist still owes money, the label might "cross-collaterize" the accounts and repay itself, or recoup from a particular album's reserve account if the account hasn't liquidated. By cross-collateralizing accounts, the label can also ask an artist to record a second album and use profits from this second album to recoup what it spent on the first. The artist might then be expected to record a third album to repay the label for what it spent on the second album, and so on.

These economic realities explain why certain rappers "sell out," or downplay more aggressive elements in their sound. For some rappers, the only way to recoup on their album and see some royalties is to broaden their audience. To do this they have to introduce more congenial, gentler, "commercial" sounds. In some cases, aggressive rappers emerge from a hiatus as singing, dancing, and smiling "entertainers." Their black audience might object, but the approach draws more paying white customers, increases record sales, and allows artists to repay what they owe their labels, managers, the IRS, producers, and their lawyers.

THE ARISTA DEAL PROVIDED NEW OFFICES ON NINETEEN STREET and Fifth Avenue and a personal assistant named Leota (pronounced "Lee-Oh-Tay") Blacknor. The office, lavishly furnished, evoked the trendy nightclub The Tunnel. The reception area had dim lighting, metallic surfaces, and glass doors. Puffy's sister Keisha sat at the reception desk. Behind her, in an office on the left, was where Puffy kept his desk; other offices formed a circle. "It wasn't really a big office," said Easy Mo Bee. But that didn't stop Puffy from working himself and his employees even harder. He now hired Mel Smith to handle promotion, Michelle Joyce as marketing director, Gwendolyn Watts as director of production services, and Kelly Green to deal with artist relations. Harve Pierre worked in street promotion and A & R, Nashiem Myrick was production coordinator, Hillary Weston worked in marketing, and Mark Pitts was taking steps to move from intern to artist manager. During this period, Mo explained, Puffy was "frantic, running around; not in a negative sense." He'd rush through the crowded office doling out assignments. "Yo do this, do that," he'd say quickly. One afternoon Mo arrived to find him rushing toward him. "Yo, what's up? Where the beat?" he snapped.

Mo forgot to bring it.

"Aw, Mo Bee go back. Go back home. Go back home right now. You gotta go get that joint. We gotta do that joint tonight: eight o' clock."

From the beginning, Puffy ran a tight ship. "Sometimes," former employee June Balloon once said, "there was too much smoking going on in the office. Puff was like, 'No more smoking, including the artists.' " Biggie arrived one day and carried a lit joint while approaching each office to greet favorite employees. While speaking, he blew marijuana smoke in every direction. Then he sat in the conference room to relax and smoke some more. A receptionist, who might or might not have been Puffy's sister Keisha, barged in and said, "Hey, no smoking in here."

Big answered, "Fire me!"

Soon Biggie had begun a running feud with this employee. During later visits, Damien Butler remembered, "Big would walk in, and as soon as he'd get off the elevator he'd take one hand and knock everything off her desk and onto the floor. He did it so much that no one would even get mad. It'd just be like, 'Big's here.' "

In the studio, Puffy worked on Biggie's music for an audience that included Big's friends in Junior M.A.F.I.A and his own producer friends from Howard University. In the middle of the night he'd stand behind the board, keeping himself awake by rocking back and forth or tapping his feet. "I ain't been to sleep in like two days," he said during one session. "We gonna do this shit."

At this point, publishing owners reduced sampling, the use of preexisting music on new songs and the foundation of hip-hop music, to nothing but a way to charge exorbitant fees for bygone music. Producers had to keep detailed records of the songs they used. They had to know who owned the publishing rights and whether ASCAP or BMI represented it. They had to know who had recorded it, what album it had appeared on, and what label had released it to stores to get a mechanical license. They had to know what part of an old record they were using—it might only be a horn or drum solo—and submit a tape of the new work that included the sample.

Easy Mo Bee originally set Biggie's song "Ready to Die" to a sample by the Young Rascals. "Check this out," Puffy said. "The sample? The owners, the publishers won't clear it." He sent Mo back to the studio.

Sitting at the board, watching Biggie record lyrics, Puffy searched for reasons to reject a lyric. If he didn't like it, he reasoned that fans wouldn't either. Some songs were coming out great, but he'd still ask a producer to stop the music. Later, Biggie said, "He treated my album like an R and B album."

He also was shaping an image.

After Biggie described how he would rob a pregnant woman on "Gimme the Loot," Puffy said, "You got to say that in a different way."

When Biggie started "Dead Wrong" by saying "Hail Mary full of grace, smack the bitch in the face," Easy Mo Bee told Puffy, "You should really think about this."

Puffy felt it was fine.

What he didn't like was Biggie's second verse, a rambling description of himself as a blunt-smoking street tough who was "smooth as a baby's ass."

He told Biggie to scrap it and come up with a better one. While Mo recorded the new verse, he saved the original on another track.

With *Ready to Die,* Puffy wanted to set a new standard for the hip-hop album. Some people felt he also was trying to inflict his salable R & B sound on Biggie. For the most part, Biggie followed directions. His friends in Junior M.A.F.I.A.—sitting in a corner of the studio with their forty-ounce beer bottles—let him know if something didn't sound good.

His lyrics on *Ready to Die,* however, confused his mother, Voletta. She had worked two jobs to provide a decent life for him, but he was rapping, "My mom ain't giving me shit." He said he had to deal drugs to survive. To Biggie, neighborhood drug dealers were his role models, and *Ready* was how he viewed the world. But even as he honored his old neighborhood on records, he privately dreamed of moving to New Jersey. He promoted his dealer image and saw albums sell but knew it was a bit misleading. He hadn't been a very good drug dealer. The neighborhood had been just as much a source of anguish as income. Setting up a drug spot was dangerous; someone always wanted to move in on your operation. To announce a takeover, they murdered someone. In later years Puffy would sanitize his image, but Biggie was open about this period during a conversation with Havelock Nelson for *Interview* magazine.

At age sixteen he saw an acquaintance shoot someone. He was part of a group chasing this man. One of his friends shot the man, and he fell.

Then a friend of his "put the gat to his head." Next "somebody screamed 'Run!' and we all ran." At other times, the "niggas gettin' hit all the time" included close friends like Cheese. Cheese was conducting a drug deal in an underground train station when "we just heard two loud shots. Sounded like cannons: boom! boom! We ran downstairs and saw Cheese just spread out." Biggie knew Cheese would die. But here he was back in the same neighborhood after signing with Bad Boy.

The one-hundred-thousand-dollar advance didn't go very far, and Biggie actually pined for the days when he sold drugs. Thanks to Puffy, he realized this behavior was immoral, but not having money on hand made him think about dealing. Making records paid the bills, but it, as he put it, "wasn't the same." He'd have to hope his album sold enough to merit a royalty payment. Moreover, in the industry, he felt lonely and bored. He couldn't relate to the "ghetto fabulous" executives. If anything, the people who kept him going were his buddy Lil' Cease and Bad Boy employee Mark Pitts, "the only nigga who would probably go all out one hundred percent for me."

Pitts had been around since the Uptown days, and when Biggie complained about his low advance from that label, somewhere between twelve and twenty thousand dollars, he said, Pitts urged him to be patient. One famous anecdote appeared in print: Pitts arrived at Biggie's apartment and found him in a stupor. He tried to rouse him, but Biggie growled, "Fuck you, I ain't doing shit." Pitts grabbed a hot rag, wiped it on his face, and literally dragged him to his feet. In 1993, Pitts left his job at Bad Boy and became Biggie's manager.

Another friend was Easy Mo Bee. During the eighteen-month recording process, Biggie lived three streets over from him. Puffy would call Mo to say, "Tell Big—" or "Go over to that nigga's house and get such and such beat." Or he'd say, "Hook up with Big, y'all get together, y'all do the beats."

While Biggie rode in his green Acura, Mo played cassettes of his newest tracks. "That's how we came up with a lot of beats besides going to the office or the studio and playing something," Mo recalled.

In the studio, Puffy saw Biggie present more ideas. "My original list of producers had all the Big Willies that Nas worked with," Biggie said. He told Puffy he wanted to record duets with Method Man of Wu-Tang and also expressed interest in "a Brooklyn-type thing" with Brooklyn group M.O.P. and Jeru Tha Damaja.

Puffy let him record hard-core duets with Brand Nubian's Sadat X ("Come On"), the Wu-Tang Clan's Ol' Dirty Bastard, and his buddy Tupac Shakur. Ultimately, he rejected these songs, and "Dead Wrong," but gave studio intern Nashiem Myrick's "Who Shot Ya," the thumbs-up.

Biggie wanted harder sounds on his album, and when it came to hard-core tracks, no one on earth could do better than DJ Premier of Gang Starr. Premier, born Christopher Martin, had an approach that evoked the days of George Martin or Holland-Dozier-Holland. He once told a reporter, "I know a lot of people say I'm slow with getting stuff done, but I'm all about quality. So if it takes that long for quality to come out, then it's just gotta take that long. You can't rush art." Only on Premier's "Unbelievable" did Biggie deviate from Puffy's formula.

Once the Premier song was in the can, Biggie wanted to continue in this vein. Said one witness: "Puff would say, 'Naw man, you got to do that shit over.' Biggie would say, 'Man, fuck that, my shit is—' Or 'Yo, I'm telling you, I'm telling you!' But that was the most arguing I saw."

Biggie understood Puffy's R & B approach but also didn't want hard-core fans calling him a sellout. At the time, anyone who rapped over R & B or up-tempo "house" music stood accused of diluting the music. When Biggie first entered the studio, said a witness, he rapped in a hyperactive, angry tone. Like many newcomers, he sounded hungry. While Biggie thought his album would feature aggressive back-to-back numbers, Puffy had other ideas. Over time, Puffy's direction resulted in softer music. "Listen to 'Gimme the Loot' or another song about relationships, like 'Friend of Mine,' " said one person present during some sessions. "Someone must have told him, 'It's cool the way you're coming in here and screaming and everything, but you remember how [a commercial artist] used to sound so debonair? How he had control and assurance and confidence?"

To Puffy, Biggie's voice changed for the better; smoother vocals made the album more accessible. But he still wanted more radio-friendly music. According to Russell Simmons, he didn't reach this conclusion on his own: "When Big left Uptown, *Ready to Die* only had one commercially viable single. When I heard it again there were many more accessible-type singles. Clive gave Puffy a lot of direction on that project."

Puffy called Biggie to the studio and had him record a softer track called "Big Poppa." This R & B–styled number was supposed to be the last song for *Ready to Die,* and promotional copies were pressed for radio deejays, said an insider, "But Puffy came with another song, and another one."

The battle over Biggie's image ended during the last few weeks of recording; Puffy had asked Biggie to return to the Hit Factory and record the more marketable song "Juicy." An insider defended Puffy's commercial approach: "If he'd never done that Big would never have reached the plateau that he did. We called records like that 'a good radio joint.' The batch of songs [Big had] recorded was really a lot of rough stuff. These songs were what he needed. 'Big Poppa' was almost like a last-minute addition. Puffy probably told himself, 'We got these songs and all this roughness. I gotta smooth this out, even this out.' And he accomplished it with 'Big Poppa,' 'One More Chance,' 'Stay With Me,' and 'Juicy.' "

One number included vocals by Faith Evans. She had been an awestruck twenty-one-year-old when Puffy discovered her in a studio session for another artist; she now saw herself as "somewhat of a veteran as far as recording goes." At age fifteen, in fact, producer Teddy Riley tried to sign her to a recording contract, but her mother, who lived with Faith in New Jersey, would not allow it. Still, she had made a name for herself through backup singing or songwriting and didn't want someone telling her, "OK, Faith, we're going to start with this part of the song."

Yet when Puffy asked her to come to the studio and sing on an album that discussed casual sex and murder, this was exactly what happened. Even worse, the album seemed to glorify murder, crime, and premarital sex. What would people in her church think? Later, she said she sang on *Ready to Die* because "her boss" Puffy made a "business decision."

In the studio, she learned that Biggie had only recorded part of his rap. She asked, "OK, Puffy, what part do you want me to sing?" Puffy told her which bars would comprise the "hook." When she was done, he explained that Biggie would return later to finish his vocal.

Soon Puffy approached producers to ask, "Yo, man, could you hook up 'Juicy'?" Mo Bee recalled, "I was like, Juicy what? 'Cause the song was called 'Juicy Fruit,' but he called it 'Juicy.' " Puffy wanted Mo to sample James Mtume's 1983 R & B hit.

"I said, 'Word?' He said, 'Yeah.' He told me to do it. I walked away thinking, it's so easy. Why he want me to do that? I didn't do it right away like he wanted me to. I could have made extra money and had my name on another track. But what he wanted me to do was so easy. He just wanted me to loop it up. 'That's it. Just loop it up.' "

The idea had more in common with MC Hammer than with the hardcore sound Biggie discussed in Mo's Acura. Ultimately, Jean "Poke" Oliver of The Trackmasterz created the track. Biggie rapped about a childhood spent reading *Word Up* magazine, listening to bygone act Rappin' Duke on Mr. Magic's radio show, drinking Private Stock malt liquor, eating sardines, and ignoring teachers who said he'd never amount to anything. Puffy received a coproduction credit and enlisted producer Pete Rock for a twelve-inch promotional version, "a more swinging type mix," Mo explained.

Puffy then asked his girl group Total to sing hooks on Big's most sellable numbers, such as "Juicy" and "One More Chance." He found this group when their manager, stylist Sybil Pennix, had called Puffy at Uptown to arrange an audition. Back then he told Pennix to bring the group by the Hit Factory. Before the meeting Keisha, Kina, and Pam sat in a car and quickly improvised a song. "We sang something with Puffy's name in it," Keisha said later. "We already had the bad girl attitude." They rehearsed while riding in an elevator. While they sang, he kept a poker face on. When they finished he left without saying a word. The group thought they flopped, but later that day he called Pennix to say he wanted to sign them to Uptown. When he left Harrell's company, he took them with him. Now they were filling Big's album with profitable elements.

By the time he felt the album was complete he had removed Nashiem's track "Who Shot Ya," added "Juicy" and "Respect," and set "Dead Wrong" aside as unusable. Now it was time to choose the first single. Biggie wanted his violent number "Machine Gun Funk" to introduce him, but Puffy explained that "Juicy" would get on radio and sell more copies. "If we drop 'Juicy,' you'll have a gold single."

As a concession to Biggie, he agreed to include "Unbelievable," centered on a vocal sample by R & B singer R. Kelly, as the B-side. The battle over his image, however, continued when it was time to release his second single. When Puffy announced that he wanted it to be the equally gentle "Big Poppa," Biggie thought, "Oh man." Still, he offered no resistance, because Puffy "started talking that money shit again." And Puffy was right. "Big Poppa" reached as many listeners as "Juicy" and gave the impression that Biggie's music was safe. Even so, Biggie did not sound happy when discussing the album later. *"Ready to Die* was ninety-five percent *The Chronic,* five percent of me," he told a film crew. "All the rest of that shit was the weed, man."

Puffy's other project was experiencing similar creative differences. In creating Bad Boy's first roster, he took great care to sign acts that would reach every target audience imaginable. Biggie was his answer to Death Row and gangsta rap, while Craig Mack was comedic in the outrageous Busta Rhymes and Redman sense. Faith was a successor to Mary J. Blige, while Total evoked the group TLC. For producers, leaping from Biggie's rough lyrics to Mack's playful style could be difficult. After recording "Flava in Ya Ear" and a soundalike titled "Get Down," Mack presented a song called "When God Comes."

Instead of burlesque, Mack was offering a searing indictment of gun-happy rappers promoting mayhem to increase sales. In short, he was attacking Biggie's style. Mo told Mack, "That's powerful, brother. I like that. I'm glad you taking the time to even do that." Mack replied: "Oh, yeah, Mo Bee, no doubt, no doubt."

They recorded the song over a sample from a jazz band cover of the Beatles' "Come Together." The sample didn't clear. Mo Bee had to decide whether to play the melody himself or use another sample. More important, Mack had to convince Puffy to include the song on his album.

In all honesty, while Mack and Mo viewed the song as a significant work, it was hardly a masterpiece. At best, Mack touched on his subject superficially, then resorted to his tired "comedian" formula. When Puffy heard the song, according to someone present, he asked, "Why you wanna do that? Why you wanna put that up in there?"

Mack wanted to be political while Puffy viewed him as a vehicle to reach another audience. Mack wanted to be radical when Puffy would probably have been happy with ten or so variations on the "Flava" for-mula. But Mack obviously had strong feelings about the song, one person claimed: Mack hinted that he wouldn't record any more music unless "When God Comes" was included on his album. Puffy included the num-ber, even if he privately felt it marred an otherwise commercial album.

In fact, hindsight would prove him right. "Flava in Ya Ear" spent an astounding fourteen weeks at Number 1 on *Billboard*'s hot rap singles chart, a record not broken until 2000 by a southern rap group, the Hot Boyz. "When God Comes" received a glowing blurb in *The Source.*

Ultimately, Puffy filled *Operation Funk Da World* with music that fit the image he wanted Mack to have. Every single after "Flava" was in the pop mode that had yielded such positive results. After "Get Down," he even joined Mack on his third single, "Getting Money with Puff." While Mack offered a few corny jokes, Puffy chanted, "Gotta get the cash, gotta get the dough."

To promote Mack and his new label, he created something called "The Big Mack Sampler." Journalists received a press kit that resembled fast-food packaging from Burger King. Inside, they found biographical fact sheets, photos of Mack and Biggie, and both of their first singles on the same cassette. "In terms of promotion and marketing, that's dope," said one person close to Puffy. "That was showing you. These are my two artists. I'm pushing them right now. Pushing them together." But even the sampler caused problems. Craig Mack's "Flava" had introduced the label, provided it with its first hit, but since then Mack had felt Puffy was not promoting him as he did Biggie. "Listen, man, I'm not taking anything away from Craig as an artist, but as the second artist, when Biggie came in, it totally overshadowed him. When you compare them," this source continued, "Biggie was the stronger artist, and the people make their choice. And everyone was going crazy over him. Craig Mack was seen as, yeah, yeah, you got that beat, but what are you gonna do next?"

The next step was to assemble guest stars for a remix of "Flava." In doing so, however, Puffy allegedly took credit for other people's work. "I don't know if it was by misprint or on purpose, but the credits on the remix said, 'Remixed by Sean "Puffy" Combs and Chucky Thompson.' Sean

'Puffy' Combs didn't push any buttons for 'Flava' or the remix. Thompson was nowhere around. If he was, he wasn't involved in production."

But nothing came of it. Puffy moved on; he hired Hype Williams, who directed Mack's video, setting artists in white outfits against white backgrounds. Puffy then asked his street team to head to 1515 Broadway, a Times Square building that housed the offices of MTV and *Billboard*. Billboard's chart manager remembered seeing "a crowd of young men and women outside with Bad Boy picket signs and bullhorns telling MTV to 'play our shit.' " Within a week, MTV had added Craig Mack's video to the playlist.[2]

Despite any misgivings Biggie may have had regarding singles, Puffy had his marketing approach down pat: Each Biggie single featured a commercial song with radio appeal backed with a harder number for the "street." The approach worked. "Juicy" sold over half a million copies. "Big Poppa" sold twice that amount. "One More Chance," backed with a remix of Biggie's duet with Method Man, "The What," sold a million copies.

The album started with Biggie reenacting his life over a medley of familiar hits, including Curtis Mayfield's "Superfly," the Sugarhill Gang's "Rapper's Delight," and the Audio Two's "Top Billin'." "Things Done Changed" offered nostalgia for earlier, less violent times in the ghetto. "Gimme the Loot" exaggerated the extent of his stint as an armed robber. "Machine Gun Funk" featured boasts and samples from "Chief Rocka" by Lords of the Underground. "Warning," set to Isaac Hayes's cover of "Walk on By," found Biggie worrying that those closest to him would set him up for a robbery. After his favorite song, "Everyday Struggle," his gangsta rap "Me and My Bitch," which was set to plodding funk, and commercial ditties like "Juicy," "Big Poppa," and "Respect," he offered a shocking album closer.

Whereas the rest of *Ready to Die* found Biggie adopting various poses for specific audiences, "Suicidal Thoughts" was honest, simple, and unforgettable. This one song, in fact, earned him a place in the annals of music history.[3]

---

2. Bad Boy would soon be providing the network with 50 percent of its black programming.
3. "We're considering taking it off the album," Biggie said in 1994, since Bad Boy feared someone "stressed out might hear that shit and might flip."

Structured as if it were a late-night telephone call between him and Puffy, the song described how sad, confused, and hopeless he had felt after losing his deal with Uptown. To make a long story short, after facing the violence in his life, the happy-go-lucky album narrator expresses remorse for his actions, then ends his life. The song ends with a gunshot and Puffy yelling, "Yo, Big! Yo, Big!"

After its release on September 13, 1994, *Rolling Stone* called *Ready to Die* the best rap debut since Ice Cube's *AmeriKKKa's Most Wanted. Vibe, Rap Pages, Spin,* and *The Source* planned to feature Biggie on their covers. But Puffy was about to meet his first rival.

At first, he and Marion "Suge" Knight were on good terms. Knight, a former football player who stood six-foot-three-inches tall and weighed over three hundred pounds, formed Death Row Records with producer Dr. Dre in 1992. Like Puffy, Suge had a peerless sense of the market. He knew what rap fans wanted to hear and how Death Row should package its music. While Dre created million-selling albums with discoveries Snoop Doggy Dogg and now the Dogg Pound, Knight chose artwork and promotional materials, singles and B-sides, and video directors and extras.

If Knight visited New York in 1994, he'd drop by Bad Boy's office. If Puffy traveled to Los Angeles, "he would come pick me up and we'd hang out," Puffy remembered.

Suge and Puffy were present when MC Hammer filmed his comeback video at his Oakland home in 1994,[4] and Puffy later admitted, "Bad Boy was kind of modeled after Death Row, because Death Row had become a movement."

What he didn't know was that Mary J. Blige and Jodeci were associating with Suge, for reasons different from his. Bad Boy was a record label, a management firm, and a production company, and one of Puffy's clients was Mary J. Blige. He was producing her second album, *My Life,* and she had handed him a demo by a rap group she'd been mentoring in Yonkers. The group, the Warlocks, would hand her demo tapes. She'd listen to them while on tour, then present opinions and songwriting sugges-

---

4.  Puffy appeared in the video. But fans, after years of his sell-out pop, rejected Hammer's gangsta rap.

tions. Jason Phillips ("Jadakiss"), David Styles ("Styles"), and Sean Jacobs ("Sheek") took direction well, incorporated suggestions, and attracted attention from other producers. If they told her about an opportunity to record a song, she'd ask, "Is the paperwork straight, is the money right?" The relationship between Puffy and Mary was good enough for her to hand him their tape.

Privately, she was dealing with a number of situations. "She conducted interviews," as *Vibe* put it, "where she did much drinking and talking, and looked like a zombie on national television." During one concert, she was reportedly so drunk, paying customers booed her off the stage. She was also dating K-Ci of Jodeci. By 1994, Jodeci was feuding with Andre Harrell and Uptown. Their debut had sold three million copies and the group wanted to renegotiate the terms of their contract. Marion "Suge" Knight stepped in to represent them, and Jodeci received a phenomenal deal. Uptown upgraded their contract and gave them creative control, a substantial retroactive payment, and an 18 percent royalty rate, standard for million-selling artists. The deal turned out so well that Knight bought Devante Swing a $250,000 Lamborghini Diablo. Soon, Mary reportedly brought Suge into her own situation. "She was signed to a little production company which went through Uptown and then to MCA," Knight told a journalist, referring to Bad Boy.

During this period, Knight claimed, he met with Puffy and Mary J. Blige in a suite at New York's Four Seasons hotel, and that Puffy arrived with an entourage, while he was alone: "I don't need to run in no packs." During this meeting, Knight added, "I told Mary to speak her mind, that she didn't have nothing to worry about, and then I told them they were letting her out of that fucked-up deal."

For a short period, Knight gave the impression that he was representing her. Yet, when *My Life* arrived in stores, label president Harrell told *Vibe* that Mary had decided not to work with Suge: "On the album credits it says Sean 'Puffy' Combs and Steve Lucas. That's who I call."

IN JULY 1994, AT A PHOTO SHOOT PUFFY HAD ORGANIZED FOR HIS roster, Biggie met Faith Evans, and became more independent. Faith, born in Florida to rock singer Helene Evans and a white musician who left the family, grew up with her aunt in New Jersey. She sang in church at the age of four, competed in beauty pageants as a teen, and attended Fordham University for a year. At nineteen, she dropped out, gave birth to her daughter Chyna, and returned to writing songs and singing backup for other artists. She was doing this when Puffy discovered her.

During the shoot, Faith sat at a table looking at photos. Biggie introduced himself, asked to see her pictures, then asked if she'd drive him home. They spent most of the next week together, attending parties, shopping in malls, and then Biggie told his mother, "I'm getting married. I met the one."

She said, "Congratulations, Christopher," then went about her business.

Biggie said, "Nobody believes me. Why don't people take me seriously?"

On the morning of August 4, 1994, he and Faith married in front of a witness and the county clerk. After the ceremony, he told his mother, "I got married today."

She already knew; an aunt had heard it on the radio and called to let her know. His mother asked if Faith was with him for his money.

He said, "I owe you five hundred dollars. I don't have any money."

"You don't, but you will." When she learned that he didn't sign a prenuptial agreement, she said, "Puffy let you get married, and you didn't sign a prenuptial agreement? Your lawyers didn't make you sign one? What kind of people do you have running your life?"

The marriage earned headlines and reflected positively on Bad Boy. Two stars getting married only strengthened the family image Puffy was beginning to promote. For the next month, Biggie lived with his mother, who continued to wonder why Faith had married him. One night, Faith called to leave a message. Voletta asked why Faith never said hello or acknowledged her. According to Voletta, Faith said, "Mrs. Wallace, Chris told me to stay away from you, that you might say something to me that we're all going to regret."

Voletta said, "Well, I need to meet you."

She didn't stop Biggie and Faith from having fun. Faith bought him a green Land Cruiser. His friend Damien drove him around. Next, neighbors saw Biggie in a burgundy Land Cruiser, then a new Lexus, then another new luxury car. Biggie also bought his daughter with Jan, T'Yanna Wallace, a costly bracelet. Finally, he moved into a loft with Faith and Chyna.

Biggie, raised an only child, saw Junior M.A.F.I.A. as a surrogate family. He said, "I'm in this game for the dough, because the more money I make, the more things I can do to get my peoples the fuck outta here." Biggie's plan was to become famous, then help his friends get their own deals. "I'm gonna be the ground and do what I gotta do and have everything ready, so as soon as I hit, I can push everybody out." Before *Ready to Die* was released, he was planning projects that wouldn't involve Puffy.

While Biggie continued to be a major part of the Bad Boy ethos, as early as 1994 he seemed to be unhappy with the label. "Well, I'm signed for a while, so I'm gonna handle my business," he told writer Louis Romain. "But I really can't see me doing this shit too much longer, because it's too foul for me. If I want to deal with some foul niggas I'd rather be on the street level, not no business shit, 'cause they could get over on me."

Biggie worked with Lance Rivera, called "Un" by his friends, on starting a label called Undeas, and put Junior M.A.F.I.A. and themselves in business. When he began to work on Junior M.A.F.I.A.'s album, instead of asking Puffy and the Hit Men to provide tracks, he reached out to Daddy-O, who produced the Audio Two's "Top Billin'," the track that made Mary's "Real Love" hot. Biggie also recruited EZ Elpee, who would later work on Bad Boy albums, Clark Kent, who would tour as Puffy's deejay, and Special Ed, the rapper on the classic single "I Got It Made."

In the studio, he helped Lil' Kim craft an image seemingly patterned after Puffy's own work with Mary—blonde hair. He also helped her write lyrics filled with references to guns, drugs, money, and sex. He appeared on incredible hits such as Junior M.A.F.I.A.'s "Player's Anthem," in which he delivered the classic chorus, "Niggas, grab ya dicks if ya love hip-hop/Bitches, rub ya titties if ya love hip-hop," and helped the group sign with Big Beat/Atlantic. The group's Clark Kent–produced debut sold half a million copies and proved Biggie didn't need Puffy or Bad Boy to draw a crowd. He appeared on Junior M.A.F.I.A.'s second single, "Get Money," and it sold twice as many copies as "Anthem." When Atlantic signed a distribution deal with Biggie's label, Undeas, and Junior M.A.F.I.A.'s debut album, *Conspiracy,* sold half a million copies, Biggie was finally achieving financial independence. He began to create Lil' Kim's *Hard Core.*

IN NOVEMBER 1994, PUFFY RELEASED *READY TO DIE* AND CRAIG Mack's album, and both counted among the year's most popular releases. Biggie's "Unbelievable" and "Juicy" and Mack's "Flava in Ya Ear" continued to dominate radio airwaves. Puffy threw himself a birthday party, the first large event since the CCNY fiasco.

That night, video monitors aired cameos he'd made in artists' videos. Puffy talking on albums had become a company trademark. In the past, producers Marley Marl, Teddy Riley, and Pete Rock had used the technique. But there was a big difference between Riley and Pete Rock saying, "Yeah, Guy, sing it one time," or "Yeah, Soul Brother number one," and Puffy filling most of a song with shameless self-promotion. While Puffy mingled with guests and listened to everyone tell him how great he was, Biggie held court at a table with Tupac Shakur. He had met Shakur during a visit to the set of John Singleton's *Poetic Justice,* where, between takes, Shakur played Biggie's "Party and Bullshit." At this point, Tupac was a former dancer for Digital Underground, recording political rap for Interscope, and in his home they smoked marijuana and discussed the industry.

When Tupac arrived in New York to film *Above the Rim,* Biggie introduced him to friends in Brooklyn, including Jacque, a man mentioned on "Party and Bullshit." Tupac let Biggie open for him at a few local shows. At Madison Square Garden, they shared a stage, and Biggie previewed a few outrageous lyrics from his album. In studios they recorded duets, including one dropped from *Ready* and another later released as "Stop the Gunfight."

On November 14, 1993, Tupac and his new friend Jacque went to Nell's, and Tupac met a young woman on the dance floor. Days later, he was kissing her in his room at New York's Parker-Meridien hotel, when the door opened. "As I started to turn around to see who it was," she later wrote in a letter printed in *Vibe,* "Tupac grabbed my head and told me 'Don't move.' " She claimed that Tupac, along with friends that Biggie introduced him to, started to rape her. "I felt hands tearing off my shoes, ripping my stockings and panties off. I couldn't move. I felt paralyzed."

She described one of Tupac's friends as a brute who said, "This bitch got a fat ass!"

After the assault, she faced Tupac and yelled, "I can't believe you did this to me!" Tupac kicked her out of the room. Before leaving, she said, "This is not the last time you're going to hear from me!"

Just then, Biggie arrived to visit his friend. Their mutual acquaintances quickly left the room, and after hearing Tupac's side of the story, Biggie wanted to do the same. They heard sirens, rushed to the window, and saw police cars racing toward the hotel. Biggie hurried to the door. Tupac dropped onto a couch and lit a joint.

In the lobby, police grabbed Biggie and handcuffed him. He was in custody until other officers brought the rape victim into the lobby and she said he didn't have anything to do with the attack. Police removed the handcuffs and let Biggie go. Police arrested Tupac and dragged him past news cameras with him saying, "I'm making money and they can't stop me."

At the table during Puffy's birthday party, Biggie introduced Tupac, in the middle of a rape trial, to his wife, Faith Evans, as his only real friend in the industry. Tupac partied with Biggie, but already felt a little jealous of his newfound fame. He later claimed that Biggie filled *Ready* with ideas Tupac had given him. The claim was preposterous. Biggie owed Tupac what Tupac's double-tracked vocals and subject matter owed Public Enemy's Chuck D, Ice Cube, Slick Rick, and even Redman. If anyone inspired Biggie, it might have been Death Row house producer Dr. Dre.[5] When Bad Boy told Biggie to create a new stage name, since another rapper was using "Biggy Smallz," he seemingly borrowed Dre's nicknames from *The Chronic,* "The Notorious D.R.E." and "Notorious One."

By month's end, Tupac and Biggie were no longer friends. On November 29, a Manhattan jury convened to deliberate the charges against Tupac in his trial for sexual abuse and sodomy charges. Meanwhile, Tupac was recording a mix-tape in a local radio deejay's home when someone—called "Booker" in *Vibe* and here as well—offered him seven thousand dollars for a vocal. Tupac was concerned: "Booker" knew

---

5.   And Dre's style evoked the work of Schooly D, Ice T, KRS-One, Rakim, and Slick Rick.

Jacque, a man Biggie introduced him to, and someone accused of partic-ipating in the sexual attack.

Since he needed money to pay for lawyers in various criminal cases, Tupac agreed to come to Quad Studios, located in Times Square. He'd record the vocal, but wanted "Booker" to pay him right after he finished. After a few telephone conversations, "Booker" agreed to have Uptown's Andre Harrell bring the seven thousand dollars to the studio.

After midnight, Tupac arrived at Quad Studios with three friends, in-cluding his tall producer Randy "Stretch" Walker, Fred Moore, and a man named Zayd. As they approached the building that housed the studio, Tupac was concerned, but relaxed when Lil' Cease, standing on a terrace above, called out in greeting. Tupac passed a man in army fatigues and a hat, and assumed he was Biggie's bodyguard, since, during travels in Brooklyn, he'd seen many people dress this way. Tupac and his friends entered the building lobby and saw a second man in fatigues at a desk with a newspaper.

Near the elevator, the two men confronted them with guns. The man yelled for the group to lie on the floor. Tupac was supposedly going for his own weapon when the men shot him. The media claims that his attack-ers hit him five times in the head and groin, but at least one person has claimed that Tupac accidentally shot himself in his privates.

The robbers began to kick Tupac and take his thirty-thousand-dollar diamond ring and ten thousand dollars' worth of gold chains. They also stole five thousand dollars' worth of jewelry from Fred Moore.

After the shooting, his friends got Tupac up to recording artist Lil' Shawn's studio session on the eighth floor. "When we got upstairs I looked around and it scared the shit out of me," Tupac said. The forty people present wouldn't face him, he claimed. "Booker" looked surprised to see him, he claimed, while Lil' Shawn supposedly burst into tears and cried, "Oh my God! Pac, you've got to sit down." Tupac also claimed that Andre Harrell averted his eyes and "Puffy was standing back too. I knew Puffy. He knew how much stuff I had done for Biggie before he came out."

Tupac was in shock that night. The robbers had shot him in the head. He saw Harrell there, remembered that Booker lured him to the studio by promising Harrell would bring seven thousand dollars to the studio, and immediately fit Harrell into the theory forming in his mind. He saw Biggie, who introduced him to Jacque, and immediately suspected that Biggie knew the shooting would happen. He saw Puffy, connected to Biggie and Harrell, and quickly included him in accusations he made in the pages of *Vibe.*

Before his death, Tupac would record a song that accused his new friend Jacque of masterminding this shooting, but for whatever reason, he told *Vibe* he believed Puffy and Harrell had set him up to be robbed and shot.

At the Hit Factory one night, a friend from *Vibe* brought Puffy an advance copy of the feature that included Tupac's accusations. After reading it, Puffy told Biggie, "We say nothing. Niggas come up to you, start questioning you, reporters start asking you shit . . . nothing." Biggie shrugged and said, "Man, whatever. What is there to say?"

Puffy had to deny these accusations. In fact, everyone Tupac mentioned in *Vibe,* including Harrell and Lil' Shawn, denied his description of events. Puffy later told *Rolling Stone* that far from being indifferent to the sight of Tupac covered in blood, he was shocked. "I mean, that's Tupac! I immediately went to him, sat him down, calmed him, had people call the ambulance."

Biggie was just as shocked. The night of the shooting, he called his mother to say, "Somebody shot my man!" He visited Tupac in the hospital the next day, when Shakur was recovering from major surgery, but the sight of Biggie, who knew Jacque, inspired Tupac to sign himself out of the hospital against medical advice. After attending a court appearance in a wheelchair, Tupac Shakur went into hiding, then reemerged in February 1995 to begin serving a four-and-a-half-year prison sentence for fondling his victim against her will and for sexual abuse. But even at this point, Biggie tried to be supportive. He asked friends in Riker's Island to watch over Tupac and get him marijuana to smoke. It didn't matter. Shakur's accusations, printed mostly in the pages of *Vibe,* grew to include Biggie.

The most Puffy and Biggie might have been guilty of was hearing rumors about who might have shot Tupac, but even this is unclear. Even so, Tupac continued to accuse them, and fans actually started to believe him.

Puffy tried to resolve the situation by writing a letter. "I want to come see you," he wrote. "I don't know if what the writer was saying in *Vibe* was true, that you really felt any of this." Either way, he added, Tupac should know he and Biggie had nothing but love for him. Tupac responded to his letter, Puffy claimed, by writing, "Well, Puff, everything's cool. It ain't no problem like that. I don't really want us to have no meeting about it like that."

During this period, *Rolling Stone* explained, Puffy became "known for brashness and arrogance—qualities apparent in his walk: a slow swagger, the pimp strut of an extremely self-assured man, fearless and confrontational, who answers only to himself."

For most of 1994, his girlfriend Misa Hylton, who worked with him at Uptown, was pregnant with his child. But in June he separated from her. "I was busy, and having a family wasn't my priority," he later explained. "She deserved to have what she wanted out of life." Even so, by June he leaped into a relationship with Kim Porter, whom he met in 1992 when she too worked at Uptown, as a receptionist. When Misa gave birth to his son, Justin Dior Combs, on December 4, he was already involved with Porter. Shortly after the birth, the *New York Times* reported, he traveled to Westchester and entered a "shoving match" with "the grandmother of his infant son, in which the police were called but the district attorney declined to prosecute."

Then on January 23, 1995, police in Washington, D.C., accused him of flashing a silver gun at a man in a parking lot. Police claimed he did so after he was handing out magazines with his name and photo on the cover in a student cafeteria and an employee asked him and a second man if they needed help. According to what employee Mario Cruz said, Puffy allegedly got upset and cursed him, left the hall, but supposedly returned to ask what time Cruz left work. Then, Cruz claimed, at 4 P.M., he saw Puffy and his friend waiting outside; Cruz said Puffy raised his shirt to show a gun, then leaped into a car, and drove away. After Cruz reported the incident to police, a District of Columbia Superior Court judge issued a warrant for Puffy's arrest on threat charges. Published reports claim that he surrendered to the FBI in New York, and they released him after he promised to appear in Washington. But he never had to go to court. A Washington judge dropped the threat charge, his lawyer in the case said later, because the case lacked merit. The media did not report on the two accusations against Puffy until years later, so Bad Boy's audience had no idea the police had accused him of "shoving" people and "flashing" a gun.

Puffy busied himself in the studio. He began to work with the group Total, who wanted success apart from serving as Biggie's backup singers.

With their manager, Sybil Pennix, Puffy replaced their baggy TLC-style sweatshirts and jeans with skintight leather, high-heeled shoes, and other gimmicks. Kina would have long hair. Keisha would wear short skirts. Pam would have androgynous short hair and an unwavering stare. Ultimately, fans wouldn't embrace Total as they had Mary J. Blige.

In the studio he had them sing over part of James Brown's "The Big Payback," a sample already used by dozens of rap acts, the girl group En Vogue, and En Vogue's many imitators. Then, despite their desire to distance themselves from Biggie, he invited Biggie onto their song "Can't You See," which appeared on the New Jersey Drive soundtrack. Next he had Bad Boy publicists write a bio that said Total held the "distinction" of being the first "bad girls," and were the "R and B lynchpins" in a "burgeoning empire."

At first, this seemed to be true. Their duet with Biggie, "Can't You See," quickly approached the half-a-million-copy sales mark and The Source included Total in a photo-heavy profile section with upcoming talents Adina Howard and Brandy. The underrated group also toured with Jodeci, Mary J. Blige, and other Bad Boy artists. But their debut was not enough to change the general perception of Total as one-hit wonders. Reporter Cheo H. Coker felt that, on their self-titled debut, the "girls, at times, seemed replaceable and anonymous, like background singers on their own tracks."[6] The public and the media continued to reject the group.

After seeing two members perform for students in a Chicago high school gym, a reporter decided, "Keisha and Kina don't sound great but they sound good enough for this house." In print, Pam claimed, "It doesn't bother me if people think we aren't great singers. At least they're thinking of us enough to talk about Total."

At the same time, Puffy was working on Faith Evans's debut album.

---

6. Which is ridiculous. Total made some Bad Boy releases hotter than they would have been without them.

Faith wrote all but one of her fifteen songs and wanted to include the melancholy ballads she favored. Despite a mature R & B sound and no rappers on the album, music magazines tagged her as a "hip-hop soul" artist. "There's nothing wrong with that," she later said. "But it's not what I set out to do."

Faith sang exceptional ballads such as "As Soon As I Get Home," but posed for photos with blonde hair, a skintight black outfit, a top hat, a walking stick, and sunglasses that inspired comparisons to Mary J. Blige. Cheryl Flowers, who worked as a producer for Bad Boy and later as Puffy's manager, explained that during this period Faith's "male managers" were "making bad decisions for her. A male rap group is very different from a single mother without a nanny. They wanted her to go blond. They've never dyed their hair, so they don't know, and Faith's fell out." Newspaper reporters also reported, erroneously, that she sang backup for Blige instead of writing songs for Blige's official second album, *My Life.* While Evans said, "I don't mind the comparisons," her liner notes hinted at displeasure. After thanking everyone at the label and all of Biggie's friends, she wrote, "Puffy, thanks for being so difficult and giving me direction."

By April of 1995, Puffy's work began to inspire headlines. One week, four of his productions appeared on *Billboard*'s Top 20 hot R & B singles chart: Biggie's "Big Poppa," Usher's "Think of You," Mary's "I'm Going Down," and Total's "Can't You See." Magazines like *Paper, Billboard,* and *Newsweek* singled him out for praise in feature stories, and *Rolling Stone* called him "Rap's new producer king." In print, he said, "When I'm hearing sounds, I'm always looking for something that's different." This was the beginning of Puffy promoting himself as a master producer.

At the same time, he was also beginning to change how his artists would dress. For the documentary *The Show,* he had joined Biggie onstage at a concert, and both had worn jeans, boots, Kangol caps, and maybe one chain each. Biggie, as usual, wore one of his beloved casual sweatshirts with a big letter "B" on it. When Puffy and Biggie attended the Soul Train Awards that year, they wore designer suits and derbies. Puffy was beginning to enjoy being in the limelight. When people cheered during *The Show,* he ignored the fact that it was because as sideman he was working to make Biggie look better. Soon Andre Harrell revealed that Puffy

was considering releasing an album called *Puff Daddy's Greatest Hits.*
"Just some arrogant shit straight out of the box," Harrell explained.

DURING A CONCERT IN CONNECTICUT, LIL' CEASE TRIED TO IMPRESS
the crowd by standing on tall speakers on stage. He did so while it was raining "and it started wobbling, 'cause I was moving too much. So I'm looking
how to get down, and Big is rhyming and looking up at me like, 'Yeah, all
right. Let's see this!' " Cease jumped down and landed on his ass. The entire audience said, "Ohhh," but Cease got to his feet and continued performing. "But Big says, 'Whoa! Stop the music! Stop the music, please!' He
says, 'Did y'all see that? He just bust his ass!' The whole fucking crowd just
started laughing. He never let shit slide no matter what you were doing."

While Tupac continued to accuse Puffy and Biggie of involvement in
his shooting during jailhouse interviews with *Vibe,* Biggie toured to support *Ready to Die.* In Sacramento, California, four or five cars—filled with
friends of rapper E-40—arrived. With angry men surrounding him and his
deejay, Biggie held a telephone and told E-40, "Yeah, it looks like your
peoples are getting ready to handle some real business." DJ Enuff was
impressed: "He always played it cool. And the same niggas who was
about to set it on us got word from E-40 that it was cool, and then wanted
to roll dice with us. They even asked him for autographs."

When he took an airline flight, "He'd literally put his head back and
open his mouth real wide and act like a saw," Damien recalled. Other
passengers would leave his aisle and he'd have extra room.

During one booking, Biggie and his friends were happy to be off the
tour bus and eating at a steakhouse. But the promoter refused to pay the
bill. After dinner they arrived at the hotel and learned that he hadn't paid for
their rooms as promised. After they got him to pay, they entered their rooms.
But the next night, they returned to the hotel and found devices on their
doors keeping them from entering their rooms. Again, the promoter hadn't
paid the hotel. For the most part, he suffered these indignities in silence.

By now, Junior M.A.F.I.A.'s debut album, *Conspiracy,* was released,
and Biggie's sound was all over the radio. He missed being with his new
wife, but also viewed money as a priority; he soon told people that

"B.I.G." was an acronym for "Business Instead of Game." Before each show he'd dress in a new custommade outfit, linen or conservative pinstripe, and an old-fashioned derby. He'd smoke a few blunts, then hear an announcer yell his name. When he and Lil' Cease stepped on stage, the crowd roared even more. DJ Enuff would spin his hits, Biggie would pace the stage, and Cease would cheer or yell specific lyrics for dramatic effect. If Puffy appeared, as he did during *The Show,* people reacted because he was supporting Biggie. On stage, Biggie had an incredible rapport with the audience. When he chanted the chorus to "Player's Anthem," women in the closest rows actually rubbed their breasts. When his friends tossed two hundred loose one-dollar bills at the audience during "Gimme the Loot," a gimmick he stopped performing after losing a five-thousand-dollar ring one night, crowds went insane. After each show, women wanted to be near him. He was overweight and married—he called himself ugly—but he was also a sex symbol.

His wife suspected this. "Half the time I couldn't go be with him on tour, so I used to have my doubts and I used to worry, what is he doing," she said.

After a show in Virginia, one telephone call to his wife turned into an argument and he hung up. She called back but he wouldn't answer. Just then, his friends arrived with groupies and paired up. One girl was the odd person out so he let her sleep in his room, "some completely innocent shit." His wife was already on a commercial flight. The next morning at eight, someone knocked on his room door and his guest asked, "Who is it?"

Faith said, "Housekeeping," and attacked the girl once she opened the door. "Oh, my God," Biggie once recalled. "Punched home girl in the face about thirty times, then got on the next flight back to New York."

"Not seeing him was terrible," she said.

Some nights, his mother would say Tupac had called for him. Tupac had included him in his accusations, but Biggie hoped to resolve things with him. Tupac hated him, but Biggie remembered when both of them were struggling. Back then, Tupac had let him sleep on his couch, and Biggie had let him stay over during trips to New York; Tupac had let Biggie coheadline concerts, and Biggie had invited him onto a duet for *Ready to Die.* Biggie would tell his mother, "Mom, please get a number, some kind of way to get in touch with him. 'Cause I want to know where this is coming from."

Between concert dates, Puffy had Biggie return to New York to film a video—his fourth—for his remix of "One More Chance," directed by Hype Williams. The remix featured Faith over DeBarge's piano from "Stay with Me," while another version used Craig G's old single "Droppin' Science." "If a song was dying out, a remix would give it that edge to live an extra few months," Deric Angelettie explained.

Instead of the mansion and yacht from "Juicy," director Hype Williams set "One More Chance" in the nightclub Nell's. One Friday morning Treach from Naughty By Nature, West Coast rapper Coolio, Mary J. Blige, Busta Rhymes and his protégé, Rampage the Last Boy Scout, waited for Hype and his crew to set up lighting. After a tracking shot of two women entering a party, Williams asked them to shake their hips a little more. He filmed Biggie, in a suit, lounging with Treach; standing near Busta and Rampage; talking to a girl at the bar. The video was a masterpiece. Between takes, Biggie wanted to take a smoke break; he pretended to storm off the set. Damien followed him down the street and around the corner, where Biggie was smoking. Meanwhile Damien's beeper kept going off and his cell phone kept ringing. It was Puffy. Biggie told him not to answer. "Puff was sick," Damien said.

By now, Big had asked Damien Butler to join former Bad Boy employee Hillary Weston and Puffy in comanaging Lil' Kim and Lil' Cease. Big would be forming his group The Commission, which he hoped to record for his label with Lance Rivera.

During this same period, Puffy began to complain about Biggie showing up late for concerts. "I'm talking about, just as they were about to announce his name, he'd walk through the door," Puffy claimed. One night Biggie arrived on time, but Puffy admitted that he'd been worried. Big told him, "I'd never not be there for you."

In June, the "One More Chance" remix gave Biggie his first true hit. Before the single, his shows drew one hundred, then three hundred, then one thousand fans. After the single, he was performing for five thousand, then ten thousand, then twenty thousand people. *Ready to Die* approached the three-million-albums sales mark; he raised his asking price for a show to twenty thousand dollars and coped with becoming the most visible figure in hip-hop. His twenty-five-year-old manager, Pitts, told *Vibe:* "I didn't know he was gonna be this large." Then: "I can't believe we blew up that quick."

Twenty-two-year-old Biggie was just as stunned: "That star shit ain't really hit me until a couple of months ago." Close to a year after its release, *Ready to Die* was still on the charts. Music magazines called him "the East Coast messiah." "Juicy" had sold half a million copies; "Big Poppa" sold a million; but "One More Chance/The What" debuted at Number 5 on the pop singles chart and tied Michael Jackson's "Scream/Childhood" as the highest debuting single of all time. It was also *Billboard*'s rap single of the year. Everyone was buying his music. He had even more reason to feel proud when the self-described "King of Pop" asked Biggie to fly to Los Angeles and appear on his song "This Time Around" from his album *HIStory.*

During the session Biggie noticed Jackson adopting a tougher tone; he included a curse word in his lyrics. Biggie recorded a verse and planned to leave. He didn't think Jackson wanted to meet him. Within minutes, he and Jackson were face-to-face. Biggie asked if the vocal was acceptable. If it needed work, he'd record another. "Make sure you use it," he said. "Please." An appearance on the Jackson album could possibly lead to a small fortune in publishing royalties, especially if *HIStory* did as well as *Thriller.*[7]

At the second annual *Source* Awards on August 3 1995, Death Row won awards for best motion picture soundtrack, producer of the year, and video of the year. After Snoop's *Doggystyle,* the label continued its winning streak with Snoop's *Murder Was the Case* and the *Above the Rim* soundtrack, which featured Tupac Shakur. By show's end, however, Suge Knight would flip on Puffy.

Suge Knight mounted the stage. "If you don't want the owner of your label on your album or in your video or on your tour, come to Death Row," he said. Members of the audience groaned. Some yelled catcalls. Puffy had committed all three acts with his artists. Suge further divided the audience by urging Tupac Shakur to keep watching his back, and by adding that Death Row was riding with him.

---

7.  *HIStory* was Jackson's worse commercial showing to date.

Puffy couldn't believe his ears. He later said, "I thought we was boys." He also didn't see anything wrong with his appearing on records or in videos. While he certainly seemed to be a camera hog, his ad-libs also had played a major part in building the Bad Boy brand. His appearances allowed him to cheer for the label, support lesser known acts, and solidify Bad Boy's image as a place where artists routinely drove new cars, wore the choicest fashions, and drank the best champagne. Instead of letting the comment slide and accepting that Knight might have been jealous of his newfound success, his ego seemed to get the best of him. He appeared on stage to say that, despite Suge's comments, he still respected him. Instead of starting "a riot" at that very moment, he added, he'd wish Suge and Death Row continued success. While the tone was conciliatory, this pose, and implying that he'd "start a riot," might have angered Knight even more.

As it was, Suge might have felt that Puffy had taken one too many pages from Death Row. The R & B sample on "Juicy" evoked Dr. Dre's house sound; *Ready to Die* was patterned after *The Chronic*; "Ready's" skits between actual songs brought Dre and Snoop's albums to mind. Then there was Biggie's stage name, "The Notorious B.I.G.," after Dre had spent much of his album calling himself "notorious," and one of Biggie's songs using a Dre lyric for its chorus.

As the show continued, Biggie accepted an award on stage, held it up, and yelled that Brooklyn was in the house, then Snoop paced the stage with a walking stick berating the audience for not loving him and Dre.

The next day, Faith filmed a video for "You Used to Love Me." Bad Boy was releasing her ballad-heavy debut, *Faith,* on August 29, 1995. Biggie, still in town, joined her on the set to celebrate their first wedding anniversary. Between takes, they laughed, hugged, and called each other pet names. The video, meanwhile, was for a downhearted number about a woman who never has enough time for her relationship. "I'll make it up to you," she sang. "Honey, I'll do what I got to do." That day, Biggie watched his wife stand near newsstands on New York City streets, looking lonely for the camera. Touring was beginning to affect his marriage, but it was also one way an artist could earn quick money.

Another was a deal he signed with Puffy. "I spent a lot and the label has to recoup first," he told *Vibe.* "That's why I sold half my publishing to Puffy.

I was br-zoke and if a nigga could make a quick quarter of a million just from signing a few papers, you gotta let it go." *Vibe* later wrote: "Puffy may have hit him off with a nice chunk but it's nothing compared with what B.I.G. might've made had he struck a publishing deal after he blew up."

To understand why the deal struck *Vibe* as controversial, a brief explanation of publishing is required. The people who compose a song or write the lyrics generally own the publishing rights, and publishing allows artists or companies to earn real money. U.S. copyright law requires any establishment playing copyrighted music to obtain permission for its use. After playing a Biggie song, radio stations had to pay BMI. The amount of radio play a song received determined how much money BMI sent Biggie's Tee Tee company and Puffy's publishing operation, Janice Combs Music. What Biggie received in publishing royalties was determined by his percentage of ownership. If he owned the entire song, he'd get every penny. If he owned half, he received 50 percent. Ultimately, publishing is one of the few ways—besides touring, merchandising, or endorsement deals—that artists earn more money. That Biggie sold part of his publishing to Puffy was problematic, because a hit like "One More Chance" could have resulted in six-figure publishing royalties. By selling the rights to an entire hit album for $250,000, he might have low-balled himself.

Soon, however, he and Puffy had to worry about Death Row Records. On September 23, 1995, Puffy, Biggie, and Junior M.A.F.I.A. traveled to the Atlanta nightclub Platinum House. Puffy said, "At that time, there wasn't really no drama." He didn't have bodyguards with him, he claimed. He left the club and sat in his limousine. He was talking to girls. "I don't see [Suge] go into the club, we don't make any contact or nothing like that." Suge, he added, got into a "beef in the club with some niggas." He "knew the majority of the club" but didn't know which person Suge "got into the beef with, what it was over, or nothing like that."

He saw people he knew leave the club. He saw Suge. He saw "everybody yelling and screaming and shit." He left his limousine, and asked Suge if he was all right. "I'm trying to see if I can help." Gunshots rang out, they both turned, and "someone's standing right behind me," said Puffy. It was Jake Robles, Suge's close friend and employee, shot twice in the stomach and once in the back. He would die in a hospital a week later. According to Puffy, Suge said, "I think you had something to do with this." Puffy said he asked, "What are you talking about? I was standing right here with you!"

While describing this event to *Vibe,* he couldn't help adding, "I really felt sorry for him in the sense that if he felt that way he was showing me his insecurity."

Later, published reports quoted witnesses saying that a member of Puffy's entourage pulled the trigger. Off-duty sheriff Chris Howard, working security at Platinum House that night, said Puffy and Suge did meet up inside the club, and that they got into a heated dispute. Howard claimed that he separated Suge and Puffy, then Robles and Puffy's bodyguard, Anthony "Wolf" Jones. Howard added that he asked Puffy, Suge, and their entourages to leave the nightclub. But since he didn't want them fighting outside, he claimed, he asked Puffy and his group to leave first. Once he saw they weren't waiting out front, he said he told Suge, "OK, coast is clear," then walked Suge outside and saw him enter a limousine.

"His partner was just about ready to get into the limo when all of a sudden Puffy's guys came from around the corner . . . and one of them had a gun," Howard added. "I chased the guy with the gun around the corner. He handed the gun off to another guy. It was a .45. By the time I got back out front, that's when the guy took a shot at Suge's partner. He shot him two or three times." After this, he claimed, the shooter entered a car filled with Puffy's friends. While he couldn't see the driver, he said everyone near Puffy that night was in the car when it drove away.

The murder of Jake Robles was a major turning point. Suge, like Tupac with his shooting, believed Puffy was involved with his friend's murder. Puffy began to travel with bodyguards and to avoid commenting on Death Row. The media implied that he feared Suge. The *New York Times Magazine* claimed that he asked Louis Farrakhan's son Mustafa to speak with Suge. He claimed that he told Mustafa, "If there's anything you can do to put an end to this bullshit, I'm with it." It didn't matter. Suge refused to meet Mustafa. When Puffy didn't show up for a music conference in Miami two weeks later, *Billboard* claimed he might have received threats from Death Row.

With tensions between Death Row and Bad Boy at an all-time high, releasing Biggie's "Who Shot Ya" might not have been the best idea. But it was exactly what arrived on the streets next. The song went from mix tapes to record stores to being Biggie's main topic during an interview with New York radio station Hot 97. Biggie tried to explain that the song wasn't about Tupac, that it described a turf war between an older drug dealer and an ambitious young rival. But the industry rumor mill was churning, and according to wags, while performing the song during a party on a boat, he supposedly included Tupac's name a few times. Most disturbing, besides Bad Boy's timing, was Biggie saying, "I wrote that motherfuckin' song way before Tupac got shot. It was supposed to be the intro to that shit Keith Murray was doing on Mary J. Blige's joint [My Life]. But Puff said it was too hard." Now Puffy appeared on the song, growling, "East Coast, motherfucker."

Biggie continued to tour. Vibe planned to include him and Faith on their cover, lounging in a convertible. He'd wear his hat and all-black drug kingpin outfit and derby, despite Ready to Die being narrated by a lowly street dealer, while Faith would look her best with blonde hair, a stylish outfit, and her gorgeous figure. At this point, they made the perfect couple and seemed to be very much in love, although Faith, lying in his arms, did seem to be pouting a little. Ultimately, she had good reason to frown. By now, Wendy Williams of Hot 97 was reporting on Biggie's affair with Lil' Kim.

The Vibe story presented a hilarious account of his concert in Cleveland that shows what his core audience felt about some of Puffy's R & B ideas. DJ Enuff started the show by playing "Big Poppa." Then Big launched into "Can't You See," and the crowd roared until Total emerged from backstage to sing their hook. One person tried to throw water at the group. When they finished the crowd threw pennies and half of a frankfurter. Biggie wisely stuck to hip-hop, but for an encore he performed "One More Chance." The crowd went wild.

By the time the issue reached stands, however, Tupac Shakur was free from prison, signed to Death Row, and claiming he had slept with Faith. The hip-hop audience was shocked. Tupac claimed he had met her in Los Angeles while she was working with an R & B group. Faith said she had a drink with him. Death Row had it in for Bad Boy, but she felt that as the "lowest on the totem pole" she could restore peace. Over a drink, she said she tried to tell Tupac that Puffy and Biggie had nothing to do with his shooting. She also sang on one of his new songs but said he couldn't use the vocal without Bad Boy's permission. Tupac's accusations made Biggie look like a cuckold. He wanted to respond, but Puffy wouldn't allow it, he said, " 'cause Puff don't get down like that."

Tupac continued to tell the media he had slept with Biggie's wife, while Biggie continued promoting his new well-dressed "player" image on tour.

*Vanity Fair* claimed that Puffy responded to Tupac joining Death Row by asking an old friend named Zip to refer him to bodyguards. It's important to note that Sean "Puffy" Combs always has denied employing gang members for security purposes. Yet published reports claimed that, after Biggie's show in Anaheim, California, Zip arrived at Big's penthouse at the Fairfield Inn with over twenty members of the Southside Crips street gang. Zip supposedly introduced the group, including Dwayne Keith Davis, alias "Keefee D," and his nephew Orlando Anderson, also known as "Baby Lane," to Puffy and Biggie. Davis allegedly described how the gang could provide security for Biggie during trips to Los Angeles. Puffy has denied employing these people for security purposes. Nevertheless, an anonymous source quoted in the *Los Angeles Times* claimed, "I was in a room full of Crip killers. Puff said, 'They're gonna be doing security for us.' "

Whether this is true is unknown. But Puffy was involved in another incident that showed his concern about security during this period. According to the New York City Police Department (NYPD), after midnight on December 4, *New York Post* photographer Gary Miller arrived on West Forty-fourth Street to investigate the presence of a Mercedes-Benz with what appeared to be a police parking permit in its front window. Miller, who once had worked as a detective with the NYPD, was snapping photos when Puffy left Daddy's House, his Arista-financed recording studio near Times Square, and demanded that Miller hand over his roll of film. As Miller told it, he showed Puffy a card that identified him as a retired police officer, but Puffy allegedly yelled, *"I don't give a fuck! I want the film. Why you taking pictures of my car?"*

According to Miller, up to ten men surrounded him while Puffy pulled a gun from under his jacket. At this point, he added, he handed Puffy the film and watched him destroy it. He then quoted Puffy as saying, "If you ever come around here again we'll kill you."

Miller went to the police that night and described a young man called "Puff." The police brought Puffy in for a lineup. Miller identified him. The police charged Puffy with criminal mischief, and Puffy was ultimately found guilty and fined one thousand dollars. Miller stands by his version of events, while Puffy denies ever pulling a gun or making threats. Later his lawyers mentioned that, during the Death Row situation, Puffy was nervous about strange men photographing his car.

# FOUR

# Going Back to Cali

A MONTH BEFORE *READY TO DIE* HIT THE STORES, BIGGIE SAID, "I feel I made an East Coast movie for niggas on both sides to recognize and respect." Now Puffy and Biggie were at the center of what music magazines called the East Coast/West Coast War. The media claimed this "war" pit rappers from both coasts against each other. For Biggie, the magazines were using a personal misunderstanding between him and Tupac to boost circulation: "Tupac never said, all you West Coast niggas need to hate the East Coast, and I never said that all you East Coast niggas need to hate the West Coast." Regardless, life soon imitated art.

On December 16, 1995, in Red Hook, Brooklyn, someone fired gunshots at a trailer being used by Death Row artists Tha Dogg Pound. Apparently, they were filming a video for "New York, New York," which presented them as giants stomping on New York.[1]

Next, an independent record promoter accused Suge and several associates of attacking him at a Christmas party thrown by Death Row. They attacked him, this man told police, because he wouldn't give them addresses for Puffy and his mother.

Finally, rumors claimed that Puffy's ex, Misa Hylton, was dating

---

1. Tha Dogg Pound's Kurupt later thanked Biggie for being "one of the first East Coast niggas to take me under his wing."

Suge. Even worse, Suge was rumored to be standing near her and holding Puffy's two-year-old son, Justin, in a magazine ad captioned, "The East Coast can't even take care of their own." Wendy Williams of Hot 97 described the ad on her radio show, but Death Row said it didn't exist; Puffy said he didn't know anything about it; and Misa told *Vibe,* "I don't do interviews."

Tupac's accusations, including those published in *Vibe*'s February 1996 edition, did not hinder Bad Boy's growth. Faith's self-titled debut remained on Billboard's R & B Top 20 for six months.

Puffy meanwhile began to seek new talent. One artist, Black Rob, born Robert Ross, had started rapping at the age of eight, after his sister handed him a homemade transcript of Jimmy Spicer's novelty single, "Super Rhymes." But at age ten, Rob had drifted into petty crime: Like Biggie, Rob had been ashamed of his old clothes and had started doing what he called "sneaky stuff." He began to steal from his mother's purse, he said years later, and subsequent beatings by her boyfriend drove him away from home. By eighteen Rob was homeless, sleeping in shelters or Times Square movie theaters, and stealing for a living. He eventually wound up in jail.

Shortly after his release from prison in 1994, Puffy met with Rob and his manager. "When I first came to Puffy's office, I kicked so many rhymes that he was just like, 'You crazy!' " Rob recalled. "But there was this one rhyme he kept telling me to kick." The lyric included the phrase "I had a big house, a Bentley coupe." While Rob kept repeating it, he claimed, Puffy was saying, "Yeah, that's right that's it."

Puffy liked his lyrics but decided that his name, "Bacardi Rob" or "Robbie-O," needed work. He asked Rob to stick with another more marketable nickname, "Black Rob," given to him by a friend after Rob developed a reputation for accepting a package from drug dealers and then taking off with it. He asked Rob to record a demo, signed him to a deal, and learned Rob was still technically under contract to a production company. Even worse, Rob claimed his manager was robbing him. "Bad Boy was sending me money to live on," Rob said. "He was robbing me for that." Puffy heard Rob's accusations and "made it his business to get on that cat's ass to find out where my money was at." Rob said he fired the manager, then spent two years trying to "get out of my production deal with his company."

Another new signing was a four-man group. Puffy learned about them from their managers and met the group in the popular nightclub 112. After signing the four teenagers, Daron, Slim, Q, and Mike, he named them after the club, 112. According to the group, Puffy tried to make them as clean-cut as the group Boyz II Men. The group concealed their dislike for this "wholesome" image, even as Boyz II Men member Wayna Morris produced one of their songs, and seventeen of their nineteen songs were ballads. Later Mike would claim, "Not trying to dis Bad Boy or Puffy or whatever, but . . . a lot of music that came out on Bad Boy in ninety-six, ninety-seven, it was 112 writing it."

Puffy signed another new artist named Mase, who grew up in Harlem without a father and, by the age of five, had dreamed of becoming an artist, a psychiatrist, and then a professional basketball player. Puffy's marketing of Mase continues to inform the work of the rap industry's top producers. Before becoming one of the biggest stars in rap, Mase had played point guard for Manhattan Center High School's basketball team and performed as "Murder Mase" with his group, Children of the Corn. Of his ten childhood friends, he later explained, eight had been murdered and two were in jail. His life was nothing to smile about: Once he carried an injured friend to a hospital but watched as the friend died before they arrived. During one winter his apartment was unheated; his fish bowl turned to ice and he couldn't use the toilet because it was "all frozen over." Like Biggie, a doctor had diagnosed his mother with cancer. Yet somehow Mase was not embittered.

Mase's original group disbanded after one member died in a car accident. Mase was attending the State University of New York at Purchase on a basketball scholarship when he met a manager named Country. Country urged him to slow his delivery to a more conversational pace, and within six months Mase and Country traveled to Atlanta where he planned to audition for producer Jermaine Dupri.

Puffy was heading to Dupri's party at the Hard Rock Café when Country introduced him to Mase. Puffy, who also had heard about him from The Lox, led Mase into Dupri's party and toward Da Brat, who was performing some of her derivative "female Snoop"–style raps. Puffy asked, "Yo, Brat, I know it's your show, I know it's Jermaine Dupri's birthday party, but can you give me the mike for one second?"

She agreed, then stepped aside, and he told the crowd: "If this guy sound good, he's gonna be a Bad Boy tonight. If he wack I want you all to boo him off the stage and make him never want to rap again." Mase grabbed the microphone and the crowd cheered, "Go, rap, rap, Shorty rap!" Puffy watched Mase begin his lyric with "Hum all you want to, come all you want to," and say that he'd "front" a woman some money, show her off, and hand her "thousands."

When he was done, the crowd gave him a standing ovation. Mase quoted Puffy as saying, "You wanna be a Bad Boy when you get to New York? Don't talk to nobody. You don't need to talk to nobody. You're gonna be signed."

Mase dropped out of college and signed with Bad Boy, where Biggie was supportive and told Country, "Yo, bring Shorty by, I wanna meet him."

Said Mase: "Biggie gave me a check before Puff gave me a big check, when it ain't have nothing to do with anything. He just wanted to see me out of the streets and wanted to see me do something for myself."

Puffy decided to include Mase on a remix of his new group 112's song "Only You." In the studio he had Mase record the verse from Dupri's party. After the session, Mase expressed misgivings about his performance. He thought he sounded like Father MC. Although Puffy asked him to remove the word "Murder" from his stage name, Mase still believed he'd be able to record tougher material. When he expressed his dissatisfaction about his sound, however, he claimed the conversation went like this:

Puffy would ask, "You wanna sign with Bad Boy?"

"Yes."

"Do you wanna be a star?"

"Yes."

"Are you willing to do what it takes to be a star?"

"Yes."

"So until I do something wrong, you don't have to ask me no questions. If it's not broke, why are we talkin' about fixing it?"

Puffy was so effective in his mentoring that Mase came to see his new softer sound as buying in rather than selling out. "So, at the time the way I was thinking was the wrong way to be thinking," Mase said later.

"'Cause I wasn't thinking on a business term. You not gonna make no money. I'm in it for the money."

Ironically, Puffy had second thoughts about including Mase on the song, Country remembered. "We had to beg Puff to put that verse on there 'cause he was just going to keep Biggie's part." He ultimately left Mase on the song, and Mase accepted that although he'd been "Murder Mase," Bad Boy already had a hard-core artist in Biggie.

On Monday, March 29, 1996, Puffy took Biggie, Junior M.A.F.I.A., and other members of what he now called his Bad Boy Family to Los Angeles to attend the tenth annual Soul Train Awards at the Shrine Auditorium. They traveled to California during a period in which Tupac was continuing to insult the label and saw Tupac make a dramatic entrance. He was hanging out of a car window yelling, "West Side!"

Regardless, Biggie and Faith performed for an audience that included Method Man, Veronica Webb, Teddy Riley, Jermaine Dupri, L.L. Cool J, and Heavy D. When Biggie stepped on stage to accept an award, some of the crowd booed. Even worse, Bad Boy's entourage encountered Tupac, Suge, and Death Row hangers-on backstage. Biggie saw the crazed expression in his old friend's eyes and thought, Yo, this nigga is really buggin' the fuck out. "He had his little goons with him, and Suge was with him, and they was, like, 'We gonna settle this now,' " Biggie told *Vibe*.

Lil' Cease, Biggie continued, was inebriated, and yelled, "Fuck you, nigga! East Coast, muthafucka!"

Tupac replied, "We on the West Side now, we gonna handle this shit."

Someone pulled a gun, Biggie said, and a Southside Crip reportedly traveling with him pulled one of his own. "It was a real sticky situation, where guns had to be drawn . . . and you can't talk under those circumstances," Biggie told writer Charlie Braxton. "I wish I could've grabbed him up, threw him in the limo and just told the limo driver to drive. At least, it would've just been me and him. It would've been a lot easier to talk to him."

Biggie thought Tupac knew who had shot him but blamed it on Biggie to raise interest in his music. "I was that edge he was looking for."

The media continued to report on the feud between the companies. Within weeks, a civil rights leader organized a meeting in Philadelphia, but

Puffy didn't attend. Suge did, claiming there was "nothing between Death Row and Bad Boy or me and Puffy," then adding, "Death Row sells volume. So how could Puffy be a threat to me or Bad Boy be a threat to Death Row?"

Matters got even worse in May, when Death Row released Tupac's scathing single "Hit 'Em Up." Patterned after Junior M.A.F.I.A.'s "Player's Anthem," the song threatened specific Bad Boy artists and employees with death and found Tupac telling Biggie: "You claim to be a player, but I fucked your wife." While Faith denied that this had happened, Tupac repeated his claim to The Source: "You know I don't kiss and tell."

Even worse, he appeared in a video with stand-ins for Biggie and Puffy. In one scene, a Puffy impersonator with a high-top fade stuck his face in the camera to raise and lower his sunglasses while a heavyset actor wearing a Kangol and jacket similar to Biggie's stared dully at the camera. In another, the actor playing Biggie crouched and faced the camera while Tupac, to his right, yelled in his face, "You claim to be a player but I bust your wife."

At this point, Biggie broke his silence. Tupac called his new song an answer to Biggie's "Who Shot Ya." Biggie reiterated that his song did not refer to Tupac. Tupac replied in print: "Even if that song ain't about me, you should be, like, I'm not putting it out 'cause he might think it's about him."

Biggie began to draw headlines because of his complicated personal life. He was dating Lil' Kim and she was feuding with Faith. Singer Missy Elliott, featured on a song Puffy produced for singer Gina Thompson, lived with Faith and called her from Daddy's House to report that Kim was there. Faith rushed to the studio and, she claimed, "beat Kim up for the first time." They also reportedly had a rematch at the Apollo Theater. Later, Faith would claim that, during this period, "Puffy found a way to use his influence on Big, telling Big, 'I heard Faith was messin' around.' Like a little devil on his shoulder."

Either way, Biggie already was dating a third woman, rapper Charli Baltimore, whom he had met when she asked him to pose with her for a photo in front of a hotel in Philadelphia. Biggie cast her in Junior M.A.F.I.A.'s "Get Money" video as what some wags called a platinum blonde "gold-digger" stand-in for Faith. After she left a rap-styled message on his answering machine, he planned to include her in his side project, The Commission, a trio he wanted to form with Jay-Z.

Puffy meanwhile was facing controversies of his own. On June 30, 1996, he arrived at the emergency room of St. Luke's–Roosevelt Hospital. Doctors treated him for a serious cut to his lower right arm that the New York Daily News described as a "slit wrist." Puffy now had to deny rumors that he had tried to commit suicide. "I was playing with my girl and I reached for a champagne glass and it broke on my bracelet, cutting my arm," he said. He had problems, he added, but none that merited suicide. Then, in July, rapper Craig Mack left Bad Boy over what Mack has called creative differences. "The problem was, like most artists, Craig wasn't getting paid and his dealings weren't really correct," one reporter claimed. And "things got so bad for Craig, he was pumping gas in Long Island. That's how broke he had become at one point. This was after his record came out. He was broke." Then police arrested Biggie on July 26 and found marijuana, infrared scopes, and illegal guns with scratched-off serial numbers in his new condominium in Teaneck, New Jersey. Finally, Biggie made more headlines with his most recent song, "Brooklyn's Finest," a duet with Jay-Z: "If Faith had twins she'd probably have two Pacs," he rapped. "Get it? Tu . . . Pac's . . ." Faith felt the song was "tasteless. Because I was having his baby and that was disrespectful to me and his baby." Biggie, she claimed, told her he knew it was wrong but was under "so much pressure from people."

During the summer, all of Puffy's hard work paid off. Bad Boy dominated radio and video. Bad Boy released 112's album on August 27, 1996, and a classic hip-hop remix of "Only You." For the video, Puffy had Mase wear a colorful Avirex jacket and stand near Biggie, the group, and a Humvee Jeep parked in the middle of Times Square at night. When MTV, Teen People, Seventeen, and Tiger Beat saw Mase flash his dimpled smile at the camera, they began to set up interviews with him.

112 also became favorites of the R & B audience. They were on the bill for a Keith Sweat concert with Bone Thugs-N-Harmony, Nas, and Foxy Brown. But a promoter told them, "Y'all ain't performing tonight. We'll give y'all tickets to the show, and y'all perform tomorrow." One member explained, "Keep in mind that we had our performance outfits on, so we were all looking alike, and I guess they didn't realize how strong 'Only You' was at the time." When the lights were turned on during an intermission, "some little girl screamed, 'That's 112!' " A crowd of girls

chased them like the Beatles in *A Hard Day's Night.* They had to hide in a bathroom for forty-five minutes to escape these fans.

Mase, meanwhile, continued to fret over his new sound. But Biggie helped him come to accept it.

Before performing at the Apollo Biggie approached Mase backstage and explained that he had to extend his show by a few minutes. Would Mase want to perform? While nervous about the audience booing him and his R & B rap off the stage, Mase said he'd do it.

After Biggie performed "Brooklyn's Finest," he told the audience, "Yo, I got somebody from the World." Harlem World was the neighborhood's nickname. To Mase's surprise, the crowd gave him a standing ovation. "Then I came out of the back rocking my verse," Mase said, "and everybody went crazy!"

After the show, Puffy appeared to tell him he had been great and to hand him the keys to a new car. Mase was stunned, but in a hurry to show it off. He immediately drove to a nearby housing project, stood in front of his brother's window, and yelled, "Hey, yo, Blink, come down! Come down now, nigga. It's on!"

Problems with Death Row caused Biggie to see hip-hop for what it had become. "I was kind of fooled because when I was looking at my *Right On* magazines and *Black Beat,"* he said in an interview, "I was thinking all the rappers were together chilling. I'm thinking everyone hung out together." Biggie now told reporters he wanted to retire from hip-hop once he made a certain amount of money; he told Lance "Un" Rivera he wanted to move to Atlanta and write a book. He was depressed.

Puffy, meanwhile, invited journalists to Daddy's House studio and said he wanted to be promoted as a six-year industry vet, ASCAP's 1996 songwriter of the year, and a businessman whose every release sold half a million copies. "How it got to this point, I really don't know," Puffy said of the feud. "I'm still trying to figure it out." He renegotiated his deal with Arista and reportedly received a six-million-dollar cash advance, a two-million-dollar recording studio, and a credit line estimated at fifty million dollars.

Soon, however, he responded to Death Row and Tupac in the pages of *Vibe.* If someone had a problem and wanted to get him, he said, this person wouldn't talk about it. "Bad boys move in silence." The only thugs he knew were in prison, or dead, or "about to be." While he wasn't a gangster, "I'm ready for it to come to a head however it gotta go down. I'm ready for it to be out my life and be over with." He hoped it could end on a positive note but felt that "it's gotten out of hand."

The insults ended on September 7, 1996, when Tupac and Suge Knight went to Las Vegas to watch the Mike Tyson–Bruce Seldon fight at the MGM Grand. After the fight, a hotel security camera filmed the Death Row entourage attacking Orlando Anderson, a reputed Crip who had attended the reported meeting in Biggie's hotel room in Anaheim. Tupac was riding with Suge in a BMW when a white Cadillac pulled up. A gunman shot Tupac four times. He died six days later. Hip-hop fans grieved and Puffy worried that the media would tie his name to the murder, especially since news stories in Los Angeles and Las Vegas included his photo.

Two days after Tupac died, police arrested Biggie. They caught him sitting in a car on a Brooklyn street smoking marijuana and charged him with drug possession. The police released him with a summons to appear in court, but the next day he was in the hospital. Lil' Cease was driving him and his girlfriend Charli Baltimore on the New Jersey Turnpike; it was raining and the brakes malfunctioned. Cease slammed head-on into a highway median. Charli reportedly flew through the windshield, lacerated her head, and broke her ankle. Biggie suffered a broken femur bone. For the next twenty-four hours, police suspected that someone might have tampered with the brakes. Biggie's mother disagreed. "We knew it was just his brakes and the rain."

Doctors transferred him to the Kessler Rehabilitation Center and he underwent physical therapy. He spent three months reflecting on his life. He saw that he was young, "doing different shows for thirty thousand dollars a piece, [and] coming home with a million and a half" in his pocket. He bought a house and car and "the company that I was keeping, they was moving too fast. Everything just came apart, you know what I'm sayin'?" He had a "streak of bad luck," wrecked his car, "had problems with my wife, that whole East Coast, West Coast thing." He decided, "My peace of mind is more important, my mom, my son, my daughter, my family, are what matters to me now."

In November, the doctors had released him, but he was still using a wheelchair.

Biggie knew Tupac's audience always would see him as the guy who hated their idol. He told reporters they could hate Christopher Wallace but enjoy the Notorious B.I.G.'s music. "I can't really speak for Puff but I kind of think he feels the same way," he added during this interview. "You know, Sean Combs and 'Puff Daddy' are two different people."

So were Biggie Smalls and Christopher Wallace. But the stay in Kessler made him realize he didn't have to stay trapped in the image. He withdrew from the industry. "It's not worth it anymore," he said publicly. "That's why I just stay in the motherfucking house."

Puffy, meanwhile, was taking steps to move from rap and R & B and toward "universal" sounds for a white audience. He signed Fuzzbubble, a studio project from two white musicians that grew to become a four-man rock band. The group's name described their "fuzzy" guitar sound and nonthreatening "bubblegum" pop melodies. He received their demo and saw a way to tap into the large white audience that enjoyed rock music. He asked to see them perform live, but the group asked, "Who is Puffy?" After they heard about his work with black artists Mary J. Blige, Biggie, Faith, and 112, they agreed to a private showcase. While he enjoyed their playing and stage presence, he requested another performance on acoustic instruments. The group dragged their guitars up to the Hit Factory and performed in the lounge; the drummer provided a back beat by pounding brushes against a tape-reel carton. Like Total, Fuzzbubble appealed to his ego: When he heard his name included in their cover of Badfinger's "Come and Get It," he laughed. But he still wanted to hear more material. As with Black Rob, he asked them to enter a studio and record a demo. Within a week, they had created six songs and he offered them a contract.

Another way he would reach white listeners was his first single, "Can't Nobody Hold Me Down." This single more than any defined the new Bad Boy sound and approach. In the studio, producers Carlos Broady and Nashiem Myrick had created an instrumental by looping, or repeating, a section of Grandmaster Flash and The Furious 5's 1981 political rap single, "The Message." They created the track for Def Jam rapper Foxy Brown, but she rejected it. Rapper Ice Cube had used the avant-garde music already without scoring a significant hit. Bad Boy's producers said they'd add new elements and make it "a hot radio joint," but then, according to Deric Angelettie, Puffy said, "Fuck it, I'm about to make an album. If they don't want it—and I'm giving them a hit in their lap [sic]—then I'll make it a hit!"

Where the original featured socially conscious descriptions of every aspect of ghetto life, his new version found him and Mase attacking critics with prissy lyrics. For its chorus, he and Mase chanted slogans patterned after Matthew Wilder's reggae-style "Break My Stride," a white pop hit from 1984. His use of "The Message" managed to bring him the white acceptance he had been seeking. This diluted version of a once proud classic would sell over two million copies and usher in a new era at Bad Boy Entertainment.

After releasing Biggie's "Big Poppa" remix, which included a gentler backing track, Puffy asked Biggie to accompany him on a trip to Los Angeles. Puffy and Mase would film a video for *Hell Up in Harlem*'s first single. In the clip, they'd ride across a desert in a convertible. Puffy would stand in a crowded nightclub with women literally pawing at his chest. He and Mase also would borrow a popular gimmick from big budget action movies, walking toward the camera with a fiery explosion behind them. Biggie was still in a wheelchair, but made the trip.

Away from the set he reminded interviewers that he and Tupac once had been best friends, he had nothing against the West Coast, and he actually was thinking of moving his family to California. But his comments did not end negative publicity surrounding Bad Boy and Puffy. Articles continued to echo the details of Death Row's vendetta.

Puffy, meanwhile, used newspaper interviews to alter his image: shifting from the tough talk in *Vibe,* right before Tupac's murder, he now said he wasn't a gangster. The white media was on his side; in him, white reporters and Buppies saw what they felt was a much more palatable black man. He was not big and muscular like Suge; he was soft-spoken and acquiescent; he didn't harbor political views; and his music was less threatening than Death Row releases. He was also a good dancer. Major newspapers began to depict the "feud" as a one-sided attack from Death Row. Reporters didn't yet know that bouncer Curtis Howard had offered a different version of the Jake Robles murder. If anything, white reporters heard his new pop style, saw his new friendly pop rapper Mase, and began to present Marion "Suge" Knight as a bully who had targeted Puffy for no reason.

By now, newspapers and the police claimed that Bad Boy had ties to the Southside Crips. Puffy needed a break from the drama. In December he paid for his old friends from Howard to accompany him to Trinidad.[2] He asked them to bring sampling equipment and a portable sequencing studio. For the next month, in Caribbean Sound Basin studios, Puffy worked with Deric Angelettie, Stevie "J" Jordan, Ron Lawrence, Nashiem Myrick, Carlos Broady, and engineer Doug Wilson on new songs. He didn't let artists join them, and forbid producers from throwing parties. As Deric remembered, "We went down there so focused and hyped because Puff sat us down and said, 'I'm giving y'all the opportunity to do B.I.G.'s whole album.' We was like, Whoa, let's do it. Rarely do producers get to go somewhere and focus. We came up with 'The World Is Filled,' 'Downfall,' and 'What's Beef,' just to name a few."

Each day they recorded up to five instrumentals, or 90 percent of what would be Biggie's own Tupac-style double CD. Angelettie and Ron Lawrence produced "Hypnotize." Stevie J. wrote music for "Mo Money, Mo Problems." Nashiem Myrick and Carlos Broady recorded "Somebody's Gotta Die." They also produced tracks for Biggie's "Nasty Boy" and Faith Evans's "I Just Can't." By the time they returned to New York they had an estimated forty to one hundred instrumentals ready to go. They also saw themselves as a production group loyal to their charismatic, strong-willed benefactor, Puffy.

At Bad Boy, Biggie heard some tracks. Minutes into "Hypnotize," set to Herb Alpert's oldie "Rise," he pulled Angelettie aside and whispered, "Biggie, Biggie, Biggie can't you see? Sometimes your words just hypnotize me." He added that he was already mentally composing a third verse for the song. When Angelettie asked to hear it, Big said he needed twenty

---

2. A published rumor claimed that Biggie was so broke in 1996 that Faith had to buy their Christmas presents.

minutes. Twenty minutes later, he recited three verses and said "Hypnotize" should be his first single.

The trip to Trinidad had meant that Bad Boy would no longer be dependent on outside producers who resisted Puffy's new pop-style direction. He then met with producer Easy Mo Bee. "By that time Big had a lot of shows," Mo remembered. "I was seeing him less. Then it was time for the second album. Puff called me into the office and told me to play some beats, and we went through over fifty beats." He sat by a radio and played Mo's cassette. "Nothing was going on without going past Puff," Mo recalled. A few seconds into one song, he impatiently pressed fast forward. Another song began, and he moved past it. He passed another; he rejected more and more instrumentals. With each rejection he'd face Mo and offer comments like, "I want you to do that over, I don't like that, I don't feel it, it ain't got enough soul, you know."

The problem was that Mo Bee had brought a tape of *Ready*-era hardcore at a time when Puffy planned to move Biggie into the mostly white pop market. Mo played another beat, and Puffy said: "Nah." For the next: "Nah." The next: "Nah, nah, nah." Mo thought, Damn.

Puffy decided to show him the sound he wanted. He played a few of the commercial instrumentals that would be on the new album. "He was attempting to reach a whole other level of the public," Mo Bee learned. This was why, where *Ready to Die* included one duet with Method Man, the new album found Biggie collaborating with the crossover rap group Bone Thugs and Harmony, R & B singer R. Kelly, and other pop-style guest stars. Mo Bee decided to play Puffy a beat on his tape that fit the watered-down pop mode. As the R & B pop track played, Puffy sat up and excitedly said, *"Yo!"*

Biggie continued to enter the studio and describe the streets for a white pop audience. To help reach these listeners, Puffy provided tracks built around familiar sounds from Diana Ross and the Commodores and enlisted singers to provide catchy choruses.

By now, Biggie had left his old style behind. In the past he had borrowed West Coast styles from Ice Cube and Tupac and crafted a persona as an amoral street kid and crack dealer turned rapper that helped *Ready to Die* sell 1.9 million copies. Back then, fans loved and feared him and feared for his safety: He had claimed on his songs that rival dealers could kill him or that he might commit suicide. Back then, he also felt that his album would at most sell half a million copies.[3]

His new album was nothing like this. Under Puffy's guidance, he had become pretentious, flamboyant, and a bit too comfortable. He described double crosses, dead friends, and threats from other dealers, but also sang a ballad, discussed his new condominium, wristwatch, and car, then rapped, "Don't forget the publishing."

In public, Puffy attributed the new direction to personal change. For *Ready To Die,* "he wasn't really enjoying making the music as much. He was just trying to give you his story." For *Life After Death:* "He really enjoyed making the music."

More guest stars appeared. D.M.C. provided a link to the old school. R. Kelly sang rhythm-and-blues. Too Short brought lewd raps, while Lil' Kim provided more of the same. Aside from Premier, RZA of Wu-Tang, and Prodigy of Mobb Deep, Puffy and his Hit Men produced the majority of the album's 110 minutes.

For the cover shot, Biggie posed near a hearse that had his name on the license plate. After a skit that presented the final seconds of "Suicidal Thoughts" as a nightmare, Biggie set flamboyant lyrics over the new house sound, a hit parade of pop hits, including Diana Ross's 1980 hit "I'm Coming Out" and "Missing You." For "Playa Hater," he offered a straightforward ballad, while "Notorious Thugs" paired him with speed-rappers Bone Thugs and Harmony. Only on Premier's "Ten Crack Commandments" and "B.I.G. Interlude" did he sound like the social critic from "Party and Bullshit." On these songs, he listed his top ten rules for drug dealing and offered a tribute to Schooly D's pioneering gangsta rap single, "P.S.K."

Puffy also used *Life After Death* to introduce his new wave of Bad Boy signings. One new act was Carl Thomas, from a housing project on Chicago's South Side, whom Puffy discovered while dining at Chaz & Wilson's in Manhattan. Thomas sang the chorus on "The World Is Filled" in such a way, he explained, "people thought I was some old guy from Vegas with a purple suit on." Biggie truly had come a long way from his roots.

---

3.   He once joked, "You don't see no Doggy Dogg at the end of my name."

Even the *New York Times*'s Jon Pareles noticed. To him, *Life After Death* "was gangsta rap business as usual: posturing and raw thrills in accepted commercial form." Pareles added: "Even a refrain like 'time for you to die' arrives as a pop hook."

Even so, Puffy had bigger plans for his artist. His video for "Hypnotize" continued to present Biggie as a "Big Willie," instead of as the social critic of "Party and Bullshit." Director Paul Hunter filled the big budget video with mermaids, new cars, helicopters, party scenes, mansions, high-end fashions, jewelry, champagne, showgirls, and special effects. On the warehouse set, Puffy and Hunter were watching footage. Biggie stood near a cage that held a panther. A friend asked, "Whose idea was this shit?" Big answered, "Puff's. That just adds ambience, that's all."

Earlier, Puffy had explained Big's popularity as follows: "He has a straight-up black sound, like somebody's big black uncle from Brooklyn." Now, he and Biggie were filmed near each other in lavender silk suits and matching shoes as fancy as Big's new sound. Puffy, the Colonel Tom Parker to his Elvis, assured him this would help sell more albums. He was right.

In February of 1997, Puffy took Biggie to Los Angeles for a promotional tour. By now, Faith had given birth to his son Christopher Jordan but was getting closer to thirty-year-old music producer Todd Russaw. After Missy Elliott moved in with Faith, Russaw would call Elliott on the telephone or stop by to work on her album. "Right after I had my baby, he sort of revealed that he was a little attracted to me," Faith said later.

Biggie accepted this. He planned to work with Charli Baltimore and Jay-Z in his new group The Commission and his confidence was back. "I just booked, like, thirty shows for forty-five-k each, so shit is straight," he told a friend.

When they traveled in Los Angeles, they did so with extra security. While Marion "Suge" Knight was in prison for parole violation—after attacking reputed Crip Orlando Anderson in the MGM Grand hours before Tupac was shot—there was still a danger that supporters of Death Row might try to attack them.

Billboards on Sunset Boulevard promoted Tupac's posthumous film, *Gridlock'd,* and his posthumous *Makaveli* album. Five months had passed since his murder and Big was still using crutches. Even so, he managed to travel to a tattoo parlor and ask an artist to ink Psalm 27 on his arm. When Puffy saw the new tattoo, he had an artist put the same psalm in the same spot on his arm.

During this trip, Puffy recorded a few songs for what one writer called the "goodfellas" project. He wanted The Lox to try and fashion an image around Scorcese/Pileggi collaborations *Goodfellas* and *Casino,* films about organized crime figures who dressed well, lived extravagantly, and pledged loyalty to each other.

Biggie claimed that he was "managing Puffy as an artist. We're just trying to level it out. When Puff sat me down and said, 'Yo, I want you to manage me,' before I said yes, I had to ask him why." According to Biggie, Puffy had said, "Who could teach me how to be the best artist but the best artist?"

Whether Puffy really was letting Biggie manage him is unknown. What's clear is that he needed Biggie's help for his debut. The management relationship claim seemed absurd when one learned about a particular session in a recording studio in the Valley. That afternoon, Biggie planned to lay down a guide vocal, Puffy would hear this rhyme, erase it, then say it over for his debut album. Biggie sat in a chair and moved his lips in time to the beat. Someone said he should get to work, since Puffy was on the way. He stopped mumbling, hobbled over to a microphone, and recorded his verse. When he was done, he left.

Away from Puffy, he used crutches, and made it to various interviews to repeat that he had no problems with the West Coast or Tupac and even wanted to buy a house in California. But some fans couldn't forget about the feud and continued to take it out on Biggie. During his appearance at the eleventh annual Soul Train Awards, another self-aggrandizing music industry event, Biggie made it onto the stage and handed an award to singer Toni Braxton. But some people booed and jeered. Puffy now saw for himself how ineffective Biggie's interviews had been.

After the ceremony, Biggie rode in the passenger seat of a sport utility vehicle on Sunset Boulevard. This vehicle, according to the *Los Angeles Times,* was part of a ten-car caravan that included a dark Chevy Impala and a Mercedes 500. When the caravan stopped, the man called Zip emerged from the Mercedes 500 and spoke to Biggie and then to the driver of the Impala.

The next afternoon, Biggie reportedly traveled with Southside Crips to a Compton park and a basketball tournament.[4] The media also had reported on a police affidavit that claimed Bad Boy hired Crips as bodyguards. That afternoon, some Southside Crips reportedly warned Biggie about an older member upset with him over an unpaid debt.

That night, Puffy and Biggie attended a party thrown by *Vibe* magazine, which had been supportive of Bad Boy, featuring him and Biggie on a cover titled, "East Vs. West." They attended, Puffy said later, because they thought it would be a private affair. According to Puffy, Biggie said, "I finished my album. I just want to celebrate with you. I just want to have a good time." Then Biggie told him, "Hopefully I can meet some people, let them know I want to do some acting."

They headed to the party and sat at a table. Puffy remembered Biggie asking, "Yo, Puff, tonight could you just sit here with me all night?" Usually, Puffy was "real hyper" and liked to walk around. But he agreed to stay near Big and "a lot of people were coming and giving us positive greetings." The deejay played Biggie's new single, "Hypnotize," and people danced and chanted "Bad Boy."

Shortly before 1:00 A.M., the party ended because fire marshals complained about fire codes. Biggie hobbled with his cane, having left the crutches at home for tonight, and stood outside of Petersen's Automotive Museum for five minutes. Puffy said they discussed his album and posed for photos with fans. Reputed Crip Dwayne "Keefee D" Davis later told police he spoke with Biggie around this time, his lawyer Edi M. O. Faal said. After a few minutes, Puffy said it was time to go. "My car was in front, Biggie's was in the middle, and then another security vehicle was behind, which had the off-duty officers in," Puffy explained. Why he wasn't in the car with Biggie is unknown, but that night, six off-duty police officers provided security.

The three vehicles left the parking lot and turned onto Wilshire Boulevard. They stopped at a red light at the end of the street. "I was looking straight ahead basically, and I just heard shots ring out and when

---

4. Afeni Shakur, Tupac's mother, also felt Anderson had killed Tupac; she filed a wrongful death lawsuit against him and planned to see him in court in September 1998, but Anderson was murdered before then and the case never went to trial.

the shots rang out I immediately did the human reaction. I just ducked down and everybody in the car ducked down." According to the police, a dark Chevy Impala had stopped outside of Biggie's window and opened fire with a gun. *New Times* reported that a prison informant told police the shooter might be a man named "Amir," or a Southside Crip whose name "might be Kenny or Keeky."

A half-hour later, a doctor at Cedars-Sinai Hospital pronounced Biggie dead. He was twenty-four years old. His hip-hop career was one of the most successful and one of the shortest. Puffy claimed that he had asked Damien Butler to call Voletta Wallace, but that Damien started crying. "So I had to tell her. I had to calm her down, try to get somebody over to the house."

Voletta, however, remembered Damien calling. She didn't mention Puffy being on the telephone. Either way, security guards took Puffy to his hotel room. The next morning, people told him to leave Los Angeles immediately. He was soon at the airport, he said. At the boarding gate, he broke down in tears. While boarding the plane, he thought, "He's getting left here. He's at the morgue, just laying there." He thought: "My man is in a morgue, all fucked up." He wished Biggie could be near him during the flight back to New York. Police have yet to produce a suspect in the murder of Biggie Smalls.

# FIVE

# No Way Out

WHEN SEAN "PUFFY" COMBS ARRIVED AT THE FRANK E. CAMPBELL Funeral Home on the Upper East Side of Manhattan, he saw 350 mourners, many of them famous, had showed up to pay their last respects. Voletta read a passage from the Bible. Faith, who seemingly had been heading for a divorce, offered a rendition of "Walk With Me, Lord" so stirring some mourners burst into tears. Then Puffy went to the altar and eulogized Biggie. Mourners passed the casket to see Biggie in his white suit as The Lox's new song "We'll Always Love Big Poppa" played. The Lox reportedly had signed to Bad Boy as songwriters, but this single was one of the most powerful works the label had ever released. Producer Dame Grease provides a mournful instrumental and a chorus filled with the tiny voices of heavyhearted children. The Lox delivered heartfelt lyrics about Biggie in heaven; the details of his career; his underreported positive influence on ghetto fashion and black self-image; the prospects for his reconciliation with Tupac in the afterlife; and the two children he left behind. They also describe how sad it is that hip-hop celebrates gun homicide when it ranks as one of the biggest causes of death for young African-American males. "Everybody stay strong, the good die young," one member rapped. "Where we from, it's all wrong. We all confused."

The Lox hit the nail right on the head. Biggie's death seemed to cause hip-hop to spiral even further off course. The hip-hop audience was inconsolable. Seeing Tupac Shakur and Biggie murdered within six months of each other was akin to the black community seeing Martin Luther King, Jr., and Robert Kennedy murdered within six months of each other during the late 1960s. Much of hip-hop's core black audience became disillusioned after Biggie's death.

As the motorcade passed through Biggie's old stomping grounds in Clinton Hill and Fort Greene in Brooklyn, fans wandered the streets aimlessly. For them, the aimlessness would continue for years. The media, meanwhile, believed one of Puffy's interview comments to Sia Michel of *Spin*—"We were like brothers"—and promoted Puffy as a grieving friend. Puffy appeared on television and in print to discuss Biggie. But when he did it, he did not seem as credible as The Lox, who delivered a heartfelt number without considering sales figures, personal gain, or pop chart position. Puffy would begin by discussing Biggie, then segue into his record company and upcoming solo album. "Biggie wouldn't want me to stop," he said. "Biggie wouldn't want Bad Boy to stop."

Upon its release on March 25, Biggie's double CD, *Life After Death,* debuted at Number 1 on the Albums Chart and it sold 690,000 copies in its first week.

Arista's senior director of sales and marketing Kirk Bonin said that as soon as "Hypnotize" hit the radio, they received three million orders.

The old Puffy—who had stood behind Biggie on the cover of *Vibe* or danced behind him in the documentary *The Show*—was suddenly thrust into center stage, and he wanted to be the center of attention. He had spent a lifetime trying to reach this point.

Puffy drafted a statement about the murder and seemed to use it as another vehicle for self-promotion. After identifying Biggie as a Bad Boy artist, he called Biggie a "lyrical genius," a "literary giant," and the greatest rapper of all time. Puffy also wrote that Big's problems stemmed from the fact that he had grown up without a father. Despite this, Puffy added, "Notorious B.I.G. and I both had to teach ourselves to become men." After complaining about the media dragging them into the feud, he concluded, "My music must provide the young not only with the reality of life. It must serve as an inspiration for us to create a better life."

The mainstream media did not question whether he was using Biggie's death to fuel sales. Instead, he was now the big story on MTV: During an interview, he denied using Crips as security guards. He appeared on the cover of *Rolling Stone* and presented a new image: a baseball cap, a fur coat hanging off his shoulders, and baggy jeans slung low around his hips so everyone could see his name-brand underwear. He told interviewers trite anecdotes about how Biggie refused to perform at the 1995 Soul Train Awards because he did not like the shoes he was wearing. He even attached historical significance to the tattoos on his forearms. The one that reads "Friends Forever" was for his grandmother, who died in 1994, while the psalm, which he'd rushed to get after seeing it on Biggie's arm, was now a "memorial to Biggie."

The media ate it up. The story had everything: fame, fortune, success, betrayal, murder, and loss. Biggie's mother later said, "They had a beautiful relationship. But it was a business relationship. Puffy was not Christopher's best friend."

As he told it, the idea for the Biggie tribute arrived while he was depressed at home one afternoon. He was watching MTV when The Police's black-and-white clip for "I'll Be Watching You" aired, and he was inspired to use the song for a single about Big. What actually seemed to happen was that The Lox had presented their excellent tribute single and Puffy wanted to record his own. He approached Biggie's widow, Faith, he added, and said he wanted to do the biggest tribute ever done. She was hesitant, but he won her over. He got her and producer Stevie J. into the studio and tried to set his tribute to a number of sounds. He had his black producers try to set it to a number of records by black artists. They offered one track and he vetoed it, then another. They set it to the O'Jays' "I Miss You" and it was close, but he presented The Police idea.

"I'll Be Watching You," 1984's song of the year, was a favorite at weddings, despite the fact that Sting's lyrics detailed how a stalker might serenade his prey. After producers set the bass line over a drum track, Puffy asked his ghostwriter, Dame Grease, to help move the song from its original meaning. Grease worked with Puffy on a lyric universal enough to appeal to a white audience and specific enough to reach bereaved fans. While Puffy claims the song was heartfelt, the writing session reportedly consisted of him sitting with Dame Grease for a day, writing four bars, and then telling Grease to "take it from there."

With this song he was able to rap over the soft rock music his class-mates had played during his high school years. After years of struggling in black music, hoping for "mainstream," or white, acceptance, he finally had it and couldn't let go. Whites wanted him to be a star. When Stevie J. played the final track, everyone in the studio agreed it would be a hit. Puffy then had Faith change the chorus. She felt it would be easy, that she only had to "change a few words, write a few phrases," she explained.

But Puffy was obsessed. If someone suggested changes, he ignored them. Only he knew what it should sound like. For six days he coached Faith and 112 on how to sing the chorus and gave orders to Stevie J. and two engineers during the mixing sessions. In due course, "I'll Be Missing You" entered the *Billboard* chart at Number 1, only the fifth title in the history of the Hot 100 to do so. The song also topped six *Billboard* charts for six weeks. The song's light melody and "rap," actually Puffy mumbling proverbs, made it 1997's best-selling maxisingle and a favorite of white listeners. He became the darling of the mainstream media, the MTV-approved face of rap.

At Daddy's House, he continued work on his solo album. He'd changed its title to *No Way Out* and was adding new songs that capital-ized on Big's murder and solidified his position as grieving lieutenant.

Puffy worked nonstop and expected everyone around him to do the same. He told reporters, "That's what keeps me hungry. This is a 'job.' You don't get comfortable. You keep doing what got you to this point." He told employees, "You want to live like me? Stay up till four and five in the morning doing your job. If you take this shit like it's a nine to five, you're never going to get where I am." His employees heeded the advice of their charismatic leader. They wanted to earn their own fortunes, rallied around him, and saw themselves as a family. "Like, I may do a song for The Lox and not get a dime from it," said Mase. "Do a remix for Total and won't ask them for anything, 'cause that's how we roll with each other."

Work continued on *No Way Out*. Puffy created what would become— for better or worse—the new house sound. For "Been Around the World," which was originally titled "Why Do They Hate Us," he showcased

Mase's innocuous style over Ron Lawrence and Deric Angelettie's loop of David Bowie's pop hit "Let's Dance."[1] During its hook Biggie sang Lisa Stansfield's "Been Around the World." Hip-hop purists felt it was anemic, but Puffy wanted to reach white listeners and pop radio.

He continued to promote his friendship with Biggie. Sandwiched between a Bone Thugs and Harmony–style number, his string-laden "I Love You, Baby," and his cheesy album filler "Senorita," he offered "Victory." According to the label, the song represented "how close he and the Notorious B.I.G. were." An informed listener, however, might wonder if this was a duet or a work-in-progress for Biggie's proposed side project, The Commission.

Over an unaccompanied sample from a *Rocky* movie, Biggie's ad-libs reveal that he was preparing to begin his lyrics. Puffy's voice bursts in to deliver a rhyme. Behind Puffy, however, Biggie is complaining to an engineer. "One, one two. Check me out right here, yo! You can turn the track up a little bit for me, all up in my ears. The mike is loud but the music ain't loud." Puffy raps as if they're recording together, "Yeah, right, no matter what we air-tight," while Big says, "Yeah, yeah. Now the mike is low now. Turn the mike up more. My shit is all the way up. Yeah. The music's too loud. I like that shit hot. Uh-huh, uh-huh, uh-huh; it's okay now."

Halfway through the song, Biggie begins a lyric about The Commission. "In The Commission, you ask for permission to hit him," he says. His verse ends with the phrase "another day in the life of The Commission." Puffy offers tepid raps and Busta Rhymes hoots and hollers, but whether "Victory" was for Puffy or whether he recorded new raps into spaces left empty for Commission bandmates is unclear. However, by refusing to submit to an interview for this work, he ensured that he wouldn't have to face this question. One thing, though, is certain. Biggie never mentioned Puffy being in The Commission.

During the session for "Pain" he told *Rolling Stone*'s Mikal Gilmore that the song captured how he felt when he was at home "and I'm real

---

1.  When Puffy was asked about the Bowie sample in 1998, he said, "It was Mase's idea."

upset and I'm crying." This said, Puffy entered the recording booth and delivered a lyric that mentioned his father's murder and the City College tragedy. Then he described a dream in which Biggie descended from heaven to tell him to continue making money with Bad Boy—that he should remember "the kids." From here, his voice goes from somber to chipper and he adds, "That's when I knew that Bad Boy lives."

Gilmore, who "liked him a lot" but felt "he was a hard person to get close to," nonetheless crowned Puffy the new "King of Hip-Hop." Puffy was on the cover a month after *Rolling Stone* claimed that Biggie's murder meant "Bad Boy and Death Row must now face the music."

The cover story also made him the most "magical" black musician since Michael Jackson or MC Hammer.

He intended to introduce new artists while media interest was at its highest. According to Andre Harrell: "He's able to spend money on a video for Big that will introduce Puffy, which in turn will produce a video where Puffy introduces Mase. And then Mase introduces The Lox, and so on . . ."

In April 1997, he went to a golf course to film a scene for the "Mo' Money, Mo' Problems" video. That sun-drenched afternoon, Mase, wearing a suit on an immaculately trimmed golf course, pretends to interview Puffy, who is impersonating a Tiger Woods–style golf champion while fans look on. Backstage, however, a minor dispute erupted. Puffy had shown Mase the silver, reflective suit he wanted him to wear. Mase objected. "The first thing that came to my mind when Puff showed me the outfit for 'Mo' Money, Mo' Problems' was when Easy E dissed Dr. Dre and had him in the video with that glitter suit on," Mase admitted. "I said, 'I'm not gonna wear that! You got me looking like the Temptations.' " Ultimately, Mase did wear it, and the so-called shiny suit became Bad Boy's new image, the crossover look of choice, and the reason many hard-core artists viewed the label with contempt.

In the video they also wear shiny red spaceman suits and float in an antigravity chamber. Biggie appears on a monitor behind them; the song stops and footage of him delivering a paranoid rant, of how wealth causes jealousy, fills the screen. Puffy and Mase then appear in identical "shiny suits" to dance, shake near each other, and shove their faces into the camera. Later that month Puffy directed a video for The Lox's "We'll Always Love Big Poppa." For this clip the hard-core group sat on the stoop of a Harlem brownstone and eulogized Big with famous guest stars Faith, Fat Joe, two-thirds of Salt N' Pepa, and Craig Mack. Everyone looks inconsolable. The difference between the two videos is astounding.

Puffy filmed another video two weeks later. In it he wears a fancy suit and rides a sleek motorcycle down a picturesque highway. Although he fell from the bike and injured his arm, the show went on. Styled in an angelic white suit, he crossed an Elysian field crowded with black and white children in matching white outfits. Then, at night, he appears in a snazzy black outfit and tap-dances in the rain on an empty street. Fans ate it up, especially his white ones. It was pure Michael Jackson. His sphere of influence began to extend past his minions and lackeys at the label. The white media singled him out for glory. Even Hype Williams, director of the "Missing You" video, began to put on airs, saying that the video was "a visual interpretation of how Mr. Combs feels at the present time." Biggie did not appear anywhere in this video.

MTV felt Puffy would continue to earn them high ratings. In an endless stream of profiles and news stories, Puffy promoted his new image to a worldwide audience that usually supported such trifling crossover artists as Will Smith, Young MC, and MC Hammer. During one MTV profile, he claimed that an interview with Fox News would be his last; he would stop speaking publicly and become as reclusive as Michael Jackson. This wasn't true at all, but it added a little drama to another obsequious segment. On Fox, when the anchorperson asked his opinion on why Biggie was murdered, Puffy evaded the issue, though the question was harmless. When the interview ended, however, Puffy threw a tantrum, ripping the Fox microphone off his shirt and ranting while leaving the building. "I'm so heated right now, I don't want to talk right here," he said. "I'm feeling nothing, there's nothing going on, I don't want to argue with the dude. I need to . . . Wooooeee!" His publicist endured it. "You're not listening," he snapped. "I did enough stuff. I told everybody what I wanted to tell everybody. Now I just want to go make my music." He continued, "I saw it coming from the get-go! I was reading the prestuff and I was looking at you like, 'I told you! I told you!' Do not even fuck with that news that . . . what is that called? What kind of programming is that?" Within days, however, Puffy broke his vow of silence, telling a black reporter, "To be honest, I really want to do country."

BIGGIE USED TO STAND UP TO PUFFY. WITH HIM GONE, PUFFY WAS free to make rap or watered down hip-hop for whites and to assume total control of Bad Boy. In the studio, he kept artists as busy as worker ants and they were happy to do it, feeling they were supporting a black man in business. Faith recorded another album; Mase and The Lox churned out songs. If he needed them, he had them contribute to his work, enabling him to profit whether he worked with or without them. By now, Hype Williams and Busta Rhymes were eager to work and be included in the glow of the mainstream spotlight. Thanks to Puffy's marketing and cross-promotion genius, the telephones at the office and studio never stopped ringing.

In the studio he'd have producers and engineers spend fifteen hours mixing just one song. He'd ask them to change entire sections. If something as tiny as a high-hat noise, played by a drummer tapping a cymbal over his beat, sounded off, he demanded another mix. When old friend Deric Angelettie played him an instrumental for "Do You Know," he asked Angelettie to sit with him. "I hear strings here," he said. "I hear it getting dramatic here, I hear it doing this and doing that." Angelettie and coproducer J-Dub felt his revision turned their raw hard-core track into crossover pop. But soon his influence had them reversing their opinions. Angelettie later would claim that Puffy's strings would make it a "great R & B record."

Puffy now truly had the magic touch. He was no longer the man who, after Big's murder, said, "I want out of this. I never planned on this." He was now the white media's chosen one. Even *Rolling Stone* predicted he would be rap's biggest star. Already, three of his fifteen songs were major pop hits. "Can't Nobody Hold Me Down" topped six *Billboard* charts for three months and was *Soundscan*'s best-selling single of the year. "It's All About the Benjamins" was hot, and would be even hotter once he remixed it for white fans. His album would move Bad Boy past Biggie and into a lucrative crossover phase. It would begin his reign as the second coming of MC Hammer. In fact, the similarities between the two were staggering. Both were dancers turned label owners who would tour with entourages called "The Family." Puffy had decided to credit his album to "Puff Daddy & The Family," with The Lox, Mase, and Black Rob standing behind him on the cover as if they were a backup group. Like Hammer, Puffy also would produce most of his "spin-off" groups, sell millions of albums, and have extraordinary success in marketing watered-down rap to white audiences. But Puffy would outdo him. He would be able to maintain his ties to a black audience by reminding everyone that he was Biggie's good friend. He even threw in a "personal letter" to Biggie on his liner notes. "Not a second passes that you're not on my mind," it read. "I would do anything to turn back the hands of time and bring you back."

He had the Midas touch. He even had the media eating out of his hand. He could do almost anything and not endanger sales. Missing a public appearance upset fans but also created demand. In fact, a day before *No Way Out* hit the stores, he was to appear at a Virgin Records store in Manhattan.

Hundreds of young fans waited on line for hours. They continued to wait even after midnight, in a downpour. Instead of appearing, Puffy sent his street team in Bad Boy jackets to wave promotional signs. Fans had to settle for the life-size cardboard cutout of him in the store window. The next day, undaunted, his fans started buying his album, and it debuted at Number 1, with first week sales of over 560,000 copies. His single "I'll Be Missing You" was still America's Number 1 single. Biggie's "Mo' Money, Mo' Problems," featuring Puffy's voice as well, was Number 2. Russell Simmons called him "the hottest nigga there is." MTV said, "The only chart safe from the Puff Daddy onslaught is the modern rock singles chart." He already was trying to top that one as well.

Big's murder left the playing field wide open for someone who promoted flashy costumes, conservative songwriting, Hammer-style dancing, and familiar melodies. *Rolling Stone* and MTV continued to promote him, but a few critics attacked, ridiculing his "Mafioso" pose, corporate pretensions, songwriting, and production. They described his use of classic songs as uninspired and demeaning to Bowie, The Police, Roberta Flack, and American composer Samuel Barber, who reportedly went unnamed even though Puffy had used "Agnus Dei" to introduce "I'll Be Missing You."

*Billboard* wrote that his album proved "commercial success doesn't neces-sarily equal artistic merit." *Time* magazine named him "the hottest pro-ducer in hip-hop," but called the album "an uneven work." Fans loved him. They didn't care that he presented himself as a friendly, harmless Tiger Woods–type, while "It's All About the Benjamins" and "Young G's" found him describing watches, cars, and rings, singing, "I have nice things," then adding: "Get your own, nigga. That's what I did!" They didn't notice that, after campaigning to avoid the Bad Boy/Death Row "feud," he spent most of *No Way Out* describing his heroic role in the battle. As long as he had his fans, *Billboard,* MTV, *Rolling Stone, Time,* and *Newsweek* would have to continue promoting him. Bad reviews didn't change a thing.

By August 28, Fleetwood Mac's reunion album, *The Dance,* knocked *No Way Out* from the Number 1 spot on the pop chart and "I'll Be Miss-ing You" dropped from Number 2 to Number 3 on the singles chart. How-ever, Biggie's "Mo' Money, Mo' Problems" continued to be the Number 1 single in America. Puffy had to keep it going.

Originally the plan had been to release three other albums in 1997: Faith's second album and debuts by Mase and The Lox. *No Way Out's* status as a huge hit delayed progress on other albums because of inces-sant interviews. At Bad Boy, employees could not make major decisions without his input. Instead, they went as far as they could on the three al-bums without his presence. They created marketing strategies, arranged publicity events, sifted through proposals and treatments, and hired video directors and more, but they could not move past the point where Puffy accepted or rejected ideas. If he showed up during this period, it report-edly was to discuss his European tour, new singles by himself and Biggie, and his plans to shoot two more Biggie-related videos. Even when general manager Jeff Burroughs called with information about various projects, Puffy would say he couldn't deal with it now.

Puffy did, however, keep his appointments in the studio. Artists on other labels were paying $150,000 for a single instrumental. He didn't see that his main strength—his drive for success—was becoming a liability. In one meeting with Jeff Burroughs, who tried to discuss various album projects, Puffy said, "I'm not doing anything before the MTV Awards except rehearsing for the show. That's the only thing I'm gonna focus on."

Burroughs said, "But if we don't shoot either the Faith or Mase video before then we won't be able to have them both ready when the singles drop."

"I'm not doing anything before MTV."

"But then we're gonna be late with the video."

"I don't care."

"Puff, you're not listening. We're gonna get fucked up if we're late with one of their videos—"

"I don't care. I know what I'm doing, and until you can go into that studio and come out with a Number one song, we're not talking about it anymore."

Burroughs left the room.


PUFFY APPEARED ON MTV'S "VIDEO MUSIC AWARDS" ON WEDNES-day, September 4, 1997, and entered that "magical" arena reserved for crossover stars like Michael Jackson and MC Hammer. That night he wore a baggy T-shirt; baggy light-colored pants, a gold chain, and sun-glasses. His dancers wore light-colored suits, and a thirty-two-person gospel choir wore white robes as they swayed in the background. Then Faith Evans emerged from backstage and Sting rose from a hole in the floor to join her as huge video monitors showed photos of Biggie in a suit. While Sting struggled beneath Faith's spirited vocal, Puffy tried to steal the show with his dance routine from the video. All the while, his sidemen in suits kneeled on the stage and faced the heavens. It was crossover music history in the making.

Puffy promoted himself to the entire world as Biggie's grieving friend. When Biggie received the award for best rap video, Puffy brought Voletta Wallace on stage with him. When Biggie won another award, Biggie's wife, Faith, joined him on stage, only to step aside as he delivered yet an-other eulogy. The MTV awards promoted the image of Bad Boy as a fam-ily united by the murder.

Other artists wanting the magic to rub off on them vied for his atten-tion. In 1996, Puffy had remixed Mariah Carey's song "Fantasy" by in-cluding a vocal from guest star Ol' Dirty Bastard and a melody from The

Tom Tom Club's eighties dance hit "Genius of Love." Now he told reporters she wanted the "same formula" for her new single, "Honey." But Carey was independent. Before entering the studio, she would have her lyrics and melodies already written. In this way, she hoped to avoid an overbearing producer intruding on her creative process. In the studio, Puffy, Stevie J., and rapper Q-Tip of A Tribe Called Quest offered suggestions. After Q-Tip told her to keep a sample playing throughout the entire song, Puffy said, "I think we should have a bridge."

Carey replied: "Ahh, I don't think we should have a bridge."

Puffy responded, "I'm telling you, we should have a bridge."

Stevie J. and Carey then created a bridge around the words "hey deejay." Carey wanted it to appear midway through the song, and he agreed, as long as it also started the song. Next, they filmed a two-million-dollar video that shattered her wholesome image and helped position Bad Boy as a pop/rap powerhouse. Instead of the light-skinned diva in flashy gowns, the video for "Honey" presented her as a secret agent in stiletto heels and a bikini. She played a hostage in a mansion. An actor with more than a passing resemblance to her then estranged husband, Sony executive Tommy Mottola, played her captor. She then escapes from the house, leaps on a Jet Ski, and is involved in a high-speed chase until Mase throws a rope down from his helicopter and rescues her. The video then cuts to her dancing with sailors behind her and The Lox surrounding her and Puffy in a corridor and mouthing a gruff lyric. The camera films her leaving the ocean in Puerto Rico and leaping into the arms of a younger man, but doesn't end until Puffy manages to shove his face into the camera a few times. Soon after, comedian Chris Rock patterned a routine around what had now become Puffy's video direction. After interviewing Arsenio Hall on his HBO talk show, Rock screened a "Puff Daddy remix" of the conversation showing Puffy standing in front of the two men.

During the last week of September, Carey's *Butterfly* debuted at Number 1 on the pop chart with first week sales of over 235,000 copies. Puffy started working with L.L. Cool J on *Phenomenon* and wondered about the people around him. If he told a joke, everyone laughed, he told Smokey Fontaine; he wondered if people kissed his ass because he was, as he put it, "the leader." Even as Bad Boy artists increasingly were starting to see themselves as a tight-knit "Family," Puffy began to feel he wasn't "part of the gang."

He also told a reporter that he worked late into the night because he wanted to win. "This is why I don't go out to the Hamptons."

Yet, that summer, he would rent a large home in the Hamptons near rich neighbors like Donna Karan. He would lounge at home in plush, white terry-cloth robes and publicly in Italian suits, diamond watches, and platinum chains. He would throw star-studded parties and worked his way into the socialite Hamptons circle by hosting charity events. He now would watch his big-budget videos on a giant-screen television set in his master bedroom or gather his thoughts while facing gorgeous sunsets outside of his picture windows overlooking the Atlantic. When rap magazines questioned his move into crossover rap, or mentioned that his peers in hip-hop felt he was ruining the genre, he would say, "It's fucked up. We niggas don't root for each other."

HIS NEXT PROJECT, *HARLEM WORLD,* CHANGED THE BAD BOY sound even more. Biggie's booming voice no longer defined the label. Mase's gentle lisp and tepid raps replaced emotionally resonant works like *Ready to Die.* Bad Boy now specialized in flat voices over nostalgic pop, rock, or disco of the past. Even more preposterous was label marketing that insinuated that Mase could fill the void caused by Big's death. Mase denied in interviews that he tried to do this, but rapped, on "Take What's Yours," that he would "take [listeners] back where Biggie took 'em before." Either way, his use of Biggie's themes and guests, including Lil' Kim, was marred by his Puffy-like habit of following strong points with such filler as "it's all about money, hoes, and clothes and shit." Hard-core listeners felt that, compared to Biggie, Mase didn't measure up.

Mase, however, also had the support of the major media; high-profile videos like Biggie's "Mo' Money, Mo' Problems" and Mariah's "Honey" introduced his good-humored crossover-minded persona. Now in the studio, it was hard to believe he'd once worried that his vocal on the Total single made him sound like Father MC.

Instead of protesting, Mase agreed to Puffy's ideas for songs like "Do

You Wanna Get $" and "Will They Die for You." He mumbled foolish lyrics over Hit Men tracks set to eighties dance hits like Teena Marie's "Square Biz," and even sang the lyrics to Culture Club's "Do You Really Want To Hurt Me." Yet, even as he appeared in a series of videos and promoted possessions over people, and the glitzy Bad Boy lifestyle, Mase began to retreat from the new house sound. He tried to rebel by distancing himself from pop samples during interviews and hiring outside producers Jermaine Dupri and The Neptunes. But his defiance only led to these producers filling their contributions with their own dull pop samples.

While "24 Hours" presented The Lox, their friend DMX, born Earl Simmons, and aggressive hard-core, most of *Harlem World* found Total, Puffy, Kelly Price, Lil' Kim, Lil' Cease, Jay-Z, and Busta Rhymes marring songs with formulaic crossover rap. Puffy even included "Jealous Guys," a faithful cover of New Edition's ballad "Jealous Girl," as his album closer and sang on it with 112 and Mase.

Sessions yielded just the sort of music Puffy needed to propel Mase into suburbia. His first single made use of the tired old Kool & The Gang chestnut "Hollywood Swinging." It was perfect for pop radio. The video was even better. It was filmed on a set in front of a hotel in Las Vegas with flashing neon lights, explosions, and voluptuous female dancers in revealing shorts. When he handed Mase another shiny suit, Mase asked, "Is you crazy? What is this, my image?"

Indeed it was. Puffy reminded him that his ideas exceeded Mase's goal of selling a half-million copies. In fact, within a year Mase had earned more than he had in six years as a "hard-core" rapper. And back then, Mase never saw a dime. "Fuck it," Mase told himself. "I may as well run with it—as long as I don't have to kiss anybody's ass. Just make mines baggy and put a pair of Nike Airs with it!" When he called his mother, it was to say, "We about to be rich, Ma!"

But not every artist appreciated the new direction. The Lox, who faithfully ghostwrote some of Puffy's memorable crossover lyrics, wanted their own album to feature what Jadakiss called that "back-to-the-street sound of hip-hop." Puffy, however, wanted what they brought to Mariah's "Honey," and Deric Angelettie was "constantly putting in his two cents on the production level," Jadakiss said.

Thus, much of their debut, *Money Power & Respect,* presented tedious lyrics, lackluster tracks, and dated ideas. Producers tried to fill "Goin' Be Some Shit," "Livin' the Life," "Everybody Wanna Rat," "The Heist," and "Not to Be Fucked With" with dull drums and piano notes that suggested harder groups like The Wu-Tang Clan and Mobb Deep. "Can't Stop Won't Stop" used a played-out Spoonie Gee melody and found Puffy chanting his name during their chorus, while "So Right" was a familiar dance-track run through Hit Men samplers. To round it off, "I Wanna Thank You" was simply watered-down gospel. Only on their high-pitched "Money Power Respect," their low-key "Get This $," and their mellow "Bitches From Eastwick" did producers fuse their hard-core lyrics to appropriate music. As The Lox told it, they were battling over their image in the studio. "There were times we was wondering if we was even gonna come out," Jadakiss said later. "But we just sat down and did what Puffy wanted us to, and—"

Most of their album found guest stars bringing pop-rap sensibilities, and The Lox found themselves moving from hard-core group to pretty-boy rappers in silver suits. Dame Grease, cowriter of "I'll Be Missing You," produced six songs. Kelly Price sang R & B choruses. Puffy and Angelettie were the executive producers, and the group claimed they bowed to pressure and rapped about cars, money, women, champagne, and nightclubs, fully representing the new Bad Boy image.


PUFFY CONTINUED TO BE THE DARLING OF THE MAINSTREAM media, a crossover prodigy who had tapped into exactly what whites wanted from black music. A remix version of Biggie's "Been Around the World" soon followed. This video has Puffy, Mase, and an R & B singer in a white-walled space with Biggie's image on a video monitor behind them. Biggie's "Sky's the Limit" used the same mansion and swimming pool image seen in "Juicy" but featured children playing Puffy and Biggie. "It's All About the Benjamins Volume II" found Puffy battling dancer Savion Glover in a tap-dancing contest. A second video for "Benjamins" completed his transformation from black artist to crossover entertainer.

This version, set to earsplitting rock guitars, came about after he met guitarist Dave Grohl at a party. Puffy had become such a mainstream figure that Grohl, former drummer for Nirvana, knew of him. Within a week an MTV camera crew arrived at Daddy's House studios and filmed Puffy and Grohl during a recording session. Even rock musicians felt that Puffy held the secret to a hit song. By now, Puffy was on his way to being involved in 40 percent of the year's top *Billboard* hits. Americans watching MTV saw Grohl sit with a guitar and Puffy prod him toward a melody no different from his original "Benjamins." Once Grohl played the riff featured on his album, Puffy said, *"That* sounds like a record."

The video, shot in Los Angeles, begins with Puffy in a tuxedo and thick glasses warbling R.E.M.'s "Everybody Hurts" on stage at a high school prom. Then deafening rock music kicks in, and fans see him in Hammerlike shades and tight black clothing, holding a microphone stand and striking poses à la Robert Plant. Even Lil' Kim joined in the crossover mania, appearing with new shoulder-length blonde hair, blue contact lenses, and a revealing black leather outfit. The video ends with a mob of white students charging through a school hallway, ransacking anything in their path—a scene familiar to anyone who has seen *Rock 'N' Roll High School.*

By October 28, 1997, Puffy announced that he would tour. While he had everyone's interest, he released Mase's debut *Harlem World* and saw it become an immediate hit, selling a million copies in a month. Although he no longer had to invoke Biggie to draw customers, he announced that he would have *Born Again*, another Biggie album, in stores within a year. "We go from his first demo tapes, the songs that he's made, to unreleased songs that were never put on record, to like maybe two or three new songs that nobody's ever heard," he claimed. He again made headlines by announcing that *No Way Out* would be his only album. He would produce for other artists, he said, unless there were issues he needed to discuss. After playing the media as skillfully as Prince during his *Purple Rain* heyday, Puffy took his show on the road and staged each concert as a tribute to Biggie.

On November 7, he unveiled a show in Albany's Pepsi Arena that included acts that had either written or performed most of the Top 10 singles in America. On stage, a huge neon sign read "PUFF DADDY & THE FAMILY." Three big video monitors, a number of smoke machines, a few choreographed dance numbers, costume changes, and explosions rounded out the performance. Rapper Foxy Brown began the show by urging segments of the audience to yell at each other. Mase performed his hit "Can't Nobody Hold Me Down." 112 performed a few Boyz II Men–style ditties, then Lil' Kim hit the stage in a skimpy outfit.

Then, the coup de grace: As Isaac Hayes's timeless "Theme From Shaft" blared from speakers and singers chanted Puffy's name, ropes lowered him from the ceiling as if it were a Broadway production. Puffy then stepped on stage and launched into back-to-back hits "I'll Be Missing You," "It's All About the Benjamins," and his part of Big's "Mo' Money, Mo' Problems." Each night, Biggie was as much a part of the show as anyone else. Everyone invoked his name or dedicated songs to him as his image played on video screens, leading the crowd to hold lighters and sway back and forth in homage. All Puffy needed, one critic felt, was for the audience to sing John Lennon's "Give Peace a Chance."

Nonetheless, the *No Way Out* tour made Puffy even more of a crossover superstar. When he appeared on stage in his black leather jacket, matching pants, shades, and white shirt, he was dressed like a rock star but giving his white fans a primer on hip-hop culture. "That's why white kids will never let him go," Kierna Mayo once said. On the road, he rapped in aggressive tones, engaged in hip-hop call and response routines, and gave "shout-outs," or acknowledgments, to peers or boroughs in New York City. When Lil' Kim stepped on stage to perform their he-said-she-said bickering routine, he abandoned his squeaky clean MTV image by asking male attendees to raise their middle fingers and yell, "Fuck you, bitch!"

Other elements also deviated from the sanitized MTV-version of Bad Boy. When Foxy Brown performed, her brother "Pretty Boy" joined her in what one reporter called an "incestuous" rap. Puffy would go from discussing oral sex with Lil' Kim, in front of an audience that included children, to delivering a fiery sermon or pulling a cell phone out and saying he wanted to give Biggie a call. Fans did not know whether to laugh or be appalled.

After what had happened to Biggie, security became a major issue for Puffy. He traveled with a few hard rocks, and several police departments claimed that they left guns behind at various stops. After the November

10 show in Moline, Illinois, a limousine driver found two loaded stolen guns in the Rolls-Royce Puffy had leased. After they returned the car, someone called the driver, claiming to represent Puffy, and saying they had left something in the car. They asked if the driver could "ship them" the weapons. Instead, the driver handed the guns over to the police.

On November 16, the entourage stayed at the Ritz Carlton in Cleveland. A guest in the next room heard what sounded like a heated dice game. At 7:15 that morning, she heard another noise. When she woke up she saw a hole in the wall of her room. She also saw a bullet which police later determined was from a 9mm or a .38-caliber on the floor. At 8:30 she called hotel security. Police arrived and learned that the bullet had come from a room registered to Paul Offord from the "Puff Daddy Rap Group." By 8:52 A.M., the police wanted to speak to them but the entourage had checked out and left town already.

There were other problems. On November 18, Jay-Z, an old friend of Biggie's whose album *In My Lifetime, Vol. 1* debuted at Number 3 on the *Billboard* charts, told reporters he loved his well-stocked tour bus. Five days later, a mechanical failure caused a fire that destroyed the vehicle. Jay and ten others had to sit out the next show. By the time the tour returned to New York—for a December 1 date at Madison Square Garden—Jay was back on the bill. That night, Puffy's concert lasted four hours. "And he had three costume changes before the first song was over," a witness told *Spin*. "It was total Elton John. Then he dropped his pants." Even so, he cut Jay's performance time by twenty minutes. Jay was unhappy. Then, during his set, there were sound problems.

After the show, Puffy went to Justin's, his restaurant, and saw Jay and his friends taking up a number of booths. Jay had rented the restaurant to throw himself a birthday party. "Just as his party was about to get under way," wrote Davey D, "Puff rolled through with his entourage and asked Jay-Z to leave so he could have a party of his own."

December 4, Jay left the tour.[2] That same night Puffy called Biggie's mother on stage at the Garden and made a big show of handing her a

---

2.   After the tour, Jay-Z focused on his own label, filmed a second video for his album, and planned his own Puffy-style tour (which within two months would feature his label's acts, tour thirty cities, and serve as the basis for another film).

check for two million dollars. This was his share of the profits from "Missing You," he said. In fact, he actually would give her three million dollars. Once they got off stage, he wrote her a second check for one million dollars. After this fans adored him even more. His image as Biggie's best friend was secure. He was the best-loved rapper in America. Even so, Jay-Z's protégé, Foxy Brown, left the tour. While MTV implied that she was kicked off after backstage arguments with Lil' Kim, booking agents claimed that she had been scheduled only to appear through December 11.

Regardless, Puffy had The Lox replace Foxy Brown and Jay-Z. By December 13, their video "If You Think I'm Jiggy," in which they sang their version of Rod Stewart's "Do Ya Think I'm Sexy," was airing on MTV. With The Lox, Mase, and Faith onboard to help sing "I'll Be Missing You," Puffy knew that the *No Way Out* tour would draw paying customers consistently. He would continue to feature the Bad Boy Family—including Black Rob—in shiny suits, performing most of the year's hits backed by Biggie on video monitors and a deejay playing Tupac's "Hail Mary" while he yelled, "Pray for Biggie! Pray for Tupac!" Through it all, everyone wore Bad Boy hockey jerseys and stood near each other while Sister Sledge's "We Are Family" played, balloons dropped from the ceiling, fireworks went off, and white suburban fans applauded and cheered.

# SIX

# Dead Wrong

*NO WAY OUT,* COUPLED WITH MEDIA INTEREST IN BIGGIE'S MUR-der, made Puffy the biggest star hip-hop had ever seen. In 1998 he was nominated for seven Grammy awards, five American Music awards, and five Soul Train awards. He performed his successful rock version of "It's All About the Benjamins" with Fuzzbubble on MTV's *NBA All-Star Bash* and the Keenan Ivory Wayans show. He even performed the song at Arista's pre-Grammy party at the Plaza Hotel. The single quickly sold a million copies and was certified platinum by the Recording Industry Association of America, while the video won an MTV Viewers Choice Award. Hollywood studios offered Puffy roles in *Lethal Weapon 4* and *Any Given Sunday,* Fox offered him a variety show, and Sony wanted him on the soundtrack to *Godzilla.* For the last Puffy teamed with rock legend Jimmy Page and struck poses in a video for their faithful cover of Led Zeppelin's "Kashmir."

After earning two hundred million dollars in 1997, he definitely did not have to continue invoking Biggie's memory to draw fans.

But when he heard about Jamal "Shyne" Barrow, a young artist from Brooklyn who sounded exactly like Biggie, he broke out his checkbook and entered a bidding war, just as the first anniversary of Biggie's murder approached.

In the year following the murder, he repeatedly denied that he had hired Crips to guard his artists during trips to Los Angeles. Rumors that he had had spread since March 18, 1997. The *Los Angeles Times* reported that the Los Angeles Police Department (LAPD) believed a Southside Crip might have killed Biggie over a personal financial dispute. On March 24, 1997, *Time* reported that the LAPD felt "the same group of Crips that Bad Boy used as bodyguards" had murdered Biggie and Tupac.

Police Officer Reggie Wright, Jr., said, "Puffy hired Southside Crips, and the Southside Crips started extorting them for more money. That's when they decided to look for [different] security." Wright added that Puffy was telling the truth about having off-duty police officers protect him, but that he had hired these officers from Inglewood after the Southside Crips tried to collect one hundred thousand dollars they felt they were owed. According to Wright, when they asked for this money, Puffy said he would only pay ten thousand dollars. "That's why Biggie Smalls is dead today." An August 1997 issue of *Time,* meanwhile, found Puffy denying that he ever had hired Crips. He said, "Never." Even as Puffy earned fifteen million dollars from a tour that eulogized Biggie every night, an unnamed source told *Vanity Fair* that Bad Boy knew exactly why Biggie had been killed, and that Puffy felt guilty about the murder. "He knows deep in his own heart he's responsible for Biggie's death."

Even as he planned a reprise of the *No Way Out* tour in March of 1998, MTV offered a segment that recounted the shooting and Biggie's death thirty minutes later. Chris Connelly added that police had impounded Dwayne Keith Davis's "dark Chevy Impala, which matched witnesses' descriptions of the car used in the Biggie shooting," but that Davis claimed that he had not driven the car in six months. Within a month, he added, the police had returned the car to Davis and said, "At this time, there is nothing to connect him to Biggie's murder." The segment continued with Detective Russell Poole saying that East Coast rappers always faced intimidation during trips to Los Angeles. "It was very real and it was very intimidating to Puffy Combs's entourage. So in order to counter that, Puffy Combs had to take measures in order to protect himself." Puffy appeared onscreen to deny using Crips, then MTV cut to Detective Poole saying, "There are some people who, although they've been cooperative . . . There are a few details, I think, that need to be shared with us."

For whatever reason, other reporters shared this opinion. Joe Domanick asked a Bad Boy publicist about the Crips, who replied, "As a family, Bad Boy did not use them." Cathy Scott of *George* magazine contacted Puffy for an interview, and his lawyer, Kenny Meiselas, said, "This is a nonstory. No one is interested anymore."

Meanwhile, Biggie's mother said that Puffy had not contributed a penny to the fifty-thousand-dollar reward she and the City of Los Angeles had offered. "Does Puffy know something about my son's death?" she asked in print. "Maybe he's afraid to talk. Maybe he's intimidated. But at least do something. Give a hint. Don't just sit back and act as if he was my son's best friend and confidant."

Undaunted, Puffy's tour continued into March. He ended his New York show by yelling, "Yo! Cut the music for a second! I got something I want to do here." The deejay lowered "We Are Family," and Lil' Kim, The Lox, Black Rob, and 112 gathered around. He had Mase step forward, and then handed him a framed platinum record for *Harlem World.* Mase handed him a quadruple-platinum plaque for *No Way Out.* This display may have been good for show business, but problems continued to develop within the Bad Boy Family.

Old friend and producer Deric Angelettie wanted to form his own label. Its first album would be by The Madd Rapper, a raspy voiced character that had first appeared on Biggie's "Kick in the Door" on *Life After Death.* As the *Village Voice* told it, Puffy tried to prevent Angelettie from using the character; he said the phrase "Madd Rapper" belonged to Bad Boy. "Deric was furious!" one of Angelettie's friends claimed. "He told Puffy, 'Man, I created the Madd Rapper.'

"But Puffy said, 'You created it on my record label. I own it. You work for me.'

"Deric was, like, 'Fuck you! You don't own the right to my character!' "

Deric, according to another source quoted in this particular article, supposedly was ready to take it to court. "It was a big falling out, adding to a lot of stress that was evident in Puffy's camp," this person claimed.[1]

Ultimately, Angelettie used the character and Puffy shared an exec-

---

1.  Angelettie has denied that this ever occurred. "There was no dispute," he said. "That was a media thing."

utive production credit. At the same time, Mase formed a record company called Harlem World. His debut album had been a hit with a pop audience but had also asked hard-core fans, "Why y'all cats wanna player hate?" Mase was still waiting for royalties and seeing critics label him a sellout. Reviews of the album ignored that one song teamed him with The Lox, Black Rob, and DMX. Instead, Mase's image remained that of crossover sensation; the man in the shiny suit who stood in front of a hotel and danced to Kool & The Gang's "Hollywood Swingin'." Another video solidified the safe crossover image: While Total sang an alluring chorus, Mase spent much of "What You Want" offering women money and saying, "Now Mase be the man wanna see you living good."

Throughout *Harlem World,* and in many of Mase's videos, Puffy offered comments like "Yeah," "Uh-huh," "Let's go," "Come on," "Don't stop." His appearances gave the impression that Mase supported Bad Boy's new money-centered philosophy and delighted in courting a white audience. A close listen to the album, however, reveals that Mase spent many of his songs complaining about his image. "Love You So" found him saying "Can't Nobody Hold Me Down" would've "did more without the censorship." Another song claimed that "the things that went three-mil, I didn't even like."

Away from Bad Boy, Mase's breakout success inspired executives from rival labels to approach him in restaurants and offer a label deal. Signing Mase would help them tap into a pop-rap market Bad Boy dominated unquestionably, they knew. For Mase, owning a label would provide more money and a way to put his group of friends, and twin sister, Stase, in business.

Mase asked Puffy to distribute his label during a time that "he was busy working out a deal with Deric Angelettie." Puffy was interested but supposedly wanted too much of the profits, so Mase entered talks with former Bad Boy employee De'Andre Maiden.

Before becoming vice president of operations for Jermaine Dupri's Sony-distributed So So Def label, Maiden had worked on *Harlem World.* Now he brokered a deal between Mase and Dupri, the producer Mase originally wanted to see during his 1996 trip to Atlanta.

After learning that use of the phrase "Harlem World" could lead to copyright problems, Mase renamed the company All Out, and saw the media claim he was leaving Bad Boy. "I would never leave Puff Daddy," Mase claimed. "He would have to try to kill my mother or something like that, something that would make me say, 'I'm leaving Bad Boy.' But as it stands right now, Bad Boy is my family."

Just as the Mase incident blew over, Puffy faced complaints from Black Rob. After Biggie's death, Rob claimed, people were "riffin'," and "throwing chairs around the office." "Puff was like, 'I'm not even doing this no more. I could do R & B and gospel all day long. I ain't gotta touch this hip-hop shit.' " Publicly Puffy claimed that Rob's album would hit stores by the end of 1998, but they were having creative differences. "As soon as somebody doesn't agree with him, their music goes on the cutting-room floor," an unnamed artist would claim later.

Rob believed the market was swinging back to hard-core lyrics. He tried to record raw music, but Puffy wanted to continue Bad Boy's run on the pop chart. Rob felt that trying to plan a commercial album was nonsense, because a record was not "commercial" until radio deejays "pick it up and make it commercial." Puffy continued to offer pop samples, Rob claimed, and he continued to refuse them because he believed that "Puff wanted me to make songs like Mase but harder. But I didn't want to [sample] David Bowie. It was nothing personal."

A & R executive Harve Pierre, who sang choruses on artists' records as "Joe Hooker," receiving songwriting credit and, presumably, royalties, helped Rob. But his solution, providing an obnoxious chorus for "I Dare You," only led to more problems. The song became a respectable hit, its video landed in rotation on MTV, and the label's street team plastered the city with promotional posters, but Puffy decided not to release Rob's album as scheduled. Rob believed he knew why. "They felt like it wasn't a Bad Boy album with everybody talking about money, cars, and houses, and B Rob is coming out of the field with, 'Fuck that car, fuck that house, I just wanna get paid and chill.' They wasn't trying to hear that, I guess." During this period, Rob told Deric Angelettie, "I know one thing. When I get my chance it's gonna be crazy, [because] none of these niggas talking all this shit will be around. The spotlight's gonna be just on me."

Another person having difficulties with Puffy was his latest girlfriend, Kim Porter. After having a child with Misa Hylton in 1994, they had separated and he began to date Porter, a tall, striking model with shoulder-length hair, a stunning figure, and radiant eyes. At the time, Porter was pregnant and expected to give birth in April of 1998. On March 30, Puffy took her and both of their sons to the Garden for a Knicks game. Before the game ended, however, he and his entourage left a very pregnant Porter with the children. Hours later she went into labor, and he appeared at the hospital, one insider said, to start "directing the whole thing, being the coach."

Within twenty-four hours the label issued a press release about how he had named his son after Biggie. But then, Puffy also had been seen mooning over Jennifer Lopez at an industry party. He had met Lopez while filming his video for "Been Around the World." In that clip she plays a princess at a ball; he wears a cream-colored suit and almost curtsies while kissing her hand. Now newspapers were calling him "her latest love match," and revealed that during his tour, she had traveled to Detroit to be with him. When Porter asked about these reports, Puffy claimed that they were untrue.

Some of Biggie's friends in Junior M.A.F.I.A. were also frustrated with his behavior. Since Biggie's murder, many people who had invoked Biggie increased interest in their own work. Lil' Kim wore one of his suits and derbies, held his walking stick, and posed near his ashes in *People* magazine. Lance Rivera, meanwhile, told a reporter he was the one who convinced Biggie to pursue a career in music. He claimed, "I influenced what Biggie rapped about; Puffy did the music and Biggie was the artist." But Puffy earned the most from tributes, tours, and videos, and did so while some group members suspected that he knew more about the murder than he said he did.

About his "Missing You" video, one member of Junior M.A.F.I.A. said: "How many times we gotta watch Duke fall off that motorcycle?" About the murder: "If I was there with Big, I'd have seen it happening. I'd have seen it."

Said another member: "I'm saying—Puff . . . I don't know about Puff."

A third added: "Some niggas I know: They think that Puff should put more interest into finding out who really killed Big. It's like, once Big died, he just dived out and collaborated on another project, and that's Mase." This person snapped his fingers. "Like that."

Biggie's murder was still a sensitive issue when Puffy learned about Shyne Barrow, but he ignored the warnings of people around him and worked hard to bring the controversial new artist to Bad Boy.

Like Mase, Puffy, and Biggie, Shyne had grown up without a father. Tall, rail-thin, somewhat gawky, and intellectual, he was born in Belize in 1980, to Frances Franklin and Dean Barrow, that nation's deputy prime minister. Dean never married Frances, Shyne claimed, but he regularly saw his politician father on television with two children from another relationship. When he tried to build a relationship, he claimed, Dean said, "I don't owe you anything, I never wanted to have you." His father, he claimed, also said his other two children were "made out of love." He was devastated.

By 1988, Shyne and his mother were living in Flatbush, Brooklyn. She worked as a housekeeper, while he found self-affirmation in hip-hop, read books, and by the age of thirteen, prosecutors claimed, participated in robberies with members of The Deceptions street gang. One robbery supposedly landed him in a detention facility for a year. Two years after his release he argued with a man who then blasted him with a shotgun. The bullet left him with a six-inch scar across his right shoulder and chest and the desire to go straight. Like Biggie, he didn't want to hurt his mother's feelings. His alleged misbehavior was causing her to become depressed, he has claimed. Shyne changed his life. He finished high school, got his diploma, and worked as a bike messenger while thrilling to albums and videos that promoted Bad Boy's new upscale image.

The bidding war for Shyne began almost immediately after he ran into Clark Kent in a barbershop in Flatbush and filled his subsequent freestyle with Biggie-like pauses and long words. After performing for Kent, Shyne met Robert "Don Pooh" Cummins, an associate producer on albums by rapper Foxy Brown. "I just saw something in him," Cummins said. "I saw a star."

Said Shyne's friend. James Barnes, present during this period: "My friend who introduced him to Don Pooh was trying to decide whether to go with Don Pooh or Jermaine Dupri." Shyne signed with Cummins, who then involved Biggie's manager, Mark Pitts, who had attended Howard University with him and later employed Cummins at his company, Bystorm. With Pitts onboard, Cummins then asked Puffy's lawyer, Kenny Meiselas, to help obtain a deal.

Puffy was interested. By 1998, rap fans were beginning to support tougher works from Jay-Z and Bad Boy needed to compete. Lance Rivera also wanted to sign Shyne, "not because he sound like Big, but because he was dope." Ten different record companies shared this opinion, including Def Jam, Interscope, and Sony. Despite the fact that Shyne had never recorded a demo tape or a hit record, and had never performed at a show, these companies tried to outbid each other.

They continued to offer six-figure cash advances, cars, homes, and complete ownership of his publishing rights, unheard of even in deals for major stars. When Sylvia Rhone of Elektra reportedly dropped out, Puffy was supposedly up against Russell Simmons and Interscope's Jimmy Iovine. "I knew that he should not be there because of the ferocity with which Puffy was coming at him," said James Barnes. "Don Pooh was very interested in Shyne, but he was humble. But Puffy was just coming on, and there was something very shady about that."

Lance Rivera revised his opinion of Shyne's rap style, which came, he said, "from him studying Big." Signing him "could be suicide to Puff, and you don't wanna lose this kid's career because of that."

Despite this, Puffy supposedly promised Shyne a million dollars, the use of his Manhattan townhouse, ownership of his publishing, enough money for a home in Jersey, and a dark-blue Range Rover. Bad Boy would promote his work heavily and Puffy would travel with him. The offer was historic, and indicative of how large hip-hop had become. In 1997, Bad Boy had had its best year yet. In 1998, hip-hop acts would sell over eighty-one million albums. Puffy continued to woo Shyne. He invited him to a four-star hotel in Manhattan. "Puffy just hit him up with a Rolex watch," Barnes claimed, "and Shyne just stayed there with him at the hotel." He reportedly bought Shyne fancy clothing and diamond-encrusted jewelry similar to his own. It worked. Shyne signed with Bad Boy, thereby changing the nature of a rap advance. Before, if an artist left the bargaining table with fifty thousand dollars they had been lucky. One hundred and seventy-five thousand dollars was a fortune. Shyne signed for "at least $1 million," *Newsweek* reported, and Mark Pitts claimed: "Now a lot of people say, I want a Shyne deal."

# SEVEN

# Mo' Money, Mo' Problems

PUFFY GROOMED SHYNE TO BE HIS NEW SIDEKICK. SHYNE WAS awestruck when they flew to California. "That was when he was, like, the Michael Jackson of hip-hop," Shyne said later. "I went everywhere with him. That was the relationship. I was just watching Michael Jackson at work. Combs was one of the biggest people in the world, and I was just going along for that joyride."

They began to dress alike and spend money together. For the trip out west, Shyne received an undisclosed weekly living allowance on a Friday. By Monday, an insider recalled, he had called the accounting office to request more money. "Yo, I had to get my iceberg shit," the insider remembered him saying, "I had to get my man some things, I had to put him down."

His attitude fit with the label, and Puffy continued to mentor him. He asked Shyne to spend as much time as possible in Daddy's House studio. "I was there all the time, because one day I hoped to be on the level of a Michael Jackson," Shyne told Peter Noel. "I was gonna study everything Combs did, just try to be around him as much as possible to absorb some of that energy and see what it was that got him to the level he is at right now."

Some artists, unhappy with Puffy for various reasons, shared these sentiments. Except they hung around because they felt they might learn enough to one day strike out on their own. During 1998, many people connected with the label were living extravagantly. The image of success reflected well on the company and on Puffy himself. Despite not having a record in stores, Shyne was able to spend ten thousand dollars on a bracelet for Puffy, according to an insider. Another night, he blew six hundred dollars on a meal at Mr. Chow's; he shared his booth with three women and greeted everyone from Jay-Z to Johnnie Cochran. "I don't know how well-documented this was, but Puffy wasn't giving Biggie any money in the beginning," one former *Source* writer claimed. That Puffy "throws a million dollars at Shyne for sounding like Biggie" caused labelmates to resent him.

Shyne supposedly had an attitude, but Bad Boy employees tolerated it. Puffy believed Shyne would do well for the company and by now his employees were acting more like a cult than a staff. "They jump back and forth between loving and hating this guy, and their Stockholm syndrome allows Puffy to blatantly disrespect people, including the fans buying his records, by doing dumb shit like signing Shyne and claiming, 'This is the next Biggie.' There ain't no next Biggie. Shyne was a person. He was somebody's child, not a commodity."

Shyne continued to infuriate people. When the office telephone rang, some employees dreaded taking his calls. An insider called Lady felt that "a lot of hype said he sounded like Biggie and he believed it."

Other people, including Puffy's friend Bethann Hardison, mother of sitcom star Kadeim, a mentor and adviser to young celebrities and a respected figure in the fashion industry, saw him differently. After meeting Shyne for dinner at the urging of a record executive involved in the bidding war, Hardison felt he was "a special young man. He didn't seem intimidating. He was a nice young man who was bright and engaging," she said.

Signing a Biggie-like artist led to scrutiny from the industry. "Everybody wanted to claim they smoked a blunt with Biggie," one person felt. " 'Yeah, I smoked some blunts with Biggie, yeah, I stood next to Biggie, yeah, Biggie bit my sandwich.' Everybody wanted to have a little piece of Biggie, and this poor kid had to suffer for that."

Shyne told a reporter, "Puffy saw me and saw dollar signs. Let's just be real." One day at Violator Management's offices, a popular street-level deejay asked his manager about "the Biggie thing." According to the deejay, Shyne said, "I guess we sound the same, but that's not what I'm trying to do."

Bad Boy publicity, however, continued to promote his "deep and husky" voice. Producers also encouraged the style. "I'm being cultivated," Shyne said, but the pressure soon got to him. When Puffy offered a car, it began a series of events that ended in death. Said an insider named E, "Shyne wanted a six hundred but Puffy was only willing to lease a Range and they went back and forth with that process." Shyne then asked for a six-series Mercedes. According to Lady, who worked for Shyne's accountant, the Mercedes dealer told him "your credit limit will only allow you to get the five-series model, as far as monthly payments."

Shyne said, "I want a six," and presented what he felt was an ingenious solution. He would accept the five-series car, but pay the dealer to attach an emblem from the six-series model, a number of sources claimed. Within a week of receiving the Mercedes, however, he totaled it while driving home from a nightclub with two friends and his cousin. Shyne drove off a road and crashed; one friend died and his cousin sustained injuries that left him in a wheelchair. Shyne walked away from the wreckage with nothing but minor scratches. The *Village Voice* claimed, "They were all drunk."

Lady remembered: "After the car crash, he was distraught. He was depressed. He'd call the office because he wanted to pay for the funeral." She added: "It really shook him."

But rumors about Shyne described an arrogant pretender to the throne. Wags said he was a spoiled brat with tough guy pretensions and a million-dollar deal; a cheapskate who contributed a mere one thousand dollars to his friend's funeral, then laughed and joked as the coffin was lowered into the ground. Next, people claimed that when someone robbed him of a Rolex Puffy had given him, as James Barnes told it, "His main focus was, 'Puff better get me another Rolex.' "

Even worse, after spending a million to sign him, Puffy felt Shyne needed a scolding. In front of a reporter, he said, "You've got to stop writing rhymes without listening first to the music tracks. The lyrics don't match the melodic flow. Do you understand what I mean by writing to the beat?" He added: "I need a star, not just a rapper." One person said, "There are so many lessons you could learn from this. There's a little sympathy. He's a young kid who got caught up."

For his part, Shyne later said, 1998 was the worst year of his life. "Every time I went in the studio it was garbage."

In July of 1998, rumors that claimed many of Puffy's well-known rap mogul friends were gay grew to include him and Mase. Puffy and Mase already had presented themselves as a team. He now wore earrings in both ears and expressed interest in having a fashion line. He and Mase stood near each other on stage and dropped their pants to rap in boxer shorts. Both performed sissified dances in videos and rapped like a hip-hop interpretation of *La Câge Aux Folles,* represented by the banter on "Can't Nobody Hold Me Down."

After an unnamed star appeared in the fanzine article "CONFESSION OF A GAY RAPPER," Hot 97 radio deejay Wendy Williams implied that Puffy and Mase were lovers, despite Puffy's children with Misa Hylton and Kim Porter, and his regular appearances in videos with half-naked women. Police, meanwhile, accused Mase of patronizing a female prostitute on April 9, 1998, and arrested him. In court he pled guilty to a reduced charge of disorderly conduct, and a judge ordered him to pay a two-hundred-dollar fine by June 9. Mase told the magazine *Sister 2 Sister* that he left Daddy's House that night, entered his new black Mercedes, and drove toward the Hit Factory. At a red light, while he watched a crowd outside a restaurant, cops surrounded his car and accused him of trying to pick up a hooker. The court reduced the charge to disorderly conduct, he added, because he never spoke to anyone near his car. He was a "laid-back gentleman" who never chased women; they chased him. Even so, Wendy Williams accused Puffy and Mase of being homosexuals. Fans considered their high-fashion image, Puffy with earrings in both ears, Mase lisping, a Diana Ross sample on "Mo' Money Mo' Problems" yelling "I'm Coming Out," and their loose-limb dance moves, and were open to believing her. Williams offered what she called "proof" on her Web site. A series of photos showed Puffy at an outdoor party, seemingly intoxicated. One photograph found him, back to the camera, lowering his heart-covered boxers to show his ass. Another found him lying on his back, clutching what appeared to be another male on top of him. A third showed him and Mase with faces, as the site put it, "too close for comfort." For Williams's listeners, this last picture spoke a thousand words—especially when rumors claimed that Mase was living in his home.

Puffy tried to ignore the rumors, but they became more prevalent. Finally, during an interview with fans online, someone asked him what the craziest rumor about him was. He answered: "I'm gay." When *Vibe* asked about the photo with Mase, he said, "Picture me being motherfucking gay. I can't even fathom that."

Though Wendy Williams left Hot 97, she continued to tarnish his manly image. Worst of all, this rumor surfaced when his group Total was flirting with gay and lesbian themes on their second album; one interlude had one member asking another if she had ever kissed a woman.[1]

During this same period he called a meeting with his artists. Recalled Black Rob: "Puffy was like, That was my man, and I was there, and I don't really want to do this no more, y'all." As he expressed sadness about Biggie, his artists reclined in their seats with arms crossed over their chests. Mase, Rob said, "[was] working with Jermaine Dupri; he didn't give a flying cat's ass what happened. Lox: They wanted to be with Ruff Ryders anyway." To hear Rob tell it, instead of everyone rallying around him, as they'd done for *No Way Out,* the meeting ended with "everybody getting up like, 'Yeah man, I guess it's over.' "

However, instead of "retiring," he asked Arista to renegotiate the terms of the distribution deal. "I told them they had to make things right," he said. "I wanted to be very, very rich, right away."

Arista granted his wish: They agreed to give him a reported fifty-million-dollar advance against future earnings. Even as the media reported on the deal, Faith Evans used an interview to characterize his business practices as deceitful. She told *Elle* magazine that she still had not been paid royalties for her three-year-old debut album, which had sold 850,000 copies, or a "dime's worth of royalties" for "I'll Be Missing You," his tribute to her late husband, Biggie. *Elle's* reporter wrote "the phrase 'deal with the Devil' springs to mind," and Faith added that she wanted more publishing rights and creative control.

The label responded by saying that they were withholding her royal-

---

1.    Puffy told *Vibe* the group wasn't "K. D. Lang or Ellen DeGeneres or no shit like that."

ties during "negotiations." Puffy, meanwhile, responded in terms that left some newspaper reporters appalled. "In Faith's instance, everything's a joint decision," he said. "Legally, it's a different story—I have final say." By turning a negotiation into a fight over position, he risked alienating someone whose help he'd need for the posthumous Biggie album he kept promising.[2] Faith was also one of Bad Boy's few artists with long-term sales potential. Eventually they reached a solution, but she was still unhappy. "It's definitely more of a business relationship than a personal one," she said.

She agreed to return to the studio and complete her album, but resisted his ideas and self-promoting ad-libs. She abandoned samples and enlisted R & B producers Kenneth "Baby Face" Edmonds and David Foster to help create maudlin ballads. Near the end of recording, however, Puffy executed a series of moves that consciously or not resulted in him emerging as the star of her album. When he filled "Love Like This" and "Sunny Day" with samples, she didn't mind. These were only two songs; the rest of the album reflected a more sophisticated direction. During the final session, he said the album needed another marketable work. Preferably, something lighter in tone and more pop-oriented. She wrote "All Night Long" for a track he fashioned from an old disco record by Chic.

He released his production "Love Like This" as the first single, and it became a radio hit. Faith's video was also in rotation on MTV and BET. "Love Like This" was one of two great songs on the album. He followed this number with the second, his other production, "All Night Long," and joined her in an extravagant video that inspired the media to focus on his contributions. In addition, the video allowed him to describe himself as Bad Boy's visionary, and to claim that all was well between her and his company.[3] For Faith, however, the two popular singles turned her battle for creative control into nothing but a return to the image she'd tried to outgrow.

Ironically, Puffy then decided to commemorate Bad Boy's fifth an-

---

2.  By 1998, Faith Evans was the coexecutor of Biggie's estate. She originally had received everything, but handed 50 percent of the estate to Biggie's mother.

3.  His two singles inspired MTV to call her "one of the most talented soul singers around" and helped *Keeping the Faith* sell over three million copies.

niversary with a greatest hits album. By releasing the album he would see almost pure profit—talent costs were minimal. He also would sell the public many of the same songs, repackaged for his self-promoting *Puff Daddy: Changing the Sound of Modern Music* CD and work with one of the few Bad Boy artists who didn't resent him—eleven-year-old singer Jerome.

Why Puffy now focused on R & B albums when rap sales had reached an all-time high is unknown, but by doing so, he miscalculated the market, with disastrous results. While he prepared second albums by Total, Faith, and 112, other rap labels filled the void. No Limit Records, run by Puffy-like entrepreneur Percy "Master P" Miller, released a staggering twenty-eight albums in 1998, and Def Jam took in nearly two hundred million dollars. Bad Boy meanwhile experienced a 75 percent drop in revenue right after Arista handed him a fifty-million-dollar advance against future earnings.

Even as the market continued to change, he kept promoting his tired crossover image. For MTV he joined Jerome in a video, and told an interviewer, "They're calling him Junior Puff." He failed to realize that Bad Boy was no longer a serious player in the rap game. He'd forgotten that hardcore rap was what had allowed him to buy that home in the Hamptons. In fact, half of the songs on his greatest hits collection featured Biggie.

Instead of releasing a rap album, he spent time partying in East Hampton, focusing on other businesses, or promoting himself, and became increasingly out of touch with the streets. He had come to believe that a rapper should think like a businessperson but act like a rock star. This was why he paraded around in furs, flaunted his gaudy platinum jewelry, and came to resemble a black interpretation of eighties Euro trash. Many of his black fans were long gone. His new image now appalled his supportive white media.

As sales continued to nose-dive, he hired his former boss and mentor Andre Harrell, now thirty-six years old, who had just lost an estimated hundred million dollars of Motown's money during his twenty-two months running that company. Instead of suggesting that he reopen the lines of communication with his artists, Harrell suggested ways in which Puffy could further insulate himself: He instituted a hierarchy, with corner offices, and emphasized weekly meetings and results. "We're restructuring and hiring more seasoned executives," Harrell said. "Some of the performers have gotten bigger than the executives. We've hired one to two more senior people." When Harrell said he needed "time to be the artist so he can put out his next album and not have to worry about doing all the things a president of a company needs to do," Puffy agreed.

Yet, even as he kept Harrell away from Arista executives and tried to figure out how his former mentor would work with label president Jeff Burroughs and Puffy's manager, Benny Medina, producer Stevie "J" Jordan left Bad Boy.

Puffy's habit of implying that he alone was responsible for the music when his input was sometimes limited to orders given over a cell phone had alienated Jordan. His name had appeared near Jordan's in credits for *No Way Out* numbers such as "Victory," "Is This the End," "Friend," and "Can't Nobody Hold Me Down," and Jordan helped create his biggest hit, "I'll Be Missing You." Most recently they had shared credit for two songs on Total's second album.

Since his Uptown days, Puffy had faced accusations of including his own name in album credits whether he actually had worked on a track or not. Unknown to the public, one insider said, there had been a "credit struggle" over Craig Mack's "Flava In Ya Ear" remix. Puffy's remix of Mary J. Blige's hit "I'm Going Down," this person claimed, had included Easy Mo Bee's track for Biggie's "Warning" without crediting or paying the producer. Mo never complained about this, the source stressed, and never complained when Puffy, for his contribution to a Motown anniversary album, used another of Mo's tracks without crediting him. This time, the insider claimed, "Puffy did a remix of the Jackson Five's 'I Want You Back' featuring Black Rob. The verses with Black Rob had Black Moon's 'Who Got the Props' behind them. When it got to the chorus, and they brought in Michael Jackson, the beat from 'Going Back to Cali' comes in."

Now Jordan was making similar claims to *Vibe* magazine. "There's a lot of times when the track would be finished and [Puffy] would come in and be like, 'Just put a cymbal here,' and then [he'd get] a co-production credit," Jordan told *Vibe*. "At first it was like, Damn! He ain't really doing shit to be getting this co-production!" Still, he would remind himself that Puffy was giving him a great opportunity. "So it was like, well, I'll take it."

When *Vibe* asked about Jordan, Puffy admitted that songwriting credits sometimes had upset him. "But I'm not perfect," he stressed. "Some-thing may fall through the cracks. It may be a messed-up credit. But it's nothing that would ever be intentional." Either way, Stevie left the Hit Men during a period when Puffy needed hot beats for Mase's second album and, despite telling MTV that *No Way Out* would be his only re-lease, for his own second album as "Puff Daddy."

In December of 1998, he decided that another working vacation in the Bahamas was in order. He flew Deric Angelettie, his last few Hit Men, and new producers Buckwild, EZ Elpee, Jack Knight, and Mario Winans to Nassau and booked studio time at Compass Point Studios. He nursed the hope that this trip would re-create the magic of the original, which led the Hit Men to produce most of Biggie's second album. Yet he ignored the fact that the original voyage had yielded such useful results for specific reasons. Back then, there were no artists and no parties. This time, Lil' Kim, Cease, Mase, and Shyne joined them and, as Jermaine Hall put it, "parties were unavoidable."

# EIGHT

# Things Done Changed

PUFFY SEEMED TO HAVE FORGOTTEN THAT BIGGIE'S DEATH HAD helped fuel sales of *No Way Out.* Before Biggie was gunned down, he had had to stand behind Biggie in photos, videos, or on stage; he had been the agitator in the background saying things that got Biggie deeper into a feud with the West Coast. Puffy failed to see that Biggie's interview on "Pain," his hook to "Been Around the World," and his vocals for "Victory," "Young G's," and "It's All About the Benjamins [Remix]" might have been *No Way Out*'s main appeal.

Puffy came to believe his own hype, that he was the star people wanted to see. His high sales and production of 33 percent of 1997's top *Billboard* hits led Arista to the same conclusion. When he received the fifty-million-dollar advance, he entered another phase of his life.

Rap magazines presented him as a mogul, despite the fact that sales were low, and the fifty-million-dollar advance meant Bad Boy was indebted to Arista until the distributor recouped from Bad Boy's share of the profits.[1] Privately Puffy knew he needed to continue earning. He started working on four albums at once, but made them among the most expensive in the business. The original estimated cost for the albums was five

---

1. In 2001, Bad Boy remains in debt, since Arista has yet to recoup a reported thirty million dollars.

million dollars. He would spend even more on videos, marketing, and promotion. By now, he was traveling with an entourage. "The daily cost," *Forbes* reported, "as much as $55,000."

For his second album alone he paid to fly his producers to the Bahamas, but created only four usable tracks. A month later he flew his producers to Atlanta, then to Miami for a seven-day party, then to New York, then back to Atlanta. He spent millions on traveling with his mother, his two sons, a new girlfriend, an ex, two personal assistants, Shyne, a personal photographer, a video cameraman, twenty producers, engineers, songwriters, a bodyguard, and his biographer. Even if he was only flying to Atlanta to perform at a concert, he dragged this entourage with him. It was astounding, vulgar, and sad, but mostly it was extremely expensive. Yet he felt he could offset costs by selling seventy of the one hundred tracks his producers had recorded between parties in Nassau. Yet even this solution would cost money. Before presenting a track he would add final touches. Studio sessions to record them could cost another $100,000. Instead of budgeting, he bought himself a $375,000 Bentley convertible, had it flown from Britain to New York, then had it shipped to Atlanta so he could show it off during his concert. Then he flew his large entourage down on a private Gulfstream III and packed them into three Lincoln Continental limousines. He took them to the upscale Swissotel, where he booked them seventy rooms and he stayed in their two-thousand-dollar-a-night Presidential Suite.

He was way out of touch with the streets, but none of his yes-men dared to tell him this. When he presented half-baked ideas, everyone swore they were hot. During a late-night studio session he listened to a track an outside producer had submitted for his second album. He rejected it and told his followers, "I need some crazy, ridiculous joints, joints that'll make 'em dance." He played a demo by the unknown Nashville trio G-Style and started doing what *Forbes* called "a wacky kind of Egyptian dance move." Puffy explained he wanted to "bring the group, a few Bad Boy soldiers and the Bentleys into Tennessee, Georgia, Virginia and Louisiana." He wanted to imitate Master P's No Limit "soldiers." He seemed to have moved from setting the trends to trying desperately to imitate them.

Nevertheless, in the spring of 1999, Bad Boy returned to the hip-hop genre. On April 13 he released a remix of Total's "Sittin' Home" and introduced his much touted Shyne as "the man y'all been waiting to hear." Shyne's lyrics had improved. One witness said, "Songs where he sounded less like Big kind of got kicked back," and producers told him, "Do these vocals over." The Total remix found him "coming out like he and Puff were crazy close, sort of like Big and Puff, but you never heard of this guy before."

The single managed to attract attention in rap's most competitive period ever. In 1995, record labels had released less than five hundred rap records; in 1999, that amount was almost double. That year, 997 rap albums were vying for the same audience. Puffy also tried to recapture his audience by appearing with Nas, a Queens-based rapper whose 1994 album *Illmatic* had revived East Coast rap as much as *Ready to Die* and The Wu-Tang Clan. On the set of Nas's video for "Hate Me Now," Puffy watched a shirtless Nas lug a cross on his back while an irate crowd jeered. Then Hype Williams asked him to take his place on a huge cross and yell the chorus, "You can hate me now." He did, then mouthed his dialogue: "I think I like this." Later, many people said he was excited about the concept; one even credited him with creating the crucifixion sequence. During editing sessions, however, he had second thoughts. Some people suggested that he feared tarnishing his image with white rap fans, though, one person said, "People see him as the new MC Hammer." In fact, even Vanilla Ice made disparaging remarks about him.[2]

Still, during editing, he asked Nas if he was nervous about the scene. "He was saying that maybe we should let other people see it and get their opinions," Nas explained. Puffy reportedly consulted with his minister, feeling the mock crucifixion was blasphemous. He asked Steve Stoute (Nas's manager) to remove the scene. Stoute worked for Interscope and was president of Track Masters Entertainment, which represented the producer of Biggie's "Juicy." He probably would have cut the scene if Nas's label, Columbia, had not already sent a copy to MTV. On April 15, two days after releasing Total's single to stores, he saw the crucifixion air on *Total Request Live*.

"He blew up," an insider said publicly. "As soon as he saw it, he got

---

2. He said, "You got Puffy doing the same shit I did fucking nine years ago. It's like, 'Come on, get something new going.' "

up, grabbed some of his security guys, and left the office." Since the Death Row troubles, he had kept his bodyguards close. Two men were with him when he arrived at Stoute's sixth-floor private office at Universal Records. Stoute was meeting with two executives when Puffy, according to a witness, said, "Y'all get the fuck out of here. Y'all got nothing to do with this." When they left, Puffy and his men trashed the office, shoved Stoute out of his chair, and shoved his desk over when he was on the floor. They were on him so fast that he barely had time to cover his head, Stoute said; they punched and kicked him, but he stayed in a fetal position and rolled around. The blows, he claimed, kept coming. They used a telephone, then a champagne bottle. "His desk was turned over," said a witness. "His chair was on the floor. His CDs, tapes, and DATs were all over the floor."

Puffy and his men left Stoute lying on his back with blood covering his face, one arm, and the walls of the office.

Hours later, Puffy arrived at the Limelight nightclub to celebrate the launch of *Notorious* magazine, in which he had invested money. He entered through the backdoor and a reporter asked about the attack on Stoute. "I heard that rumor too," he answered. "I don't even really know where it came from." Asked if he had been involved: "Not to my knowledge."

Publicists tried to justify the attack by saying Columbia had submitted an unapproved version of the video to MTV. MTV stopped airing the video. Puffy vanished, but the police kept looking for him. The Stoute attack happened when the mainstream media considered Puffy a pop rapper so All-American he could perform "Take Me Out to the Ballgame" for the Chicago Cubs.

He reappeared two days later to surrender to the NYPD. He wore an expensive, oversized black suit, a white shirt, and a silver tie, with diamond earrings. Hours later, in Manhattan Criminal Court for his arraignment, he signed autographs for court officers. After charging him with second-degree assault, prosecutors pointed out his 1996 conviction for criminal mischief. After the judge set bail for fifteen thousand dollars cash, his lawyer opened a brown briefcase, counted out the money, and then led him away in silence. On the way out, Puffy stopped to sign an autograph for a seven-year-old girl, telling her, "Be good."

On Tuesday, April 20, five days after Puffy had attacked Stoute, Mase's new management firm, Magic Johnson Music, released a statement that announced Mase's retirement. It was effective immediately. He would appear only at spoken word performances.

For Puffy, the announcement could not have come at a worse time. He and Kim Porter, the mother of his son Christian Casey Combs, had ended their engagement. "I don't think she sees me as her boyfriend anymore, and that's been that way for some months," he told the *Daily News.* The CCNY tragedy also had returned to the headlines, and in December he would face a victim named Nicole Levy in Manhattan Supreme Court. The media continued to denounce him for attacking Stoute, and he was facing up to seven years in prison. Even worse, second albums by 112, Total, and Faith Evans had flopped. All of this, and his East Hampton lifestyle, had created what he now saw as a serious image problem.

Then there was the fact that Mase always was good for a surefire pop hit: *Harlem World* had debuted at Number 1 on the pop and R & B charts and had sold over 270,000 copies its first week. *Double Up* followed the same formula.

Puffy had to tell reporters that the departure was a shock, even as Mase's management claimed he knew it was a long time coming. In fact, his new manager said, Mase had announced his decision to leave while he and Puffy were in the recording studio; Mase had four more songs to record but decided to speak up. Puffy reportedly was shocked but asked him to at least complete the album and record a video for its first single. This Mase did "against his will," his manager added.

In print, Mase claimed that various people had inspired his decision to retire: One friend had overcome an illness by having faith in Jesus Christ. On the set of a music video, Tia and Tamara Mowry of the sitcom *Sister, Sister* had spoken about religion to the point where he felt God was reaching out to him.

At the same time, he told other reporters, he was no longer having fun. He was tired of people suggesting how his music should sound; tired of rejecting suggestions and hearing people say "I'm too damn big for [my] britches."

People wondered if it was a publicity stunt. Within days, everyone realized Bad Boy's most mainstream artist—so nonthreatening he could be interviewed in *Teen People* and record for the soundtrack of *The Rugrats Movie*—had retired just before he had to promote his next album.[3]

While his manager originally had believed that religion would not prevent Mase from accepting offers for "four or five movie parts" and "two deals with TV," he learned that Mase meant he was leaving the *entire* entertainment industry. There would be no movies. He would enroll in Clark Atlanta University, and then form S.A.N.E. Ministries, an acronym for Saving A Nation Endangered, to draw people to church.

During interviews, Mase said people at Bad Boy had urged him to reconsider. Some, like Lil' Cease, were upset. In the past, Mase had said he would feature Cease on his album because Biggie would have wanted this. Now, Cease told a reporter, "he lost a lot of love with that shit. You're not rapping anymore because you found God? What does that have to do with rap?" When he called Mase, Cease added, he left various telephone numbers, but Mase never responded. While he couldn't fault his decision to go to God, "He can't go to Brooklyn. I'm scared for him to even come around here."

Mase added that he would no longer write songs for his sister's group, Harlem World, or work with his label, All Out Records. The truth about his involvement with the label was revealed: "I wasn't really the owner of the company. I just was giving advice. If somebody still want me to advise them, I'll still do that."

As the week after his announcement continued, he explained his departure in terms that seemingly referred to Puffy's 1998 meeting with his artists. "People say that they were going to leave music and never went public with it," Mase said. "It just was rumored. I just wanted to be the first one that actually stands on his word." Another interview found him taking another swipe: "People ask me how my style is different from Puffy's style, and I tell them Puffy's style is my style. I wrote his album and mine."

He was tired of "all this fake shit, with people kissing your ass today that didn't even speak to you last month." Yet he was willing to promote his final album and publicly claim that he had decided to retire *after* he

---

3. Bad Boy was preparing to release his first single, "Get Ready" (featuring Teddy Riley and BLACKstreet).

finished recording. "So this decision had no effect on the music that's gonna be portrayed or already recorded."

He continued to tell reporters he would miss Puffy; he was grateful; he would have liked to have recorded with Biggie, Michael Jackson, or Janet Jackson, but that that was besides the point. He would use his fame to benefit those less fortunate. This had nagged at him since a woman from CNN had asked, "What have you done to give back to the community?" He had hosted basketball programs for at-risk youth, created scholarship funds, and organized Easter carnivals for children in poor neighborhoods. Becoming a minister seemed to him the next logical step. More important, though, his retirement would send a message: "All [the] money in the world won't bring back Mase."

On Hot 97 he included Biggie and Tupac among his reasons for leaving. "I just felt that they both were at a stage to where they wanted to do something else. Biggie was about to do something else besides just doing the music with Puff." Tupac, he added, reportedly had planned to leave Death Row. "So I feel as if me, as myself, I'm just trying to do something that two great rappers never got a chance to do, and I feel by me doing this, I'm breaking a pattern."

During another interview, he added, "It's not going to be understandable to everybody. Maybe in three years it will be."

Three years later, the reasons behind Mase's departure were still unclear, and an unnamed source questioned in the *Village Voice* how he was able to obtain his release immediately before Bad Boy released his second album. "Puffy does not let people out of their contract so easily," this person said. "He had Mase under contract for a long time. You let somebody walk into your office and say, 'I don't want to be under contract no more,' and you just say, 'Okay, go ahead'? I think Mase had something over him, some little secret that Puffy did not want to get out, and he used it as a bargaining chip to get out of that record deal." This person added that Mase entering the church might have saved his life. "When you're with the Lord, they think twice about doing you [harm]. Think about it. He's the only one who got out on top."

Mase's departure was so sudden that when *Double Up* arrived in the stores, fans still saw him on the cover of *Vibe*'s June/July issue with three women and a diamond-covered religious medallion around his neck. His departure also left Puffy alone. When Biggie died, Mase had stepped into the role of sidekick and helped him reach more listeners. "Can't Nobody Hold Me Down," a Number 1 hit, paved the way for *No Way Out*'s success. During the tour and in videos, Mase was by his side. When Wendy Williams posted photos on her site and leveled accusations on her radio show, Mase continued to be there. With Mase gone, for the first time since Biggie's murder, Puffy would have to be on his own. He would have to talk more, promote the albums and his company, and open himself up to a hostile media. He would have to work harder to persuade fans to buy his next album. *No Way Out*'s success had raised expectations. Reviewers would be harder. "So I prepared myself for that," Puffy said. Even so, what happened next stunned him.

By May 1999, The Lox also were unhappy with Bad Boy, and they were now spending more time with Ruff Ryders's rising stars. This relationship became so close that in reporting on Ruff Ryders's compilation album, MTV identified the label as "home to such acts as DMX, The Lox, and the newcomer Eve."

Though their debut, *Money Power & Respect,* reached Number 3 on the pop charts, the group felt Bad Boy had betrayed them. They were still upset about their video for "If You Think I'm Jiggy" presenting them as suit-wearing pop stars who rapped about groupies in nightclubs and chanting a chorus patterned after Rod Stewart's "Do Ya Think I'm Sexy." "We were watered-down," Sheek insisted. "Bad Boy's image was flossy."

Ruff Ryders, meanwhile, profited from a harder sound. The Lox still had well-established ties with the people who ran this management-company-turned-label. In fact, Ruff Ryders had managed them from the beginning, when Bad Boy "was hot," Jadakiss said. Back then, "Big was out, 'One More Chance.' That was crazy. You wanted to sign with Bad Boy. It felt like the right thing."

Over the years, The Lox had remained loyal to the aspiring Ruff Ryders camp; they had helped unknown client DMX by having him on Mase's "24 Hours To Live" and their own "Money, Power, Respect." After these appearances, Bad Boy's A & R director, Deric Angelettie, wanted to offer a deal but "we missed signing DMX by two days," he once said. "He was a day from finalizing the deal with Def Jam when I said, 'Let's sign him to Bad Boy.' "

After DMX signed to Def Jam and helped that label earn two hundred million dollars in 1998, Ruff Ryders formed a record company, signed a distribution deal with Interscope, then invited The Lox onto *Ride or Die Volume 1.* Bad Boy let them appear, Sheek explained; Puffy "knew that's our family. From day one, Ruff Ryders was our family."

But by then, the group resented Bad Boy and Puffy. "When the CEO becomes an artist, it's over," Jadakiss said later. "Because when he drops an album around the time you drop it, it's gonna get pushed more. The promotional budget is gonna be more for him."

The Lox felt that a combination of big egos, personal opinions, and bad timing had hindered sales of their Bad Boy debut. Meanwhile, Ruff Ryders, whose albums without pop samples sold millions of copies, could easily have moved five million copies of *Money, Power & Respect,* Sheek felt. Besides, The Lox felt that Bad Boy hadn't paid them enough for an album certified gold by the RIAA. Their attorney, L. Londell McMillan, then best known for freeing Prince from his contract with Warner, felt "recoupment" clauses in their contracts were to blame. "The artist has to recoup whatever funds the label spends on samples and half of all promotions," McMillan explained. "And when you don't have control on how much is spent, you can end up with less money than you should."

The Lox asked Bad Boy to release them from their contract. "We had numerous amounts of meetings, lawyers, and it wasn't going nowhere," one member said. "You can only have so many meetings and all that, so we had to take it to the streets."

The trio was to perform at an outdoor concert for Hot 97. Backstage, they wore matching T-shirts marked with the phrase "Let the Lox Go." The sentence also appeared on picket signs and posters they carried on stage. During their gig, they explained the strife with Bad Boy to a bewildered audience—which reportedly included Puffy, who was granting an interview to a film crew a few feet away.

At this point, music magazines claimed The Lox was Puffy's only hard-core act. Black Rob and Shyne were on the sidelines. When fans saw The Lox leave, they felt it meant that Bad Boy was no longer a place for artists who refused to adopt nonthreatening pop styles. Puffy had to appear on Hot 97 to give his side of the story: He said he would release the group from their contract. His publicist, Juanita Stephens, confirmed it for *Rolling Stone* but offered no details. In subsequent interviews, he complimented The Lox, then claimed that this sort of thing was normal. If a record company had twenty acts, two or three would want to leave, he explained. Away from the pundits, he sold their contract to Ruff Ryders for a reported $2.5 million. The group's lawyer thanked him for "accommodating The Lox in this extraordinary situation," and the group agreed to appear in a video for Biggie's posthumous single, "Notorious." They also would continue to lob more insults at him, Bad Boy, and its crossover image.

# NINE

# Forever

PUFFY CONTINUED RECORDING A SECOND ALBUM HE HOPED would prove to rap fans that he was more than a pampered millionaire who pledged allegiance to the ghetto but preferred hanging with rich whites in East Hampton, Long Island. He also tried to attack the reporters who denounced him for beating Steve Stoute with the help of two body- guards. Whenever his name was mentioned in the media, it was tied to the attack on Stoute, the departures of Mase and The Lox, and Bad Boy's plummeting sales. By the summer of 1999, Stoute was vowing to do whatever it took to have Puffy put behind bars. "I'm embarrassed and I'm scared," Stoute told reporter Angela Allen. "But I've got to do it. I'm scared of him. But I have to defend the record industry. It's the record industry vs. Sean 'Puffy' Combs. Everybody is afraid of him. He has a dark history."

As the year continued, Puffy abandoned the happy-go-lucky pop pose from *No Way Out* and presented the persona from Nas's "Hate Me Now," the angry young rapper battling jealous critics. *Forever* began with sound bites that described Biggie's murder then his own surrender to the police. He adopted a messianic pose that infuriated music reviewers: "What can mere mortals do to me? Yes, the Lord is for me. He will help me. I will look in triumph at those who hate me." He concluded: "Lord, forgive them for they know not what they do."

In the studio, he tried to draw on the same talents that made him a production legend. When he heard Ron Lawrence's track for "Angels With Dirty Faces," he liked the sample from Earth, Wind, and Fire's 1977 hit "Fantasy," but hired the group's horn section to replay the melody. His cover of Public Enemy's "Public Enemy No. 1" changed the original political message into an assault on his critics. The Madd Rapper skit was another reversal: Instead of Rapper insulting Bad Boy, he describes a dream in which Puffy robbed him.

On his expletive-laden "What You Want," he claims to carry a 9mm for "haters plotting," compares himself to Lauryn Hill, and quotes Jay-Z's "Streets Is Watching." He calls a peer a "clone with a production deal," then claims he and his hard-core detractors were "from the same 'hood." He then told listeners they could achieve success, then presented more death threats.

"I'll Do This For You" found Puffy imitating Biggie's wordplay to Mase's merry manner and Jay-Z's cynicism. His song "Get Off," set to an obscure work by the disco-era group Foxy, tried to match the original Hit Men, down to Kelly Price's Faith-like chorus, but evoked his imitators. His feel-good lyric segued first into threats—"When I got problems I send a dark van"—then paranoia—"Cats in the street treat me like a marked man." For "Do You Like It, Do You Want It," instead of simply copying Jay-Z, he included Jay, and both sang that even millionaire rappers have the blues.

"Satisfy You" found him claiming he wanted someone to love him for more than his riches. "All this money don't mean shit if you ain't got nobody to share it with," he said. "Love rules the world. You feel me?" Then a Club Nouveau sample, already used on The Luniz's 1995 hit "I Got 5 on It," played, and R. Kelly sang, "Give it to me" to a girl already in a relationship. "Is This the End's" harrowing speed-rap, set to trendy southern "bounce," alluded to him seeing his "whole empire crumble into pieces," "killers on our asses," and police chasing him in his car. *No Way Out* was to *Forever* what Sly and the Family Stone's "Everybody Is a Star" or "You Can Make It If You Try" was to *There's a Riot Goin' On.*

Puffy introduced "I Hear Voices" with "Sometimes I don't think you motherfuckers understand where I'm coming from, where I'm trying to get to." He introduced "Fake Thugs Dedication," his cover of MC Lyte's eighties' single "Paper Thin," by saying, "This one right here goes out to all the fake thugs out there" and included Redman yelling, "Fuck you, you, and you" during its chorus.

Listeners next heard the interlude "Diddy Speaks," in which he justified his crossover approach and thrashed his hard-core critics.[1] In tones that conveyed either depletion or debauchery, he said he had entered the industry to "represent for all the niggas." In the early 1990s, he claimed, there were few "young black niggas up in the music industry doing their thing." Instead, "niggas was getting jerked and ripped off," so he wanted to work hard and show the world that young black men could run record companies. When he became successful, however, "the niggas I was doing it for, them was the niggas flipping on me. I'm doing it for all of us, you know. Shit. Shit is fucked up."

This seemed to infuriate critics the most. This and the fact that his song "Gangsta Shit" opened with Al Pacino, in *Scarface,* calling everybody "a bunch of assholes."

Musically, the song bore more than a passing resemblance to Shyne's own "Gangsta Shit." Though Shyne's version was faster, it presented a similar rap style, bass pulse, and sampled drone. Whether Puffy imitated Shyne or the other way around is unknown. Shyne's version went unreleased, while Puffy's featured a performance by Mark Curry, a new artist brought to the label by Black Rob.

Another of Rob's discoveries, G Dep, appeared on "Pain" (a new song, not from his debut). This *Ready to Die*–style revenge fantasy was set to a piano sample popularized by the hard-core group Mobb Deep. As Puffy rapped about letters from jail, G Dep popped in to deliver manic backup vocals similar to Biggie's on "Gimme the Loot."

"Reverse" presented more hard-core posturing. Over a decent track, Puffy rapped, "I bust six out the roof of my Bentley coupe/head shots so motherfuckers can't regroup/can't regroup, I'll be damned if you/get more points than me, sell more joints than me." Shyne followed, and for a brief moment it seemed as though Bad Boy would be able to compete. With Shyne, Puffy sounded aggressive and convincing; he'd gone beyond the outdated house sound. Shyne also seemed to inspire Busta Rhymes and

---

1. About "Diddy," a variation on Daddy, Puffy said, "My man Biggie gave me that name."

Sauce Money to deliver better material. If Puffy had teamed with Shyne on more songs, he might have escaped what happened next. But within minutes, southern rapper Cee-Lo of Goodie Mob marred the song with his blundering "southern-style" lyrics.

This more than anything seemed the most offensive thing about *Forever*. Popular guest stars like Busta, Jay-Z, Nas, Beanie Sigel, and Lil' Kim offered tougher material. Menacing new artists Shyne, G Dep, and Hurricane G repositioned him as a street-tough gunman. An early vocal of Biggie (which also would appear on the third Biggie album) lent "Real Niggas" much needed street credibility. With this roundup Puffy could have vied for a spot in the hard-core market.

Instead, he tried to revive the *No Way Out* pop image he'd shattered when he beat up Steve Stoute. He tried again to re-create his friendly pop image with "Best Friend," a gospel cover of Christopher Cross's "Sailing." Yet he knew fans would shun this album like the plague if it were the first single. He decided that instead of a pop remake, "PE 2000" would be his first single, and that he would film three videos for the song. Although three seemed excessive when only one version would actually appear on *Forever*, Puffy hoped to exploit an upsurge in sales of Spanish and rock music. He also might have felt that "PE 2000" had the potential to be as popular as his aggressive mega-hit, "It's All About the Benjamins."

Either way, he was wrong. "PE 2000," while energetic, was nowhere near as accepted, and costs for the three videos were high, especially since a different director created each with a "trendsetting" thirty-two-camera shoot. One version shot in L.A. required black helicopters, a white Ferrari, and for police to close a stretch of freeway. The rock version presented an on-stage performance with Chuck D of Public Enemy, who had sued Bad Boy in 1998 over the unauthorized use of his voice on Biggie's "Ten Crack Commandments." The Spanish version used footage of Puffy riding a float during the Puerto Rican Day parade, where Jennifer Lopez had served as grand marshal, while the hip-hop version found him turning on a pedestal while rapping and performing Hammer-like dance moves. This last version also showed him standing in front of a Kentucky Fried Chicken store in Harlem, a scene that director Martin Weisz felt wasted the one hundred thousand dollars it cost to shoot. While Puffy hoped the scene would restore his street credibility, his director asked himself, "Why do this bullshit? No ghetto kid from Harlem is gonna buy Puffy. They think he sold out. It's more like the sixteen-year-old white girls in the Hamptons, baby!" Ultimately, Weisz filmed the shot but claimed Puffy did not "feel comfortable there. He stayed an hour and left."

Tuesday, July 13, Puffy was in Los Angeles, in a local nightclub with two hundred guests, including reporters and executives of Bad Boy, Arista, and BMG. For two hours the crowd waited for him to start the show. Many, however, lost patience and left before the video retrospective of his career began, and people heard him say, "I want this to be an album to go down in history." BMG executives reportedly were concerned about costs, but Clive Davis mingled with guests in the crowd, telling them *Forever* would "set everyone on their ear."

Puffy began to play his new material. He followed English and Spanish versions of his first single, "PE 2000," with his proposed second single, "Do You Want It," his duet with Jay-Z. Up next was "Satisfy You," his rap ballad with R. Kelly, then "I'll Do This for You," which he said would be his third single. After an early version of "Angels With Dirty Faces," which featured a rap by Mase, he ended the session with "My Best Friend."[2]

Ultimately, radio didn't respond well to "PE 2000." The song failed to reach the pop charts, and it peaked at Number 34 on the R & B chart. It was only the twenty-fifth most-played video on MTV. That the all-important first single failed to crack the pop chart was especially distressing, because the first single usually fueled sales of an album.

In August of 1999, Puffy hit the road on a tour of thirty important markets to try and ingratiate himself to the same media he'd disparaged on his album. When he most needed the media's support, he alienated them by avoiding discussions of Stoute and Jennifer Lopez, interrupting interviews to field business calls on his cell phone, and keeping his bodyguards close. The stop in Detroit was reportedly an unmitigated disaster. According to a report filed with the Detroit police, his bodyguards allegedly attacked an interviewer. This incident supposedly occurred on Au-

2. A press release claimed this song was "in the tradition of 'Missing You' " and was "a guaranteed international smash."

gust 10, after Puffy and his bodyguards arrived for an interview with Roger Mills at radio station WCHQ. Mills, he saw, had camera operator Anthony Wichowski filming their conversation. Everything was fine, Wichowski told police, until "the host asked Sean Combs what he thought about a rumor that Mr. Combs was in some way responsible for Notorious B.I.G.'s death." Puffy's publicist asked Mills if he would be willing to sell the tape, Mills and Wichowski claimed; Mills said no, and then three members of Puffy's entourage demanded it. Mills and Wichowski followed them out to their Jeep. "Three guys entered the Jeep, and one grabbed and pulled on my right arm, hitting at my hands, trying to pull my hands off the camera," Mills said. Puffy's guards allegedly grabbed the tape and destroyed it while standing outside of the radio station.

As the tour continued, Puffy continued to avoid talking about Stoute. His actions, however, spoke louder than words. In Smith Point in the Hamptons, while shooting a video for "Satisfy You," a reporter from *Rolling Stone* watched him explode over sweaters. "These look corny," he told a stylist. "Bring me some turtlenecks." The stylist brought sweaters. "Why he bring me all these mock necks? This is hip-hop. I can't look like a dick head!" He wanted white jackets. The stylist went to find some. Puffy followed, grabbed the jackets, and threw them in the air. "I don't want none of this shit!" He later said, "I was just very mad. I wanted to burn the whole fuckin' bus. I get to the snapping point sometimes."

Another alleged outburst occurred after he left the set of ABC's *Good Morning America*. His publicist had asked Elizabeth Vargas to focus on the new CD. Vargas's third question was about his arrest for beating Stoute. He left the studio feeling he had been "set up." He added, "I hate when motherfuckers [start] lying. That's what got me in trouble in the first place: motherfuckers lying."

Despite his energetic twenty-six-day promotional tour of radio stations, *Forever* had dismal first-week sales. It sold 205,343 copies and did not debut at Number 1. Christina Aguilera's self-titled album outsold him, and the media claimed his career was over. "I'm cool with whatever," he claimed in print, "but I'm being real honest about that. I, I can't do that to myself, the first week's numbers, they too crazy, you know what I'm saying?" Clive Davis took the blame for the low sales: Arista had delayed shipping "clean" versions of the album to the family-oriented "rack" outlets that account for 30 percent of the market, he said. Second-week sales were only 119,000 copies. Bad Boy rushed his gentle "Satisfy You," rather than his duet with Jay-Z, into stores as his next single, but even this couldn't stop *Forever* from slipping on the charts.[3]

"The most aggravating thing about *Forever* is that we're supposed to feel sorry for an unhappy millionaire," one critic wrote. Another said, "If Puffy were to be true to himself, he'd have to rap about making dollars, appearing on *Page Six* and getting his Bentley armor-plated." MTV called *Forever* "a crime against hip-hop and music in general." *Entertainment Weekly* called him paranoid and compared him to Richard Nixon. Another critic said: "Next time, Combs should stick to what he does best, namely making hits for other people."

During its third week in stores, *Forever* dropped to Number 13 without selling half a million copies. Instead of the grand thirty-five-city tour he'd planned, Puffy had to defend Bad Boy's reputation in the media. He told MTV that rumors of the company failing were "ridiculous," but the backlash continued. One Sony executive told *New York* magazine: "A lot of people in the industry are saying Puffy did this [Stoute beating] on purpose to get his ghetto credibility back. He did it to have the kids on the street respect him again." This person added, "No one cares about the Bad Boy insignia anymore. White kids are only gonna buy what black kids buy and Puffy thinks that by doing this he'll win them back."

No one cared about *Forever.* The big story was the attack on Stoute. The matter finally ended in early September. Before heading to court, Puffy promoted a gospel album called *Thank You,* claiming that Mase and singer Tonya Blount would appear on its first single, "I Love Him." The *New York Daily News,* meanwhile, claimed that he struck a deal with Stoute; for half a million dollars, they said, Stoute would drop charges against him. Puffy denied this; he said that getting Stoute to drop the charges cost nothing but "a hug and a handshake." On Wednesday, September 8, 1999, he entered the criminal court building in lower Manhattan. He wore a pinstriped suit and faced the judge. The judge glared at

---

3.  "Satisfy You" debuted at Number 2 on the Hot 100 chart, but soon fell to Number 27.

him and told him to remove his hands from his pockets. "Mr. Combs," he added, "do you remember me?"

"Can't say I do," Puffy answered.

The judge, who'd investigated the CCNY tragedy, left it at that. Instead of felony assault, Puffy pled guilty to second-degree harassment, a legal violation below a misdemeanor and not technically a crime. The judge sentenced him to a day in an anger management program. "You have a very interesting history," he said. "Let's hope we never meet again."

# TEN

# Born Again

DESPITE SCATHING REVIEWS, PUFFY HAD NO INTENTION OF QUIT-ting or giving up. He continued to promote himself as an influential su-perstar. In September of 1999, he arrived in Miami in an enormous jet with the words "Puffy Daddy Forever" and "PD" painted on its side. His manager, Steve Lucas, and Bad Boy's VP of marketing, Ron Gilyard, waited in a black Town Car. Police officers on motorcycles formed a mo-torcade. He left the plane with six duffel bags, shopping bags from Prada and Gucci, a car seat, a bodyguard, his son with Kim Porter, a nanny, and a female flight attendant. At this point, Puffy encouraged media outlets like BET to include his new post-Mase sidekick, Shyne, in coverage, to set the stage for his album, which was set to follow *Forever.* As he made his way off the plane in Miami, Ron Gilyard told a reporter, "He's fly like that."

His employees stayed loyal even as he became increasingly demand-ing, eccentric, defensive, and disconnected from the streets. During an in-terview, one of his yes-men dared to knock on a door. He yelled, *"You must be a stupid, stupid motherfucker."* He had a barber flown into town to do his hair "just right" and continued to yell at what *Vibe* called the "constantly shifting group of men" that ran his errands, protected him, and agreed with everything he said.

*Vibe* magazine ran a cover story that described him as a disordered has-been who refused to believe his pop-rap gravy train had run its course. The article detailed how, while editing his video for "Satisfy You" in Los Angeles, he had spent thirty minutes insisting that an editor alter a scene in which his skin looked ashy. It also described him fixing himself a drink at 2:00 A.M. and dropping a liquor bottle that "smashed" on the floor; he responded to charges that he had lost his audience by yelling, *"It will never, never, never, never be over! Never, motherfuckers, never."*

Arista now reportedly was concerned about costs, and business reporters called Clive Davis to ask about the fifty-million-dollar advance. Davis also was having his own problems: BMG was said to be unhappy with Arista's lower than expected 1998 profits. Despite Arista posting earnings of twenty-five million dollars for 1999, BMG head Strauss Zelnick reportedly told Davis to boost the bottom line. An unnamed music executive told the *New York Post* that Zelnick wanted sixty-five-year-old Davis to leave BMG's Arista when his contract with BMG was up for renewal in June 2000. "Strauss can't say Clive is too old," the unnamed executive felt. "He certainly can't say he doesn't know what he's doing. But what he can say is, 'His numbers are off.' It's the oldest trick in the book."

Bad Boy was partially responsible for the numbers being off, the *Post* claimed. "Bad Boy's spending is out-of-control," the insider added. "They run up huge expenses for marketing, parties and plastic surgery. . . . Costs like that were OK when Bad Boy was on top, but they have to exercise some control."

Puffy needed a year-end sales boost. Shyne's album was set aside; everyone focused on *Born Again,* a posthumous album by Biggie. Said label insider E: "That *Born Again* shit was out of desperation. They'd been working on that for some time but never put a release date on it until after Mase and The Lox broke out."

By now, many of Puffy's artists felt neglected. "Of the nearly dozen new recordings reportedly slated for release this year, only one besides Puffy's has made it into record-store bins," *Newsweek* reported.

His artists believed that he spent most of 1999 looking out for Number 1: attending parties; promoting *Forever* and his various projects, including Sean John clothing, *Notorious* magazine, and his restaurant, Justin's. "I applaud Puffy's success, but I do feel it took away a lot of attention in terms of work and thought put into other artists," Faith Evans said. According to Deric Angelettie: "Our new artists had to take the background for a minute." Shyne's album was pushed back; the same with Fuzzbubble's rock album and Jerome's R & B debut. Black Rob was another casualty. By now, Rob had set his hard-core pretensions aside; he did what Puffy wanted. He even featured Jennifer Lopez on his song "Spanish Fly" and Puffy on a song named after him, "P. D. World Tour." Still, Puffy insisted that he needed better songs. He asked him to return to the studio. Rob said, "My album is tight, and I shouldn't have to do this." Regardless, he entered a studio with new A & R person Bobby Springsteen, as well as Harve Pierre, who saved the day. Pierre brought him an idea he developed while riding in a car one night. Each sentence, he explained, would end with the word "Whoa," his version of Juvenile's "Ha." Said Bobby Springsteen: "Harve came up with the concept, told Rob about it, and Rob wrote some shit." After recording "Whoa," to a track by Buckwild, they also produced a terrible Spanish pop number called "Espacio."

Faith, meanwhile, was furious. Less than a year after she'd renegotiated her contract, she hired The Lox's lawyer to help her gain full control of her music-publishing rights. She also complained about the amount of money Bad Boy had spent on recording and promoting her second album—then had billed to her—as well as someone claiming she had cosmetic surgery. In the *New York Daily News,* she said, "I'm disappointed. I am not happy."

Harrell claimed that her complaints were a normal part of any contract negotiation and predicted that she would stay with the label. "Faith is our first lady, our biggest-selling female artist," he said. "We will no doubt resolve this and move forward."

The feud with Evans really could not have come at a worse time. Puffy was still uncertain if he had full rights to all of the material that he wanted to include on *Born Again.* He needed Faith on his side. Yet, *Black Beat* wrote: "Bottom line, she wants off the label, which has experienced a well-documented dip in overall sales over the past year or so." Other artists like Fuzzbubble and Jerome also wanted to leave. And now the group Total was ready to disband.

Puffy gave Faith a better royalty rate and the Biggie estate, which she controlled with Voletta Wallace, a substantial cash payment. He then worked to get the Born Again CD in stores by December. At the same time, *Newsweek* said, he was also "consumed with making a smash hit out of *Forever.*" He hoped that releasing his third single, the syrupy "Best Friend," in December would jump-start sales.

WHEN IT WAS TIME TO RELEASE HIS SECOND ALBUM, PUFFY AGAIN began to discuss Biggie in print. Before critics heard Biggie on *Forever,* Puffy claimed that only recently had he overcome his fear of hearing Biggie's voice. He said that, after the murder, he had avoided Biggie's tapes because he didn't know how he would react to his voice and that this delayed the release of *Born Again;* no one could get him to work on it. Yet, for *Forever*'s "Real Niggas," he not only retrieved the tapes from the vault, he played them, and, he said, felt good about hearing Biggie's voice again. It was special, he added. It was as if Biggie were "right there." In fact, Puffy said that hearing his voice made Puffy admit to himself that he really missed Biggie, adding, "When I heard his voice it lit me up."

In the studio, he moved *Born Again* away from what he had been promising since 1997. Originally he had said that the album would present new material and narration from Biggie's mother; it would start with his demo and focus on every phase of his career; it would not be a greatest hits or remix album. *Born Again* instead would feature music "never heard before or songs that have never been released."

However, by mid-1999, he said that remixes of "Party and Bullshit" and "Who Shot Ya" would appear on the album, which would arrive in July. In August, he added that it would feature previously unreleased material, but that producers were "updating" the music. He continued to claim that *Born Again* would feature only tracks Biggie had finished and loved. "The only person that rejected tracks was me. And none of these were rejected tracks."

After two years of amending his claims, he told *The Source* that *Born Again* would consist *mostly* of unreleased demo tracks. He did not publicize that some of these "unreleased" vocals already had been included on old singles and remixes by lesser known artists, or on Biggie's first album,

*Ready to Die.* Instead of questioning why Puffy had changed the plan, *The Source* claimed *Born Again* would be "a project worthy of the three-CD set Biggie had envisioned for himself before he passed on."

For years, Bad Boy had kept a veil of secrecy around the project. "The first step was basically getting with the producers, getting music for the vocals we had, going through hundreds of tracks, and trying different things," said Bobby Springsteen. Puffy and Harve Pierre added "additional production."

This was when Easy Mo Bee met with Springsteen and played him fifty instrumentals. "He was sitting there and saying, 'That's hot, that's hot, that's hot,' " said Mo. "He picked out at least sixteen beats, but they never got on *Born Again.*" During a telephone conversation with his former manager, Francesca Spero, who was production manager on the album, he learned that other material did. According to Mo, Spero played a few songs and asked him, "Didn't you do these in ninety-four or ninety-three or something like that?" Mo recognized some and said, "Fran, ain't those the lyrics from 'Dead Wrong'?

"She said, 'Yeah.'

"Or rather, I had to remind her of it because it had been a while. Maybe she didn't remember." He added: "They put in Chucky Thompson's beat but left the vocals there." Thompson's track used the same Al Green drum sample he had brought to *Life After Death*'s "What's Beef" and later to Mary J. Blige's *Mary,* for her song "Time"; he'd increased the tempo, added orchestra strikes, and delivered a timeless instrumental.

Mo also noticed a verse that Puffy had asked Biggie to remove from the original "Dead Wrong." The verse appeared on "Hope You Niggas Sleep," a new song set to a bustling track by Cash Money Records producer Mannie Fresh.[1] Unfortunately, in this song Puffy alternated between promoting Bad Boy and cheering for his rival Cash Money and their most popular group, The Hot Boyz.

Two other songs, meanwhile, made use of one performance Biggie had recorded for a duet with Fatman Scoop. The first verse of the Fatman

---

1. Mo was the only person credited on liner notes as producer of original sessions that yielded vocals.

song and its chorus appeared on Puffy's "Real Niggas" on *Forever,* while the song's third verse provided Biggie's contribution to *Born Again*'s "Notorious." The new song "Biggie," meanwhile, recycled a lyric Biggie had recorded for Heavy D's "Let's Get It On." In the original, Heavy D, Tupac, and Grand Puba joined him, and Biggie ended his verse with a four-bar lyric mentioning the title of Heavy's song. The four-bar lyric, without chorus, was now the new song "Biggie."

The DJ Premier track "Rap Phenomenon," meanwhile, evoked Biggie's classic "Ten Crack Commandments" as much as it did Gang Starr singles. "Premier told us he was going to take a long time," Pierre had said. "He's not rushing shit for Biggie. He's going to make sure that shit is crazy." For lyrics, Premier used Biggie's two verses from Howard alumnus Tracey Lee's 1997 song "Keep Your Hands High," which was released by Mark Pitts's Bystorm. On Lee's record, Biggie had ended his first verse with the words: "Leave most in the blood they layin' in, ask Tray and them." His second verse on the Lee single began with "What, what." Premier created a seamless flow by removing the words "What what," and pasting the second verse to the tail end of the first. Method Man, the only guest on *Ready to Die,* then appeared with Redman to offer middling lyrics.

Clark Kent, who had produced Junior M.A.F.I.A.'s hit "Player's Anthem" and Jay-Z's "Brooklyn's Finest," overhauled his track for "Come On Motherfucker," a number Puffy had rejected for *Ready to Die.* Yet Harve Pierre bickered with him for fifteen minutes over whether Kent should include a sampled gunshot. "We need more drama," Pierre said. "Puff is going to want more drama."

Kent said, "Nah, listen," played the song again, debated with Pierre for another fifteen minutes, then did what Pierre wanted.

Soon, Puffy invited a reporter from *The Source* to hear a few works, and a few employees sat around trying to look happy. Harve Pierre said, "We're trying to get this album tight. Right now there's just a lot of rough ideas." Mark Pitts, *Born Again*'s associate executive producer, claimed Puffy wouldn't ruin the album with "slick A & R shit," that Bad Boy knew "how much this project means to Biggie's family; and they know one person can't take all the credit."

Bobby Springsteen added, "We're not trying to change the direction of

Biggie: we're giving you the party records, the dramatic records and the straight hip-hop joints. It's classic Big."

Yet, it seemed Puffy was doing just that—changing Biggie's direction and continuing the move to pop that he'd begun with *Life After Death*. Similarly, he seemed to be inviting guests onto this "tribute" that would help Bad Boy tap into audiences that had abandoned the label's watered-down sound. He even tried to call Will Smith's manager. "Will is going to be on the new version of 'Party and Bullshit,' with Faith singing the chorus," Pierre told a reporter. Smith, another crossover rapper known for squeaky clean dance-rap, felt it was strange that Bad Boy would call him for the album. Pierre added, "People might think it's an odd combination, but when it drops the whole world will love it." Then Bad Boy asked former Fugee Lauryn Hill to record a tribute song, and Puffy made his most controversial decision. He asked Dr. Dre's newest protégé, white rapper Eminem, to perform on the lead single, "Dead Wrong." For one, Biggie had never heard of him; Eminem became famous with white fans after his murder. For another, Eminem's whiny voice and self-conscious lyrics, which mostly insulted harmless boy bands and Christina Aguilera, seemed a bit incongruent with Biggie's straightforward, authentic hip-hop.

By including him, Puffy caused even more of Biggie's fans to suspect him of using *Born Again* to make a fast buck and recapture a white audience he'd lost to other labels. As the guest list swelled, Lil' Cease questioned some of the choices. "It just felt wrong 'cause he wasn't there," he said.

Many things felt wrong, including Shyne recording for Bad Boy. Said one deejay: "I was in a studio session with Lil' Kim, and people had [many] negative things to say about Shyne." Junior M.A.F.I.A., he claimed, did not want a copycat on the market. "Especially if he was exploiting Big and making money off of his name."

As *Born Again* continued to change, Cease said of Biggie: "I don't think nobody can fill his shoes." Lil' Kim also began to have qualms about the album. Said insider E: "Even that 'Notorious' song on *Born Again:* She was on that but wouldn't support the album."

Friday October 1, 1999, Puffy was in Florida promoting *Forever.* Shyne was recording in Daddy's House. Lil' Cease and members of Junior M.A.F.I.A. arrived. "They weren't there just chillin' and talkin' shit," one person said. It was rumored that they traveled from Brooklyn to confront Shyne and "Puff to try to end the shit." They began to "pester" Shyne and "push him around and tell him to get the fuck out of here." There was reportedly a confrontation and shots rang out in front of the studio.

Shyne left the scene before the police arrived, he added, while Lil' Kim and the group, including Damien Butler, who reportedly argued with him in a bar next to the studio, granted interviews to a New York television station.

Bethann Hardison, however, denied that Shyne did any shooting that night. According to her, someone insulted Shyne outside of Daddy's House; he responded, and then tried to walk away; a third person tried to instigate a problem by telling Shyne's opponent, "You gonna let him say that? He didn't say nothing! He didn't even answer you right."

"Next thing you know, one or two people walked up on him," she said. They started "fighting, with a couple of people kicking and punching him. He's down; another one or two join in, and they're kicking and punching him." Bystanders wanted to break it up, but these people jumped him and Shyne lost consciousness.

Within a day, MTV claimed that Shyne was "the intended target of the incident," but to this day no one really knows what happened.

Bethann Hardison met with Shyne during this period. "I didn't see any bruises or anything," she said, "which is amazing, because someone else who had been there was amazed that he walked away." When she gave him a friendly hug, she also did not notice a gun on him. What she did notice was that "he didn't seem the same." When he spoke, he now ended his sentences with the slang phrase, "You know what I'm saying." He did not discuss the incident, but she said she suspected that he was repressing anger. "Honestly, in my heart," she concluded, "I do believe that what happened between the last day of September had an effect. From that point on, his back was slightly up."

Within four weeks, Puffy was accused of performing his own act of violence. On Halloween night, he and Jennifer Lopez attended the Garden of Hedonism party at the nightclub Lot 61. By now, Puffy had grown a bit protective of his relationship with Lopez. When a writer from *Vibe* called to get a quote for a cover story on Lopez during this period, Puffy was quoted as saying, "I swear to God, my name better not even be in Honey's article."

As he was leaving the Halloween party, a fashion publicist named Edwin Perez claimed that, when Puffy saw him speaking with Lopez, he walked up and hit him in the face, near his right cheek. By the time the NYPD arrived, Puffy was gone. Perez filed a police report that said "he was startled but didn't need an ambulance; but he did say that he was in fear for his safety." Puffy denied hitting Perez less than two months after a judge had sentenced him to a day in an anger management class. His representatives claimed it was mistaken identity.

Through all this, *Born Again* continued to take shape. By now, Puffy had remixed "Long Kiss Goodnight" from *Life After Death,* added vocals from Mobb Deep, and called it "Tonight." He also included Biggie's protégés Lil' Kim and Lil' Cease on a few numbers. "Can I Get Witcha" and "Biggie" found Lil' Cease delivering pop rap and hard-core. Puffy seemingly had justified his *Forever*-like production approach to Cease. "They didn't just make it a New York album," Cease said publicly. Lil' Kim, meanwhile, rapped on "Notorious," which featured buoyant pop raps that evoked "Mo' Money, Mo' Problems," and the label's *No Way Out* heyday. As in the early days, Biggie cracked a few jokes, Puffy delivered a light rap about money, and Kim called other female rappers "hoes" who benefited from delays in her second album.

Cease, Damien Butler, and Voletta Wallace served as consultants but ultimately could do nothing to prevent Puffy from turning *Born Again* into "slick A and R shit." Biggie's classic mix-tape performance "Road to the Riches," set to a medley of Dr. Dre–produced beats from *The Chronic* and other Death Row albums, now featured overbearing keyboards. Even worse, Puffy recorded a "new" version of "Everyday Struggle." The original had been Biggie's favorite from *Ready.* Now it was called "I Really Want To Show You," and featured ho-hum R & B, former Jodeci members K-Ci and Jo-Jo rehashing their old single "Come and Talk to Me," and a lukewarm performance by Nas. "Big Booty Hoes" followed, featuring a crude, sexually explicit lyric from self-styled "pimp rapper" Too Short.

Some observers in the industry questioned Puffy's approach to creating the album. Said one frequent visitor to Daddy's House, "What's sad is that it was a bad reflection on Biggie." Tupac's posthumous works had worked wonders for his label Death Row; new albums presented songs as he had recorded them. "Biggie's album was just vocals, they just used the vocals, man, and that really took away from him. I think if Puffy had even B-level songs that were Biggie's own music, they would've been in business, with a much hotter album. But to make it this thing, putting all these people on that Biggie wouldn't make records with, didn't seem like a natural progression."

Hearing Big's voice on speakers, and studio employees discussing "Big's session" in Studio A, disturbed Damien Butler. And the album already was dated because some of Biggie's lyrics were six years old and referenced long-gone stars Bobby Brown and House of Pain. Still, Puffy continued to set Biggie's early lyrics to new music, creating a Biggie album after his death, when the rapper wasn't around to offer input or veto questionable decisions.

Harve Pierre told *The Source,* "I get mixed feelings when I hear Biggie's voice. Sometimes I get hype and dance around the room, just wildin' out to the music. Then it hits me for a second . . . damn; Biggie's not even here. I go back and forth." Engineer Paul Logus said, "A lot of this stuff is Biggie before he knew Puffy and the whole Bad Boy camp. He was hungry." While mixing the album, Logus felt it was "weird for me to be working on a track that he didn't originally rhyme on."

Regardless, Bad Boy continued to claim that Puffy's motivation for releasing the album was artistic, not financial. Yet, Puffy did not attend the *Born Again* listening party held at Justin's. On Tuesday, November 23, he was busy promoting *Forever* on the *Tonight Show,* even as the backlash against him grew.

By December 8, a day after *Born Again*'s release, the *Washington Post* reported on "The Deflation of Puffy Combs" and implied that he was a "presumptive has-been" at the age of thirty. *Forever* had gone from debuting at Number 2 in August to Number 83 on the Top 200 albums chart. It had sold 990,000 copies—less than a third of *No Way Out*'s 3.4 million units.

When he appeared at rock-rap group Korn's concert at the Apollo—to position himself for a rock rap EP he planned to release as "P-Diddy"—

the audience chanted "Puffy sucks." Web sites also had started to denounce him.

He was losing ground even in the mainstream: He went unmentioned in *Fortune* magazine's list of America's forty richest under forty, while No Limit's Master P appeared at Number 28. He was included on *Forbes*'s list, at Number 16, with earnings of $53.5 million in 1998, but Master P outdid him there as well, at Number 11 with $56.5 million. Even as he continued to pretend that there wasn't a backlash, promoting himself in *GQ* or *Vibe,* the Stoute beating, and departures by Mase and The Lox took their toll on Puffy. Then there was dating Jennifer Lopez, partying in the Hamptons, blowing six hundred thousand dollars on a birthday party, wearing a seersucker suit and straw hat at his East Hampton Labor Day bash, and sharing the cover of *Forbes* with Jerry Seinfeld.

To add to his despair, critics attacked *Born Again.* Writer Kevin Powell said, "This is not Biggie's work. This is regression." The *Washington Post* said " 'Dead Wrong' seems to suggest sex with prepubescent girls." *Vibe* asked, "Would Biggie have approved of Puff resurrecting his memory with *Born Again* if he was alive?" *Westword* said, "A few of these cameos, like Lil' Kim's, make sense given Biggie's history, but come on—what the hell is Eminem doing on the album?" *Rolling Stone:* "The simple fact is that B.I.G. may have released all of his best stuff during his lifetime." MTV: "As a matter of fact, it's not even a good Biggie album—he's virtually a guest star on what's been made a compilation by either lack of material or desperation for commercial recouping." VH-1 called it "grave robbing" and "the hip-hop equivalent of *Weekend at Bernie's.*"

Another critic noted that Voletta Wallace's comments over The Lox's "We'll Always Love Big Poppa" had been "cut off in mid-speech as if she's some rambling nobody at an awards show." Despite these reviews, Biggie's fans remained loyal. *Born Again* opened at Number 1 and sold 485,000 copies in its first week, twice as many as *Forever.*

# ELEVEN

# Whoa!

HIS NEW IMAGE AS THE MOST BELITTLED FIGURE IN MUSIC DID NOT stop Puffy from promoting himself as an esteemed rapper. In December he filmed a video for Biggie's "Notorious." He planned to appear with Jennifer Lopez on MTV on New Year's Eve. He appeared at the VH1/Vogue Fashion awards in a fur, sunglasses, and over one million dollars worth of borrowed diamonds. After entertaining the mostly white audience, he and Lopez attended a party, grabbed microphones, and rapped along with *Born Again.* It was pathetic: Him and his pampered movie star girlfriend pretending to be "hard-core" at rap events; exchanging such gifts as a white mink coat, an antique diamond bracelet, and a forty-thousand-dollar ring, and drinking expensive champagne like tap water. Puffy was achieving success in new circles for reasons other than hip-hop. The mainstream media focused on his fur coats and diamond studs, his fashion spread in *Vogue* and his telling that magazine, "I got the softest feet in the world."

Puffy's relationship with Lopez, in fact, created as much publicity as Biggie's murder. Newspapers described how he and Jennifer had their feet X-rayed at the Hospital for Special Surgery; he produced her moronic album *On the 6;* she appeared on the cover of *Notorious* magazine, and they held hands at the MTV awards. Some people preferred his new image. Said openly gay *Vibe* editor in chief Emil Wilbekin: "He brought a rock and roll edge to hip-hop and made it very glamorous."

In hip-hop circles, however, Puffy Combs lost all credibility. Hip-hop fans came to see him as a poser who had a chauffeur in a Bentley drive him to socialite charity events and a fraud who wore white suits with Biggie-like derbies and moved away from black people, into a fourteen-million-dollar Manhattan mansion and a palatial East Hampton home.

Yet he kept trying to promote a "hard-core" image. He did it although he was one of the few people bringing many bodyguards to events like Jay-Z's listening party at Irving Plaza. He also kept trying to ingratiate himself to rich white people. He performed at a costume party at the Metropolitan Museum of Art. Instead of sitting at a table and dining with everyone else, he had to get on stage and yell, "Come on, put your hands in the air, don't be afraid." That some wealthy whites focused on their dinner did not seem to bother him.

By the time he and Jennifer Lopez drove to Manhattan from East Hampton on December 27, 1999, Puffy had lost his audience. He believed, however, that his other successful businesses, which included Sean John clothing, would help him achieve his goal of becoming the next David Geffen. He believed that hip-hop fans continued to view him and his nine-figure empire with respect, and that his Versace furs, Prada shoes, well-maintained hairstyle, and diamond jewelry would continue to impress them. He did not seem to accept that many youths actually considered him a disagreeable has-been.

At around 11:00 P.M., forty-two-year-old driver Wardel Fenderson—a bespectacled father of three—pulled the Navigator out front, and Puffy led Lopez into the backseat. Fenderson claimed later that when he glanced over his shoulder, he saw "Mr. Combs holding in his hand a black handgun. I thought, What in God's name is he doing holding a gun?" Still, the driver kept silent and tried to register concern by making eye contact with him.

Within minutes they were at Club New York, on the corner of Eighth Avenue and West Forty-fourth Street. "I greeted him at the door," said owner Michael Bergos. "He was very gracious and polite." The owner led Puffy, Lopez, and bodyguard Anthony "Wolf" Jones to the VIP section. Security guards did not search them. He sat on a couch, listened to R & B, hip-hop, and reggae, and continued to order Veuve Cliquot champagne. One person later claimed he ordered twenty-four bottles for his group.

Soon he and Lopez went to the dance floor and, surrounded by guards, they danced. Then, back in the VIP section, he tried to show off by dancing on a small coffee table and raising his arms in triumph.

That night, Shyne was present. His album was scheduled for a first-quarter release; he felt he was going to be the label's next star and Bad Boy would regain its hard-core audience. In the studio he had rapped to R&B, Caribbean melodies, and flamenco guitars. He'd also allowed one person, probably Puffy, to hum a generic melody over one track. One number described a drug dealer betrayed by the woman he loves, on which he sang the old KRS-One lyric "The girls look so good." His song "Gangsta Shit" discussed Nicky Barnes, women with guns in their hosiery, boiling coke, and aiming guns.

Another mimicked Biggie: promoting Brooklyn, singing lyrics about "European cars, European clothes," describing tropical settings like Brazil, and spelling his name out in raps. Others revived the Bad Boy formula, such as when he sang Gloria Estefan's "Bad Boys," speed-rapped like Biggie on *Life After Death,* and presented his weak take on Biggie's "Juicy." Over an Mtume-style R & B sample, Shyne reminisced about his own mother, his violent Brooklyn streets, and bonding with Puffy: "Then I linked with Puff, deal inked with Puff, now I fly jets and buy minks with Puff." Puffy wanted to release the album, but again, on December 27, 1999, everything changed.

Jennifer wanted to leave the club, but he insisted on staying. This didn't stop her; she headed for the exit without him. Barmaid Monica Caban handed him a four-thousand-dollar check and later claimed, "I was told I wasn't getting a tip because none was left for me."[1]

Puffy and Anthony "Wolf" Jones crossed the crowded nightclub. As he approached the bar, fans called out. He stopped to shake a few hands. One person, witness Julius Jones later said, "didn't smack him five. That's what started it." The man was Matthew Allen, also known as "Scar."

"I arrived at Club New York between midnight and twelve-thirty P.M. on the night of Sunday, December twenty-sixth, into Monday December twenty-seventh," Scar later wrote. "I had been to Club New York many

---

1. Puffy claimed he had left a tip.

times before, always on Sunday nights. Before that night, I had seen Puffy many times, many locations." They'd never had any problems. They would even greet each other. "I had also seen Shyne many times and we would have conversations. Shyne and I never had any problems with each other before that night." Before Puffy reached the bar, Allen claimed that he and Shyne had spent much of the night discussing Shyne's upcoming album. "While they were leaving," Allen added, "Puffy was saying goodbye and high-fiving everybody." While reaching out, Puffy shoved him. Allen dropped his drink. "At the time I didn't realize who it was who had just knocked me and so as I turned around I pushed him off of me and realized it was Puffy.

"He started saying, 'What's up' and I said, 'Fuck you.' At that point, we were about arm's length apart and facing each other, when his crew held him back and my friends grabbed me."

The NYPD said they got in each other's faces and traded insults. Allen yelled, "I'll kill you," and Puffy looked confused.

"We started screaming at each other back and forth, Puffy was in front of me and Shyne was off to my right. At some point, I turned to Shyne and said words to the effect of, 'Yo, I'll see you in Brooklyn.' " Next, someone at the bar threw ten dollar and twenty dollar bills at Puffy's face and yelled, "You're not the only one here with money."

Allen wrote: "It was a lot of money and it came down like snow."

The crowd around them either surged forward or retreated; bouncers arrived to break it up. They told Puffy and Wolf Jones to leave; a prosecutor quoted them as saying, "Nah. We ain't leavin'."

Shyne stooped over and rose with a gun in hand, and fired it. "At that point, Puffy had a gun in his right hand as I was running out," Allen explained. "I could see both Shyne and Puffy firing guns. The reason I know both Shyne and Puffy fired is because I saw the fire coming out of their guns."

A witness said Jones ran over and asked Shyne: *"What is wrong with you? What is going on with you?"*

Robert Thompson was shot in his right shoulder. He fell to the floor and heard three more shots, he later claimed. He saw Shyne holding a gun. Natania Reuben, shot that night in the face, later would claim Puffy fired a gun. A bullet passed through her cheek, nose, and the back of her head.[2] Julius Jones also later claimed he saw a gun in Puffy's right hand. "It was black, an automatic." He added: "I thought, 'What the fuck? Damn!' " Then Jones, shot in the shoulder, also fell to the floor. Another person, Tarnisha Smith, claimed Puffy ran by her with a gun in one hand.

Puffy denies carrying a gun that night.

Shyne, meanwhile, ran from the club and saw two police officers a few feet away. After making eye contact, he ran into the path of an oncoming limousine. The officers yelled, "Police! Don't move! Let me see your hands!" When he raised his hands, his coat fell open. The police saw a gun in his waistband. While they arrested him, Puffy, Jones, and Jennifer Lopez arrived at the Navigator parked outside.

They entered and Lopez said Shyne had "busted off," fired a gun, the driver said, and that Puffy and Jones yelled, "Get out of here." The driver saw a police car blocking the end of the street, but Puffy and Jones, he claimed, ordered him to drive past it. Puffy yelled, "Trap, trap, open the trap," prosecutors claimed. The driver did not know how to open the secret compartments, he said; Puffy and Jones began to panic. The Navigator leaped onto the sidewalk and swerved around the police car. The police car reversed and followed. At this point, prosecutors said, Puffy threw a black 9mm semiautomatic gun out of a window, then the Navigator turned onto Eighth Avenue. The driver raced through eleven red lights with a police car on its tail. Near Fifty-fourth Street, a second police car charged toward the Navigator, so the driver finally had to pull over. The police pulled each occupant out one at a time.

Puffy was in the rear seat, said Officer Joseph Libraro; he had his hands between his knees as if trying to hide something and wouldn't stop moving his hands until Libraro yelled, "Get your hands up" two or three times. Puffy took his time in doing so, he said.

Officers then handcuffed him, Jones, and his driver, while Jennifer tried to walk away. A sergeant recalled: "I said, 'Jennifer, Jennifer, come back here, come back here,' and she said, 'I'm going home, I'm going

---

2. Dr. John A. Perrotti later quoted Reuben as saying, in the emergency room that night, "I was shot by Puffy."

home.' " She walked into the path of another officer and said she was leaving in a limousine. This officer said she was under arrest. She said, "It's not my gun."

The Navigator was empty when Officer William Meyer found a 9mm handgun under the right front passenger seat. Next, an agent from the Drug Enforcement Administration discovered a secret compartment in the rear of the vehicle, where Puffy and Jennifer had been sitting; inside, he found traces of cocaine. The police asked the four of them about the gun in the Navigator. Since no one admitted to owning it, everyone was arrested. At this point, a prosecutor claimed, Puffy told his driver, "I can't go to jail, I'm Puff Daddy."

Each passenger was driven to a nearby precinct in a separate car. During his ride, Puffy asked the sergeant about Lopez. "I said, 'She's being arrested because there's a gun in the car and no one is admitting to it,' " the sergeant testified later. "And he asked, 'What would happen if someone admits to it?' I said, 'Most likely they'll be charged with it, but that's the DA's decision. But right now no one is admitting to it.' " Puffy, the sergeant added, said, "Deal. When we get back to the precinct, I'm going to let you know whose gun it is."

At the Midtown North precinct, Puffy, his driver, and bodyguard Anthony "Wolf" Jones stood before the desk sergeant to fill out initial arrest paperwork. Puffy whispered something in Jones's ear, and then to Fenderson, the driver, said Sergeant Michael Reilly. "Then Mr. Combs looked back at Mr. Jones and gave him a look, and Mr. Jones shook his head from side to side, which I took as a 'no.' Then [Puffy] looked at Mr. Fenderson and he didn't say anything." After more whispering and facial gestures, Reilly continued, Jones would not make eye contact with Puffy. From here, the prosecutor claimed, he and Jones "relentlessly" asked the driver to claim the gun in the Navigator; Puffy offered a cash bribe, and a forty-thousand-dollar ring as collateral and told the driver it was worth three hundred thousand dollars. Sergeant Reilly yelled, "Cut it out! Stop it!"

In the holding cell, however, they reportedly continued to pressure the driver to approach Officer William Meyer, who had found the gun, to say, "The gun was mine." Within hours, however, without them knowing,

Fenderson had told the police that "the gun was not his, that he wasn't going to take the rap for anybody," Meyer recalled.

Police officers drove Puffy and the others to Midtown South. They remained in custody for fourteen hours; Jennifer thought she'd be charged. After being handcuffed to a bench, locked alone in a cell, and then fingerprinted, one police officer claimed, "She was crying all over the place, in the squad room." She saw Puffy, and reportedly yelled, "Look at the trouble you got me into."

By 4:00 P.M. the next afternoon, however, the Manhattan district attorney's office dropped gun possession charges against her. She would have to testify before a grand jury. "Puffy got paranoid when Lopez was cut loose," a source told the New York Post. Before long, he was released on ten thousand dollars bail. He entered a room filled with reporters, sat at a table, faced a microphone, and said, "Under no circumstances whatsoever did I have anything to do with a shooting. I do not own a gun nor did I possess a gun that night."

# PART 3

# NOTHING LASTS FOREVER

"When you start making a whole bunch of money and your lifestyle starts moving too fast, it gotta be up to you to slow that shit down."

—*Biggie Smalls*

# TWELVE

# All a Dream

THE ARREST SHOWED PUFFY HOW MUCH THE MEDIA HAD COME TO dislike him. Every major newspaper reported the shooting in terms that implied he was fractionally to blame. He realized that much more was now at stake than his popularity. The NYPD and district attorney believed he was a criminal who belonged in jail. Three days after his release, Puffy allegedly began to pressure the driver. By this point, he had paid Fenderson's ten-thousand-dollar bail and paid for his attorney. Now, Fenderson claimed, Puffy and his entourage called twelve times to urge him to take credit for the gun found in the Navigator. Next, he said, Puffy invited him to his apartment. Fenderson testified that he went there and told Puffy, "I can't work for you anymore, and I can't take the rap for your gun."

A day later, Puffy called Fenderson again. He had learned that the driver had lost his job driving for an investment banker and his family. Fenderson didn't answer, so he left a message. "Hey, yo, it's P," he said. "I was just thinking about you, dog. Just hit me on my cell 'cause I'm just concerned [with] that news you hit me with earlier." He added, "I just want to make you feel, like, comfortable, you know what I'm saying, make your family feel comfortable."

The shooting incident brought him full circle—he was as much an underdog as he had been when the CCNY tragedy had filled the headlines. But the stakes were higher. The NYPD and the DA were pursuing him. He now had to adopt a new personality.

On New Year's Eve, he appeared on MTV's "2 Large New Year's Eve Party" and told the host that he couldn't let false accusations stop him from performing for his supportive "MTV family" of fans. Jennifer had testified before a twenty-three-member grand jury: She had said she had danced with him and had not seen a gun, but she also said that she hadn't been facing him when the shooting began. During a break in her testimony, meanwhile, an adviser asked, "What are you still doing with this guy? He's no good for you—he's only going to get you killed." She reportedly nodded, saying, "I know, I know, I know."

On MTV he looked like a shadow of his former self; the host was not as dazzled; the crowd was smaller and less approving. He'd wanted to give an electrifying performance but instead looked befuddled and godforsaken performing oldies that once featured Mase or The Lox. Later he would call it his "worst show ever." Even so, the appearance allowed him to proclaim his innocence to millions of viewers.

In public, he was mild-spoken, respectful, and contrite. When a reporter traveled to his East Hampton home, he greeted him in sweats and sneakers; he had a wrinkled pillow under his arm. He did not wear his jewelry equivalent of a suit of armor: the platinum-and-diamond bracelet, his watch, his ring, the two giant crucifix medallions, and the diamond ear-studs. He didn't show off the Bentley as he had done for *Forbes*. His handlers and bodyguards were out of sight, and instead of gloating about his fortune and success, he accused the media of continuing to promote his unpopular persona.

Kevin Chappell of *Ebony* magazine preferred the new image. The media, he wrote, had transformed "a young man serious about his music and his legacy to the larger-than-life 'Puff Daddy,' a media-created megalomaniac who loves to wallow in the excesses that his fame, money and power have afforded him."

After years of histrionics, Puffy finally detached himself from his overbearing image. "There has been so much overshadowing my music," he said in 2000. "One week you'll hear that I'm messing with this girl. The next week you'll hear that I had this baby. The next week you'll hear that

I made this amount of money. The next week you'll hear that I was hang-ing out with Donald Trump. A lot of times the music gets lost. But that's all I'm trying to do is make music. That's what 'Puff Daddy' is all about."

Rapacity and gaudiness, he claimed, were always part of hip-hop. "Rap has always had a braggadocio element to it. It's just an art form."

ON JANUARY 4, HE FACED THE GRAND JURY AND SAID: "I CAME HERE today to look everybody in their eyes and tell them the truth as I know it, the God's honest truth." He mentioned his father being "killed through gunfire when I was three years old," and invoked Biggie: "My best friend got killed and one of my biggest artists got killed two and a half years ago to gunfire." He stressed that he had "two beautiful young children," and worked twenty hours a day to become a "shining example to kids and to people."

Then he distanced himself from Shyne: "I did not know Shyne was going to be there and I did not see any actions that he did." He and Lopez, he continued, should not be responsible for Shyne's thoughts or actions.

But then he bickered with Assistant District Attorney Matthew Bog-danos over whether he actually ever hit Steve Stoute with a champagne bottle. He lapsed into slang and lost his temper in front of a panel that would decide whether to indict him on felony charges of gun possession.

Outside of the courthouse he continued to proclaim his innocence and to say he believed he had done well on the stand. He did not think that his lament about not hitting Stoute with a bottle would cause jurors to believe that a side of him was capable of associating with criminals, becoming en-raged when someone threw money in his face, and entering a gunfight in a crowded nightclub. Even so, the grand jury decided to indict him for crimi-nal possession of a weapon in the second and third degrees. Investigators also were looking into three additional shootings and beatings in Manhat-tan nightclubs. They were trying to determine whether he or Jones had or-dered or committed violence against witnesses, or paid or threatened victims to drop charges. Harvey Slovis, one of Puffy's lawyers, said he was never charged or arrested for any of this, but investigators reexamined inci-dents at Justin's, Lot 61, and Carbon. In the last, a bouncer was shot and beaten in September 1998; he wanted to pursue the case, but changed his mind after a second beating. Then the *Los Angeles Times* reported that his codefendant Jones was named as a suspect in the murder of Jake Robles.[1] In February Puffy pled not guilty to the charges against him.

BACK AT BAD BOY, HE TRIED TO REPAIR THE DAMAGE CAUSED BY *FOR-ever* and his arrest. Some employees lost faith in the company. A month after general manager Jeff Burroughs left, eight to ten employees resigned, while others went on job interviews. Andre Harrell claimed the departures were part of a downsizing to make the company "more profitable," but Bobby Spring-steen recalled, "I don't look it as a downsizing. I looked at it like those were people that felt they needed to go." He added: "There was never no downsiz-ing or corporate change. It was never [anything] like that. No, not at all."

He tried to uphold his image by attending the Grammy awards in February with Jennifer Lopez, but ended up looking faded and confused. He wore a costly white suit and sunglasses while Lopez made headlines in a see-through Versace number he had suggested she wear. Before they reached their seats, however, the media reported a breaking news story. Manhattan district attorney Robert Morgenthau had announced that a grand jury also had indicted Puffy on a felony count of bribing a witness. In response, Puffy issued a statement that read: "This was done today on the night of the Grammy Awards in an attempt to embarrass me."

During the ceremony he wore his sunglasses and hoped "Satisfy You" would win the award for best rap performance by a duo or group. Instead, The Roots won. The camera zoomed in on his marked frown even as Rosie O'Donnell, hosting the show, began to insult him. "He can really Sing-Sing," she said. A new play was titled *Puffy Get Your Gun,* she added. After he and Jennifer scowled at O'Donnell, he rose from his seat and left. O'Donnell added that she really wanted to introduce Sting by saying "he spent more time with the police than Puff Daddy."

His old way of promoting himself was no longer working. He with-drew from the public and focused on improving what the *Village Voice* later called "projects that otherwise might never have seen the light of

---

1. Jones's lawyer, Michael Bachner, denies the accusation.

day." Said a disillusioned insider: "He was down in the dumps. His record sales were slumping. Everything was going down the drain." Black Rob's album suddenly became a priority.

Rob's single "Whoa" became a favorite on radio, and Puffy released a video in which Puffy joined Rob on top of a lopsided bus in nondesigner gear to perform clumsy dance moves. Shyne also appeared in the video, but only as a nonexclusive face in the crowd.

After five years of pursuing success, Rob heard Bad Boy vice president Ron Gilyard say he was now their "ghetto prince" and "top priority." While Black Rob's *Life Story* opened at Number 3 and at Number 1 on the rap and R & B charts, its first-week sales of 177,000 were still 28,343 copies fewer than *Forever. Life Story* also failed to appear on the pop chart. Even worse, Rob hurled backhanded insults in print. "I'm throwing Bad Boy on my back and keepin' 'em alive," he said. To the *New York Daily News:* "I'm the baddest Bad Boy, period." Another interview found him claiming *Life Story* would make or break Bad Boy and "Puff knows that. Everybody knows that." Another day: "Puff is a cool person. He's just not like a CEO [any] more."

Instead of ignoring this, Puffy felt the need to say, "We kept this on the low, but when we had just finished the album Rob violated his parole and had to go in and do a little bid." When Rob left prison, he added, he asked him to record fresher material. "People were saying that [the reason] it took him awhile to come out was because he didn't have the Bad Boy type of sound; that's ridiculous; look at Big, look at The Lox. They were very street-oriented, like Rob. I don't make any money by not putting Rob out. But we're only gonna put him out when it's right."

Puffy also released Carl Thomas's *Emotional.* But even Thomas said: "I've never been all under him, hanging out at clubs." To find them together "you'd have to go to the studio. When we're together, we're working, knocking out hits."

Before long, Puffy tried to be executive producer for Lil' Kim's follow-up to *Hard Core.* But Kim was harboring a grudge over *Born Again,* and about Shyne being on Bad Boy. He bought her a diamond-encrusted pendant with a Chinese symbol that meant "success," discarded material she had recorded with estranged manager Lance Rivera, and invited her to write lyrics in his East Hampton home. Yet his controlling ways upset her. Sometimes he would reach out, touch her hair, and "put it the way he likes it," she said. Other times, he would hear a lyric and say, "Change that; I don't like it. OK, now change that. No, I think you can write something better than that." Kim would have to "sit there and rewrite the same song about fifteen times," she said. Ultimately, she told him, "This has got to stop!" She took control of the album; chose her own music; wrote her own lyrics; insulted Shyne on her title track; and told *Vibe* she felt Puffy was like an "uncle who ain't shit but we love his stank ass." She compared him to "a fucking bastard" and a "spoiled brat" and told *USA Today*, "We're cool because of Biggie. I have to be honest, he's not the perfect person in my life right now."

In March, on what would have been Biggie's twenty-eighth birthday, he threw a party in a nightclub, stood by the deejay booth, and raised a birthday cake. He asked Jay-Z and Lil' Kim to blow out the candles. He hugged Biggie's mother and shouted, "Anyone who wants to do Hennessey shots in honor of Biggie, it's on Bad Boy Entertainment!"

In July he traveled to the island of Capri to attend L.A. Reid's wedding and found himself accused of assaulting Shakir Stewart, who ran Reid's Atlanta-based music publishing company. Stewart told friends that Puffy was "in a jealous rage" when he "showed up at Stewart's room with a bodyguard who stayed outside," The *New York Post* reported. Puffy had accused him of having an affair with Kim Porter, the *Post* added; Stewart denied the affair and told him to mind his own business, then Puffy "supposedly hit Stewart with a chair." Puffy's spokespeople denied that this took place, but the prosecutor in New York was investigating.

His image suffered even more when producer Dr. Dre promoted his *Up in Smoke* tour with Eminem, Snoop, and Xzibit. In print, Dre said he respected Puffy's business acumen but "as a musician, he's really hurt the art form." Each night during his tour, Dre had comedian Alex Thomas ask the crowd, "You all like Puffy?" In Philadelphia, he was there when the audience booed the mere mention of his name. Said a witness: "He looked like he wanted to cry." However, he attended another performance at the Nassau Coliseum in New York and again heard the crowd boo his name.

*   *   *

TO SAVE BAD BOY, PUFFY COMMITTED WHAT BAD BOY'S FORMER audience probably regarded as the ultimate sellout. Popular tastes had changed. Teenage singer Britney Spears was on the cover of *Forbes*'s "Highest Paid Celebrities" issue. Puffy was not listed. Caucasian rap fans now supported ready-made imitative boy bands like 'N Sync, who were to groups like New Edition what Pat Boone was to Little Richard. Puffy decided to sign a Caucasian pop group of his own. After seeing a group's dance moves and hearing their ludicrous pop during an audition at the swank Beverly Hills Hotel, he said, "I wish you guys the best of luck with your careers." A minute later, their manager said, "He wants to sign you on the spot, he's calling up his lawyers right now, he's drawing up the contract." That promoting Dream, as he called them, as part of a "New Pop America" would destroy his credibility in hip-hop did not worry him. He trotted out the song title "Pain" for the third time, had producers cover hip-hop drums with conventional pop, and got the girls in tight red leather costumes reminiscent of Total. Then his yarn-spinning publicists claimed Dream would help Bad Boy "make a definitive mark on the world of teen pop."

AT THIS POINT, ONE MATTER REPORTEDLY WAS UNDECIDED. Would Bad Boy release Shyne's album? Shyne believed that he and Puffy could still be close. They had lived together, traveled together, appeared together at a Sean John fashion show filmed by MTV; they also had bought each other gifts. After their arrests, Shyne later claimed, Puffy did not pay for his lawyer or bail. Shyne also said that Puffy was trying to distance himself by never mentioning Shyne, or his album, in public. "Honestly, he never really did anything to help me after the shooting." He added: "As soon as we were indicted, he wanted to keep me away from him. He didn't even want to put my album out." They communicated through attorneys, he said, and Puffy never asked if he needed help, if he was all right, if he needed anything.

In fact, for a short period in early 2000, Shyne's name was removed from a list of artists on the Bad Boy website. BMG reportedly had qualms about releasing his album. About the only time his name was mentioned

was when Puffy's lawyer Harvey Slovis told *Newsweek:* "There are no allegations that Shyne's action is related to Puffy at all."

After their indictments in February, Shyne asked other label executives to arbitrate. As he put it, "They wanted to do as much as they possibly could, but Combs wanted the relationship to remain minimal and not
have me publicized." Shyne said that he threatened legal action. By this
time, Bad Boy had spent millions on the project. Puffy asked Shyne to return to the studio and record new songs.

*Shyne* became yet another outmoded Bad Boy album. For "Whatcha
Gonna Do," Dee Trotman sampled "Hava Nagila." "Bang" found Yogi presenting a Ruff Ryders–like track. Mario Winans filled "The Life" with me-
dieval music and "Spend Some Cheese" with generic Jay-Z-style pop.
After self-indulgent guitar plucking, Shampelle filled "Let Me See Your
Hands" with more Jay-Z-style music. Reggae singer Barrington Levy
crooned throughout EZ Elpee's "Bad Boyz" and replaced half-witted hum-
ming on the chorus of Chucky Thompson's "Bonnie & Shyne." The rest of
the music was a mélange of bad ideas: "It's OK" featured a Run-D.M.C.–
style beat; "The Hit" sampled atrocious Worldbeat. "Get Off" included ef-
feminate singing from Slim of 112.

Lyrically, *Shyne* was no better. He started the album with a dubious
speech called "Dear America," then claimed he was one of rap's all-time
best, along with Biggie and Jay-Z. He mumbled threats on The Nep-
tunes's "Niggas Gonna Die" and mimicked Biggie's verse on "Victory"
with his own shameless work about the "Commission." His Biggie imper-
sonation had led to a muffled tone and vulgar lyrics that quoted numerous
well-known Snoop songs. If Bad Boy Entertainment ever thought that
Shyne could become the new Biggie, they were sadly mistaken. The attempt to position him as such had done nothing but ruin reputations. The
album lacked direction. It featured only two guests, Levy and Slim; the
samples were inferior; and most of the beats belonged in a garbage can.
What saved *Shyne* from becoming a complete waste of a million dollars
were his duets with Levy and "That's Gangsta." Even as the backlash
continued, and his dated pop formula marred the album, Puffy proved
that he could still deliver a compelling track. Yet to do so he had to return
to borrowing from Dre and Death Row. One night at 2:00 A.M., he and

Mario Winans created a track patterned after a Dre-produced eighties rap hit, The D.O.C.'s classic "Funky Enough." Shyne liked the music and wrote lyrics and "That's Gangsta" became one of his most expedient numbers.

The rap press did not know that relations between Shyne and Puffy had soured until a record release party in a downtown Manhattan nightclub. That night, Shyne wore a red oversized St. Louis Cardinals baseball cap pulled low over his eyes. He performed his popular black-radio hit "Bad Boyz," then performed it again, then launched into a frantic speech that thanked everyone for what he saw as ongoing support. Puffy stepped in to calm him down, and Shyne snapped, "I know I'm flipping, but fuck it, 'cause for real, I might not be here tomorrow."

Still, on November 2, he and Shyne appeared together at New York's Hammerstein Ballroom. Puffy was serving as a celebrity judge for *Blaze* magazine's MC Battle; KRS-One refereed while sixteen rappers competed for a trophy, a leather jacket, and a recording contract. Other guests included southern rapper Mystikal, old school performers Kurtis Blow and Doug E. Fresh, and A & R executives from Jive, Priority, Bad Boy, and Rawkus Records. Everything was fine until Shyne got on stage to perform. For fun, someone in the audience threw a helmet at him. His response was to leap into the audience and enter a brawl that lasted a minute. Puffy then watched as Shyne mounted the stage to yell more obscenities, and then perform with Black Rob.


ULTIMATELY, HE HAD TO FACE HIS CHILDREN. AFTER THE ARREST, he said, he would not let them see media reports about the shooting. He wanted to avoid having them see Daddy in handcuffs or tensely entering or leaving the courthouse. Yet he forgot about school; other students would be more than happy to discuss the particulars of the case. He could not call these kids to say, "Yo, don't say anything about what you saw on MTV news the other night, you know."

He had to see his children face-to-face.

One of them asked, "Daddy, did you go to jail?"

He sat them down. It was agonizing, humiliating, and unpleasant, but he explained that he had been falsely accused; that life was filled with peaks and valleys. "Daddy went out to a club and he was partying and having a good time," he said. "It was the holiday season. He was leaving." Shots rang out, he added. "Daddy had got rushed into the car, him and Jennifer. When the cops pulled him over, they had accused Daddy of having a gun." He wanted them to know he was unarmed, he said. According to him, they said they knew this. He wanted to be sure they understood, he added, so that if friends asked, they could say with absolute confidence that everyone would soon see he was innocent.

His children, he claimed, said they already had explained this to schoolmates. His heart swelled, he said; he realized that nothing was more important than family.

As the trial date drew near, he met with his children again to say that things hadn't worked out the way he thought they would. He would have to go to trial. They asked, "Is that the thing with the jury?" He nodded. "Everything is going to work out all right, because they are going to believe Daddy," he told them. "Daddy is going to make sure that they know he did not have a gun and they are going to believe Daddy." At this point, his son Justin asked, "Well, what if they don't believe you?" Later, he said this was the only comment that deeply affected him. He told Justin, "Well, if they don't believe me, I have to go to jail." But he would not allow it to happen without a fight.

# THIRTEEN

# Everyday Struggle

IN 2001, PUFFY'S MIND WAS NOT ON HIS MUSIC. IN COURT HE WAS just a "defendant" who had to keep his mouth shut while the judge listened to the attorneys quibble. Before the trial started on Monday, January 29, 2001, he tried to proclaim his innocence at press conferences and during interviews. But the judge put a stop to that by issuing a gag order. Shyne had told reporters that he was recording a "more responsible" second album. Bad Boy confirmed that it would be released in the summer or fall, but Puffy made sure everyone knew he would not be involved.

Each day Shyne became more disillusioned with him. Outside of court one day, he told reporters, "The only reason people are here is just for Puffy." Later he would claim Puffy's behavior seemed to say, "You get out of this however you can, and I'm gonna get out of this however I can." He felt that Puffy had forgotten that he was the young man who had lived with him, who had always been with him, and who had been his apprentice. He never thought, "This is the young man who was with me that night, and we are all going to get out of this together."

Shyne was arrested the night before jury selection for driving without a license and getting into an accident that sent two people to the hospital, and Puffy's lawyer asked the judge to try Puffy separately. When the judge denied the request, Puffy frowned and covered his eyes.

Then Assistant District Attorney Matthew Bogdanos discussed

Shyne's record as a juvenile offender. As part of a mob, Shyne had participated in two robberies, he'd allegedly hit a boy with "a stick that had a nail at the end," and had spent almost a year in a detention facility.

Even worse, the ADA used his opening statement to call Puffy a manipulator and a criminal. He said jurors should convict him "no matter who he is." He described the ring and the $50,000 cash bribe in the precinct; read a transcript of Puffy's message on Fenderson's machine; and said it was clear evidence of his campaign to bribe his driver. He then claimed that Puffy had fired a gun in the club, and then ran; that he had left Jennifer behind; that "it isn't until Mr. Combs gets to [his chauffeur-driven SUV] that he realizes he's fled the club without Miss Lopez." The jury sat stunned.

Puffy's lawyer Benjamin Brafman asked Puffy to stand near the defense table. He crossed his wrists under his gold cuff links and faced the jury. Brafman said, "Ladies and gentlemen, this is Sean 'Puff Daddy' Combs. You can call him Sean. You can call him Mr. Combs. You can call him Puff Daddy. You can call him just plain Puffy." They just cannot, he said, call him guilty. Puffy was on trial "because he's a superstar. Puff Daddy wouldn't be here if he was John Q. Public."

The first witness was his former bodyguard, former New York City corrections officer Curtis Howard. Howard said he never saw him with a gun the night of the shooting. Bogdanos interrupted to imply that Howard was contradicting what he had told the grand jury while under oath. When Howard left the witness stand, Bogdanos said, "Every time he 'failed' to remember something it was to benefit the defendant. He got on the stand and lied and lied and lied again and again." Brafman and Bogdanos then exchanged insults while Puffy laughed and shook his head. The next day, Puffy's lawyer said Howard's inconsistencies stemmed from his ongoing treatments for cancer, which caused "forgetfulness."

Bogdanos had a detective offer crime scene evidence and assume where everyone was standing. Puffy scowled. While leaving for lunch recess, he muttered, "Assume, assume, assume."

After lunch, barmaid Monica Caban from Club New York claimed that he had stiffed her for a tip. Everyone laughed. She could not discuss the shooting, she said, because she had hid behind the deejay booth when shots rang out. The third day of the trial, Puffy sat with his

New Testament Bible while three eyewitnesses damned Shyne but left him unscathed.

Club bouncer Hassan Mahamah said Shyne had fired his gun. Shooting victim Robert Thompson also pointed the finger at him. Shyne sat with a deadpan expression.

Next, Gavin Marchand, a twenty-four-year-old rapper known as "Pretty Boy" who had joined his sister, Foxy Brown, on stage during the *No Way Out* tour, took the stand and said he was close to Puffy. He also contradicted his grand jury testimony: Where he had said Puffy and a man known as "Scar" had argued before the shooting, he now claimed that he had seen a dispute but that Puffy had not been involved. Puffy, he claimed, had been on the other side of a crowded room. In fact, he added, his memory was fuzzy. That night, he said, he had drunk two bottles of Cristal. Under cross-examination, he said Club New York wasn't only dark that night. It was "very dark." He wasn't only drinking; he was drunk. The club was *very* crowded. Brafman asked, "Was Mr. Combs having a good time?"

Marchand said, "He's always having a good time."

February 2, Bogdanos put twenty-four-year-old Brooklyn nursing student Tarnisha Smith on the stand. She said she had seen Puffy run from the shooting scene with a "black thing" in his hand.

"What did you believe it to be?"

"A gun. What I saw was black. That's what I saw."

Puffy's lawyer focused on her faded memory, and she began to use phrases like "what I thought I saw" or "from what I can remember." Then she claimed that her girlfriends had influenced her grand jury testimony. The prosecutor pulled out a police report written hours after the shooting: While laying on an emergency room gurney after an asthma attack, she told police that Puffy had had a gun. She now claimed that she had been "on medication" and Puffy's supporters in the stands exclaimed, "Aha!" Puffy's lawyer asked, "Are you certain as you sit here today that it was a gun?"

After a long silence: "It was a long time ago."

Three days later, Bogdanos put Natania Reuben on the stand. She described how she saw Puffy's "arm coming up with a black gun" and how she had been shot in the face that night. "It felt like a flaming hot sledgehammer hitting me in the face," she sobbed. "Blood just began pouring out of my face and I looked up to the sky and said, 'Oh, God, don't take me, I'm not ready to go.' "

Puffy's supporters groaned. At the defense table, he shook his head and turned a page in his Bible.

She repeated that Puffy and Shyne had pulled guns and fired.

Puffy's lawyer tried to show the jury a taped episode of *The People's Court,* and to tell the jury Reuben had fabricated videotape evidence to help her case on the television show. The judge said he would decide the matter during lunch recess, but Puffy's publicists handed copies of the tape—and a fact sheet outlining what they described as her bad behavior on the show—to reporters. The judge denied the request, but that night, footage of her appearance on the show was included on many local news programs.

For two hours, Puffy watched his lawyer say Reuben was a liar, a welfare cheat, behind in her rent payments, and under investigation for assault, theft, and throwing a space heater through her landlord's window. But she did not change her story. His lawyer then claimed that Puffy was not wearing the silver parka she described and insisted that it would be impossible for someone to wear this sort of coat halfway down his arms and pull a gun from its folds. He spent minutes raising and lowering his jacket; then the judge said, "Mr. Brafman, put your jacket back on." Before Reuben left the stand, he implied that she stood to profit from a $150 million lawsuit she had filed against Puffy.

Wednesday February 7, twenty-eight-year-old Julius Jones testified that Puffy had a gun, during which Puffy either read his Bible, thumbed through a book of short stories, or faced Jones with indifference. His other lawyer, Johnnie Cochran, questioned Jones; Jones said he actually felt ambivalent about suing Puffy; he did not want to "bring a black man down." He would drop his seven hundred-million-dollar suit against Puffy if someone paid his seventeen thousand dollars in medical bills, he added. The ADA put Dr. John A. Perrotti on the stand, and he said that the night of the shooting, Natania Reuben had said, "I was shot by Puffy." Then he put six police officers on the stand to say that Puffy tried to bribe Wardel Fenderson at the precinct. His lawyers countered by saying that he only tried to help the police learn who'd left the gun in the Navigator.

The trial continued, and Faith Evans and Reverend Hezekiah Walker appeared to show support and tell reporters about Bad Boy's gospel album, *Thank You*. During a five-day break, the *New York Post* quoted law enforcement sources as saying that prosecutors wondered why bodyguard Curtis Howard, Foxy Brown's brother, Gavin "Pretty Boy" Marchand, and club patron Tarnisha Smith seemingly had changed their stories. Prosecutors interrogated each after they left the stand, the *Post* added. Yet the new probe was not as serious as the grand jury investigation during spring of 2000, when prosecutors wondered if Puffy's assistants, bodyguards, and artists were approaching witnesses and asking or forcing them to lie for him.

On Wednesday February 14, Valentine's Day, Puffy began to defend his image. He had publicists announce that he had broken up with Jennifer Lopez. That he was suing writer Mikal Gilmore for $325,000 and legal fees, since Gilmore, he claimed, had failed to write his biography, which was canceled in 1998 by Ballantine. At the same time, Wardel Fenderson sued him for $3 million. Club New York owner Michael Bergos sued for $1.8 million. Shooting victim Julius Jones sued him for $700 million. Shooting victim Natania Reuben sued him for anywhere between $130 to $150 million. Shooting victim Robert Thompson sued him for $50 million. A woman who rented his home in Los Angeles also sued him for unspecified damages. Another lawsuit was filed by a talent agency that claimed to have discovered Dream; they claimed they were not credited on Bad Boy's website, but damages were unspecified.

In court, his former driver, Wardel Fenderson, took the stand and testified that Puffy had carried a gun in his waistband that night. He described the chase and added that Puffy yelled, in a high-pitched, terrified voice, "Yo, dog, you know how to open the stash?" He claimed that he wanted to pull over, but Puffy and Jones had said, "Don't stop, don't pull over, keep going." He claimed that, in the precinct, Puffy had told him, "I will give you fifty thousand dollars to say the gun was yours," and "I'm Puff Daddy, I can't take this gun." In the holding cell, he added, Puffy offered the bribe again, and Wolf Jones said, "Go ahead and take the money, you know Puffy's good for it." He described the twelve subsequent phone calls and Puffy's message on his voicemail, then said he believed Puffy actually was telling him, "If fifty thousand dollars isn't enough, you name your price."

Puffy's lawyer tried to shake him up, but Fenderson said, "Don't badger the witness." Puffy's supporters groaned. After court his mother faced news cameras and said, "My son is innocent. There are two sides to every story. You've only heard one."

Puffy himself spoke with reporters. "We look forward to next week when we finally get to put our case on."

On February 22, the state rested its case, though Matthew Bogdanos added that after the defense presented their witnesses, he would have Matthew "Scar" Allen testify. Puffy and his lawyers were stunned. After agreeing to testify, Allen had fled the state. Now Bogdanos revealed that police in Maryland had arrested Allen on three outstanding warrants for unrelated charges of gun possession and aggravated harassment. Allen would testify that Puffy had fired a gun and later had tried to bribe him, his two brothers, and his "gravely ill" mother. Bogdanos added that he had also been "informed of several attempts by Mr. Combs personally to pay for their silence." The New York Times believed these allegations showed Puffy "casting a wide net of money and influence in an effort to make the Dec. 27, 1999, incident at Club New York go away."

Bogdanos added that after the shooting Puffy had approached Allen at a party; Allen asked why Puffy had shot at him; Puffy implied he would pay for his silence, that Allen should contact Wolf for more information. He quoted Puffy as saying, "Give your number to my man Wolf. I've already got a bribery on me. My boys will take care of you, but you've got to understand it's not coming from me." Bogdanos also claimed that Puffy's people kept trying to call Allen. Puffy ran into Allen and asked why he hadn't called Wolf; Puffy then sent someone else to speak with him, and Allen had left town without accepting any money. Allen also had given him a handwritten statement that said Puffy and Shyne had fired guns in Club New York and Allen's family was concerned about retaliation from Puffy and his friends.


PUFFY'S LAWYERS BEGAN HIS DEFENSE BY HAVING FIVE WITNESSES take the stand in one day to testify that they never saw him with a gun.

The witnesses included a bouncer who had tried to separate Puffy's group from Matthew Allen's friends. Then a second bouncer, Glen Beck, said he had seen Puffy was empty-handed when he ran down a stairway to reach an exit. He and his entourage had stumbled over each other, Beck added. If he had a gun in his waistband, it would have fallen out. Next, Puffy's former personal assistant, Jason Delgado, said he had seen Puffy dancing on the coffee table. "He had his hands in the air and was waving them around . . . I was able to see his boxers." There was no gun, he said, and Puffy was not wearing the silver parka Natania Reuben described; he did not have that coat until after the shooting, when Delgado claimed he brought it to the precinct after the arrest.

While Delgado spoke, Puffy turned and confidently winked at his supporters. Next, Michael Bergos and Club New York manager Eric Funk testified that they had not seen him with a gun. During cross-examination, however, Funk told the jury that it was easy to hide a gun under clothes, while Bergos claimed that Puffy's other lawyer, Johnnie Cochran, had offered help from Puffy. "Were promises made to you to assist you in having parties there?" "There was talk of that," Bergos said. "It was just an overall feeling that when things were all cleared up, they would throw business my way."

Puffy's parade of witnesses continued. His lawyers called club patron Christopher Chambers to the stand. "I was facing him," Chambers testified. "I did not see a weapon."

Chambers claimed that Puffy had flinched and ducked after the first gunshot; he became the first defense witness to testify that during the shooting Puffy was unarmed. When Chambers could not describe what anyone else was doing, Bogdanos said this was odd, then asked if Chambers looked "at anyone else except for Mr. Combs when shots went off?"

Chambers said, "Didn't notice anyone else."

Bogdanos also found it strange that Chambers had never spoken with police about what he had seen. "You told everybody but the police and the district attorney's office?" he asked.

Puffy's lawyers then called Charise Myers to the stand. Myers, a female bouncer for Club New York, claimed that Puffy could not have shot anyone since "I fell on top of Mr. Combs and other people fell on top of me."

Puffy's lawyer Cochran asked, "Did he have a gun in his hands at any point?"

"No, he didn't." Myers was the second defense witness to testify that Puffy had been unarmed during the shooting. "He looked shocked," she added. But her testimony did not fit with Chambers's version of events; Chambers never mentioned any female bouncer in the area; he only said Puffy had ducked when shots rang out.

As Shyne watched defense witnesses testify he "felt some of the witnesses lied to protect Combs," according to the *Village Voice;* Shyne demanded that Bad Boy release him from his contract. "That's when I couldn't take it anymore. I couldn't believe it. That was it. There was no way I could continue. I couldn't even look at him anymore." He added that he had remained loyal to Puffy "when it all deteriorated and crumbled." During the shooting incident, the arrest, and the prosecution, "I was right there." This was how people on the street handled things. "When you're with someone all the time, it is incumbent upon you to do that," he said. "We should go through it together. We live together. We die together. That's just the kind of person I am."

March 1, 2001, was the big day. Puffy took the witness stand to deny that he had had a gun or had offered his driver money. Before court, he squirted Visine into his eyes. The night before he had stayed up late in his lawyers' office, going over his testimony. In his conservative navy blue suit, he rose quickly and rushed to the witness stand before Brafman could even finish the sentence, "Mr. Combs would like to testify."

In the audience, his supporters, including his mother and Heavy D, watched as he identified himself to jurors. Then his lawyer asked shallow questions that allowed him to describe his childhood in Harlem and rise in the industry. When his lawyer asked how he got the nickname "Puffy," he said, "Do I have to answer that? It's a nickname. I don't want to go into details."

At the defense table, meanwhile, Shyne wondered if Puffy would place the blame on him. "I didn't know what to expect," he said later. "I didn't know what he was going to get on the stand and say."

For five hours Puffy made it a point to face the seven black members of the jury. He said Club New York was not a place of "carnage" and "mass destruction." It was a "festive, positive" hangout for black industry executives. He drank champagne, danced on a table, and tried to "feel the vibe of the people," then was leaving the club when Scar started "mouthing off." "I could tell by his body language and facial expressions it wasn't good," he added. He stopped and asked his bodyguard, Jones, what the problem was, faced Scar for a few seconds, then a female bouncer told him to leave. He did, but heard gunshots behind him and became "deathly startled." He had covered his face at the sound of the first shot since "I thought I was being shot at."

At the second shot, he said, someone knocked him down; Jones fell on top of him; he never saw a gun or Shyne; Jones pulled him off the floor; Jones shoved him toward the nightclub exit.

At the defense table, Shyne clutched his own Bible and stared in mute horror. "He proved that he was just there to save himself," he said later. "There are no boundaries to what he would do to exonerate himself. I had the Bible in front of me and I was just praying that he wouldn't continue to lie. He sort of took himself out of the situation, that [we] were never involved in meeting together that night."

His lawyer asked Puffy, "You have any greater or lesser personal relationship with Mr. Barrow than any of the other recording artists on your label?"

"The personal relationship I have with all my artists is about the same," he claimed. "I respect all my artists."


UNDER CROSS-EXAMINATION, THE PROSECUTOR ACCUSED PUFFY of rehearsing his testimony, destroying evidence in the case and threatening New York Post photographer Gary Miller with a gun outside of Daddy's House Studios in 1995. Puffy began to get upset. He admitted that he had gone over his grand jury testimony with his lawyers but denied ever threatening Gary Miller for taking pictures of his car. "That's absolutely false. Mr. Miller got up and gave me the film." At this point, Miller, a tall former police detective, stood up in the audience, and Bogdanos asked Puffy whether Miller willingly gave up the film "without any guns, without any threats, without any people surrounding him."

Puffy replied, "Without any guns, without any threats, without any people surrounding him."

Miller sat and shook his head. Bogdanos asked about a T-shirt worn that night; Puffy said he regularly gave clothing away; Bogdanos asked why he wore his driver's leather jacket at his arraignment. He said, "I just thought the black leather jacket would look better."

When Puffy Combs left the stand, Brafman looked confident. Puffy's lawyers rested their case. Puffy smiled as he left the State Supreme Court building, passing crowds of supporters outside.

The case against Shyne continued. David Cubilette, a friend of Puffy's former personal assistant, said that an unknown gunman actually had fired the first shot in the club; Shyne fired a shot into the ceiling. Club patron Tavon Terrence Jones said a man with braided hair had raised his arm and fired a gun. When Bogdanos asked if it was Puffy, this witness said, "No, sir." Shyne's lawyers rested their case.

Matthew "Scar" Allen would not testify, Bogdanos said. But NYPD Detective Joseph Sweeney would read his written statement. When Sweeney read the part about him firing a gun, Puffy shook his head and frowned.

Before long, his lawyers asked Sweeney if Allen actually had written the statement. Sweeney said Bogdanos wrote it but that it accurately summarized what Scar told them; the words were Allen's alone.

Before ending his rebuttal case, Bogdanos presented evidence that Puffy had spoken with the only two defense witnesses to testify he was unarmed during the shooting. Bogdanos introduced Puffy's telephone records and said Puffy had spoken with Christopher Chambers and Charise Myers and convinced both to alter their testimony.

Puffy wanted to see the records; he leaned over his lawyer's shoulder and pointed at certain lines. Bogdanos continued to explain that records from January 2001 showed six calls between telephones owned by Puffy and surprise witness Christopher Chambers. The records also showed a three-minute call between witness Charise Myers and Puffy's cell phone in January 2000.[1]

---

1.　On the stand, Myers denied speaking to Puffy. "Not that I know of, anyway."

Bogdanos explained that he had tried to analyze numbers for the other two witnesses who claimed Puffy had been unarmed. One had given a home number registered to a church. The other had claimed he had no home telephone and did not remember old cell phone numbers. But Bogdanos also uncovered twenty-two other phone calls between Puffy's security guard Paul Offord and witness Glen Beck, the bouncer who claimed Puffy's hands were empty when he stumbled down some stairs after the shooting. Puffy's lawyers denied that he had spoken to one witness but did not address accusations about the other. After Puffy's lawyers explained that there was no way to know what was discussed during these telephone conversations, Bogdanos told the judge, "I know this is a shocker, your honor, but some people in this case are lying."

THIS WAS NOW THE MOST SUSPENSEFUL TIME. LAWYERS FOR Shyne and Anthony Jones offered closing arguments. Shyne's attorney, Ian Niles, admitted that Shyne had had a gun that night. But he only had fired twice at the ceiling to clear a path; he had wanted to help Puffy's entourage escape Matthew "Scar" Allen, who Niles claimed had yelled, "Shyne, I'm going to kill you." Jones's lawyer said the gun found in the Navigator belonged to driver Wardel Fenderson. "He admitted the gun was his not once but twice, twenty-two minutes after he'd been arrested." After mentioning Fenderson's three-million-dollar lawsuit against Puffy, Jones's lawyer added, "He's an opportunist who's waiting for the end of this trial to collect millions of dollars."

Puffy's lawyer Benjamin Brafman spent three hours calling the case "stupid" and claiming that witnesses had testified against Puffy in order to gain from lawsuits they had filed against him. Puffy, in an off-white suit that contrasted with the dark suits worn by the lawyers and codefendants, kept his Bible open on the defense table but faced the jury. Brafman railed against the witnesses; they were "two pimps from the street, a deadbeat dad, and two people in a club with conflicting stories and lawsuits." Fenderson, he said, was "a deadbeat dad whose word is no good." He added that Fenderson owes thirty thousand dollars in child support. Julius Jones, meanwhile, was "smoking grass and drinking alcohol" that night. In contrast, Puffy was "a man who works every single day, maybe the most successful young African-American man in United States history."

Brafman explained why telephone records showed that Puffy had spoken with defense witnesses—Puffy was active in his own defense, he claimed; he regularly used his telephone to coordinate transportation for witnesses scheduled to testify. "Many found this laughable," Court TV's Harriet Ryan explained. Furthermore, other people sometimes used his telephone; they might have called the witnesses. "But that also seemed dubious," Ryan said. "His former lawyer remembered using his client's phone only once, and his former personal assistant testified that he had dialed Puffy literally thousands of times and Puffy was the only one to ever answer the cell."

Matthew Bogdanos faced the jury and played a tape of a frantic 911 call from Club New York. "This is not the Puff Daddy trial," he said, "this is not the Jennifer Lopez trial, not the Shyne or Wolf trial. Lest we forget, it's about three people shot in a club." He asked the jury to focus on "undeniable physical evidence" from ballistic experts that showed Puffy had carried a gun that night. "You can't change it. You can't spin it. You can close your eyes to it if you want, but that's what you'd be doing not to see that it was defendant Combs who fired that single shot."

He examined testimony, exhibits, and every witness that seemingly lied about Puffy not having a gun. Of Charise Myers: "Sometimes good people do bad things." About the telephone records: This case was "rampant with bribery, money, influence, and witnesses changing their testimony." The truth, he added, was bad for the defense.

At first, jurors took notes, but they stopped when he went on for hours. Many observers felt Juror Number 6 did not like him. Soon, one juror started to examine her fingernails. Another stared at the gallery. A third fiddled with his eyeglasses. He promised to finish by lunch, but was still talking three hours later. He admitted that the summation was "the longest I ever talked in my life," and said he planned to speak for another hour. Puffy received sympathetic glances from the jury. But Bogdanos wanted to show exactly why sixty witnesses and 126 court exhibits proved Puffy was guilty of gun possession and bribery. He wanted the jury to know that Puffy was guilty of arrogance, deceit, and tampering with witnesses. He wanted to explain that Puffy had fired a shot at the ceiling that night, and then, in the Navigator, wiped his fingerprints off the gun before throwing it out of a window. He wanted to show them that Puffy was smart enough to throw his gun out and that the gun found under the front passenger seat belonged to Jones. He also wanted the jury to know that witnesses had lied on the stand for Puffy. "There are people who believe that they can use money, power, influence, and benefits to change testimony," he added.

But something happened. Maybe Bogdanos sensed that he had lost the jury. Maybe he saw one juror rolling her eyes sympathetically at Puffy. No one knows. What's clear is that Bogdanos went from asking the jury to send Puffy to prison for fifteen years to saying that, despite his guilt, he sensed that the jury would "believe him [because] he is, after all, Puff Daddy." At this, Puffy shook his head. "When you have been so powerful for so long," Bogdanos added, "you begin to believe that you are above the law." He pointed at Puffy and said, "Justice cannot be bought at any price."

The jury then began deliberations. Outside of the courthouse, supporters tried to protest. They resembled one of Bad Boy's street teams, only instead of placards that told MTV to air their videos, they held signs that read "HIP HOP NEEDS YOU" and "KEEP PUFFY FREE." Despite the fact that Puffy had spent years courting a white audience and seemingly ignoring his black fans, some black court employees offered support by opening windows and chanting, "Leave him alone" when he left the building.

During the second day of deliberations, the jury asked to have almost two hours of a police ballistic expert's testimony read back to them, and for photographs of the interior of the club and actual bullets and shell casings.

Meanwhile, Puffy sat in the empty courtroom thumbing through *The Celestine Prophecy*.

The third day the jury asked to hear Officer Mark Rowley's testimony read back to them. Rowley had testified that Lopez had tried to leave the scene, and had said, "It's not my gun." This comment, Bogdanos said, proved that she had seen a gun in the SUV—the 9mm found underneath the front passenger seat. The jury then asked for a transcript of the message Puffy had left on Fenderson's machine. Then, at 6:45 P.M., the jury returned with a verdict. They began with Puffy.

When Shyne heard the individual "not guilty" verdicts, he used one hand to make the sign of the cross over himself. He had done this whenever a witness said he had fired in the nightclub. The jury acquitted Puffy of four counts of illegal possession of a gun and one count of bribery. "He was stunned at first, and then started crying," said a witness. "When the 'not guiltys' were announced, he was staring at snapshots of his kids. He had them lined up on the defense table and was sort of bracing himself with his hands and looking at the pictures of his kids." His attorneys wrapped him in tight bear hugs and supporters cheered until the judge and thirty court officers hushed them. The tearful jury also acquitted Anthony "Wolf" Jones of all charges. When they found Shyne guilty of five of the eight charges against him, the young rapper's face drooped. He looked stunned.

Puffy, meanwhile, embraced his mother and walked toward the rear of the courtroom; he stopped and faced Shyne's mother, grandmother, and supporters in the last row and said he was sorry about the verdict. Puffy's mother, teary-eyed, grabbed Shyne's mother's hand and then one of his grandmother's hands. She told both that she was also sorry. Court officers then circled Puffy and his mother and ushered them to the front of the courthouse.

Other officers surrounded Shyne. He stood behind the railing separating the defense tables from the stands and tightly hugged his mother and grandmother. After he urged them to be strong, guards led him toward a holding cell. At the same time, Puffy left the courthouse and stood in the glare of camera lights. He approached a bank of microphones. "I give all the glory to God," he said. "If it wasn't for God, I wouldn't be able to walk out here." He thanked Janice for her unflagging support. When reporters asked how he felt about Shyne, he said, "I'm going to talk about all that later. But right now, I just want to go and be with my kids." With that, he left.